not
your
*mama's™*crochet

not your mama's™ crochet

The cool and creative way to join the chain gang

by Amy Swenson

WILEY

Wiley Publishing, Inc.

For general information on our other products and services or to obtain technical support please contact our Customer Care Department within the U.S. at (800) 762-2974, outside the U.S. at (317) 572-3993 or fax (317) 572-4002.

Wiley also publishes its books in a variety of electronic formats. Some content that appears in print may not be available in electronic books. For more information about Wiley products, please visit our web site at www.wiley.com.

Library of Congress Cataloging-in-Publication data is available from the publisher upon request.

ISBN-13: 978-0-471-97381-2

ISBN-10: 0-471-97381-5

Printed in the United States of America

10 9 8 7 6 5 4 3 2 1

Book design by Elizabeth Brooks
Cover design by Troy Cummings
Interior photography by Matt Bowen
Illustrations by Joni Burns, Shelley Norris, Rashell Smith
Book production by Wiley Publishing, Inc. Composition Services

This book is dedicated to my mother, Karen Swenson, who taught me with saintly patience that crochet could be fun. Had I listened a little more closely, I may have avoided a whole bunch of holes 10 years later.

Free bonus pattern available online!

Can't get enough crochet? Access the bonus Hoop du Jour pattern (crocheted wire hoop earrings) at www.wiley.com/go/NYMcrochet.

Contents

CHAPTER SIX

Ready, Set, Crochet!

PART TWO
Projects

CHAPTER SEVEN

Jump Right in, the Water's Fine!

CHAPTER EIGHT

Fashionistas Unite!

CHAPTER NINE

Put Your Hook Where Your Heart Is: Great Gifts to Crochet

CHAPTER TEN

Bucking Tradition

Acknowledgments

This book would not be possible without the great folks at Wiley Publishing, Inc.: Roxane Cerda, Suzanne Snyder, and Kelly Henthorne. Special thanks go to Mandy Moore, technical editor extraordinaire. Not only did she have the guts to tackle my convoluted meanderings, she can also be credited with teaching me just how great yarn can be. Amy Singer, Jillian Moreno, Shannon Okey, and Kim Werker provided support and advice on the book-writing front as well as excellent excuses for procrastination. The many fantastic designers included here not only provided endless inspiration but were a true joy to work with.

My friends, co-workers, and customers who had to hear endless prattle about "the book" should be given medals of patience, or at least truckloads of free yarn. I'm hoping they're content with an autograph or two.

Finally, none of my super-sized dreams have ever, or will ever, be possible without the love and support of my partner, Sandra. During the writing and editing, she's had to clean more than her share of dirty litter boxes and do more than her share of stinky laundry. But it's okay. She's a knitter. She *gets* it. And most importantly, she *gets* me.

Introduction

◆◆◆

Crochet: Why Knot?

In many ways, the title of this book is misleading. My mother, and her mother before her, crocheted as far back as I can remember. Perhaps your mother does, too. I remember little colorful squares of acrylic scraps that she later sewed into a black and jewel-toned blanket. I remember pastel dishcloths and sparkly baby gifts. I remember an unfortunately fringed poncho from the late 1970s.

When I was barely 10, she sat down and taught me the basic stitches . . . just enough to make little spirally toys with which to taunt the family dog. A decade later, after I'd moved to San Francisco and adopted my first cats, she whipped up some of the same toys and mailed them as welcome gifts.

When my mother sits down with a copy of this book, much like you're doing at this very moment, she'll be unsurprised by its contents, and not just because she's had her ear yakked off during the writing process. The stitches and techniques of crochet have changed very little since the first documented patterns a century and a half ago.

So, in a way, it *is* my mama's crochet.

But, as much as I learned from Mom, over time, I took the familiar stitches and made them my own. I used soft merino and silk to make luscious scarves and trendy hats. I took inspiration from the ripple afghans of the early '80s and substituted luxurious hand-dyed yarns for a subtle and soft blanket under which to watch reruns of *Desperate Housewives* and *Lost*.

And you, if you're anything like me, will do the same.

How to Use This Book

Not Your Mama's Crochet is designed for beginning crocheters, as well as for those with some experience, such as my 10-year-old self, who now want to bump up their skills a notch or two. The first section of the book—chapters 1 through 6—teaches you most of the essentials: how to crochet, work with yarn, select a pattern, and choose the right size. In the second part, you'll dig into some incredible, fashionable, and fun patterns that your mama will be jealous of. When you're hooked—pun intended—you'll want to check out some other great references. For crochet fans, both new and true, Part 3 gives all the geeky details for where to go next.

From simple scarves to stunning jackets, the pattern chapters are great fun. If you've done knitting or crochet before, you'll notice we left off any difficulty ratings. It's my belief that there are no easy or hard crochet patterns. Since 99.9 percent of them use some variation of the basic stitches you learn in chapter 1, it just doesn't seem applicable. Instead, our ratings are done based on time commitment.

- ♦ **Flirtation** These projects are quick, easy, and great for experimentation.
- ♦ **Summer Fling** Takes a bit more time and more concentration, but still has a fair amount of instant gratification.
- ♦ **Love o' Your Life** Ready for commitment? Like the best relationships, you'll put a lot of work in but get a lot of enjoyment—or bragging rights—out of the final product.

In the mood for a one-nighter? Look for projects labeled "Flirtation," and you'll be done during a single chick flick. "Summer Fling" projects take a little longer. These might be better for Christmas vacation or a week at the beach. "Love o' Your Life" are the sort of projects you'll labor long for. These might take a month or more, but at the end, you'll have a true heirloom.

Why Crochet?

In the last few years, knitting has taken the crafting spotlight. Knitting as a trend. Knitting as activism. Knitting as the new yoga. Maybe you knit already. I certainly do. I knit *a lot*. I knit more than most folks could ever imagine. I knit so much that I ended up opening a yarn store just so I could talk about yarn all day (and most nights). I love that knitting lets me produce slinky body-hugging fabric far nicer than anything I could buy at the local mall.

But, I also love crochet. Crochet, to me, is pure romance.

It may sound silly if all you've seen are well-worn afghans in neon orange. But hear me out.

Picture instead, our heroine, strolling along the banks of the Seine in Paris. She's just had a glass of *vin rouge* with friends at some sidewalk café. It's one of those late summer nights where you can almost taste the approach of fall in the air. She's wearing a lovely printed dress . . . think Missoni . . . but the chill in the air has her reaching for her wrap: midnight blue cashmere. She drapes it around her shoulders and passersby can't help but notice the way the ruffled hem floats back and forth in the evening breeze. A closer inspection, perhaps from the handsome crepe seller where she stops to buy a *crepe chocolat*, reveals a delicate but simple lace made of chain-like stitches. Yes, it's crochet.

Crochet is one of the few fabric-making techniques that cannot be reproduced by a machine. Every bit of crochet you see in the world around you was produced by human hands. And, in the same way, you can put your hands to use to make something beautiful, something that embodies the same spirit of romance as a moonlit walk along the Seine.

When you take hook to yarn, you not only accomplish stitches to produce a shape, you produce an object or garment uniquely yours. You picked the yarn, you selected the right color, and you invested the time to make it come to life.

Why crochet? Why not!

• Part One •

Hooker How-To

Chapter One

◆◆◆

Crochet 101

Chances are, unless you're killing time in some waiting room and the only other choice is a 15-year-old copy of *Reader's Digest*, you picked up this book because you want to crochet. So let's get to it!

To follow along with this chapter, it'll be handy to have some yarn and a crochet hook. Chapter 3 covers all the varieties of yarn *ad nauseum*, but to start with, look for something called "Worsted" or "Aran" and a US G/4.5mm crochet hook. Make sure the yarn has a fairly smooth texture, so you will be able to see what you are doing. You may also want scissors.

The Ultimate Smack-down: Crochet versus Knitting

Since the world began, there've been historic debates. Cat versus dog. Cubs versus White Sox. Coke versus Pepsi. Crochet versus knitting. Before we continue, let's get one thing straight: Crochet and knitting are both admirable crafts. Don't let anyone, even your beloved mother, tell you otherwise.

Knitting may have gotten most of the press in recent years. But crochet is her shy little sister just waiting to debut. Maybe you already knit and are looking for something different? Or, maybe you vaguely remember crochet from your younger days and are wanting to get back into it.

The truth is, crochet and knitting have common ground. Both use some sort of implement to twist fibers together into fabric. But that's where the similarities end. The following table highlights some of the differences between the two crafts.

Knitting	Crochet
Uses two needles.	Uses one hook.
All stitches are on the needles at any point in time.	Only one stitch is worked at one time.
Can work circularly or back and forth.	Can work circularly, back and forth, three dimensionally, or free-form.
Creates a fabric that's typically as thin as the yarn that's being used.	Creates a firm fabric that's approximately three times as thick as the yarn being used. Consequently, crochet eats up more yarn for the same sized project.
With the same yarn and the same needles, every individual stitch will be identical in shape and size.	Individual crochet stitches can vary dramatically in width, thickness, and height.
Well suited to intricate and detailed multi-color knitting.	Because of the thickness of each stitch, carrying multiple colors along one row is less practical.
Allows you to work with a huge range of yarns and patterns.	Allows you to work with the same range of yarns and patterns.
Because of the uniform size of the knitting stitches, it tends to take longer to knit the same sized item than to crochet it.	Crochet tends to be quite a bit quicker than knitting, in part due to the increased height of standard crochet stitches.
Knitted fabric drapes nicely and is ideal for thin sweaters.	Crocheted fabric is quick and thick, and is great for structured garments, toys, and blankets.
Is incredibly, addictively fun and allows for a lot of creativity.	Is incredibly, addictively fun and allows for a lot of creativity.

Working with Yarn

If you just bought your yarn, it may be wound into a ball already. Chapter 3 covers more about the types of yarn and how they are packaged. For now, just remove the ball label and look for a loose end of yarn to work with, whether from the inside or the outside of the ball. If your yarn is packaged into a big twisty thing that almost resembles a Twizzler, you'll need to wind it into a ball before beginning to crochet. For instructions on how to do this, see page 43, "A Tangled Mess: How to Wind a Ball of Yarn," in chapter 3.

It's probably no surprise—if you've watched Saturday morning cartoons at all—that yarn tangles easily. To reduce the risk of your yarn building an immense tangle that will eventually consume your living room, pull out only about 3 feet of the yarn to start.

It All Starts with a Knot

In order to crochet, you need a loop. And in order to keep that loop from just falling off your hook, you need a knot. Specifically, a slipknot that is adjustable in size.

If your knot-making skills aren't up to snuff, here's a reminder:

To make a slipknot:

1. Form a ring-sized loop in the yarn, with the part of the yarn attached to the ball crossed in front of the loose end. See figure 1.
2. Bring the yarn attached to the ball up and behind the ring-sized loop. See figure 2.
3. Use your fingers to pull the yarn through the loop. Tighten into a knot by holding the top of the loop with one hand and pulling on both ends with the other hand. See figure 3.

Et voila! A slipknot! Now, insert your crochet hook into the loop and pull on both ends to tighten. The loop should be just big enough to slide loosely along the body of the hook.

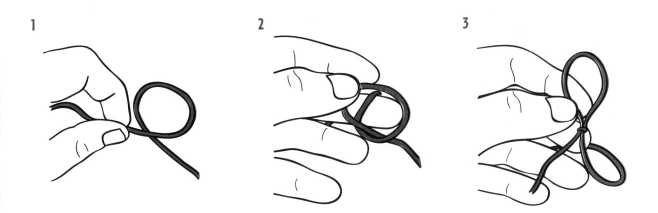

Ch-ch-chains of Love

You've got your hook; you've got your slipknot. Now it's time to make a little chain, the most fundamental of all crochet stitches. Chain stitch is abbreviated as "ch" and is typically the base of any crochet project. For this reason, it's often called a *foundation chain.*

Every crocheter's technique is a bit different. It won't take you long to figure out what finger position and motions work the best for you. But to start with, try it this way. Why? Because I tell you so, that's why.

1. Open your left palm and bring the yarn across your palm and between your first and middle finger. See figure 1.

2. Close your fist. The yarn should be caught by your last three fingers.

3. Extend your index finger and thumb like you're a kid pretending to be an outlaw. Bring the yarn forward over your index finger and use your thumb and middle finger to hold on to the bottom of the slipknot.

4. With your right hand, hold the hook so the loop is about an inch from the end of the hook. You're now ready to chain! See figure 2.

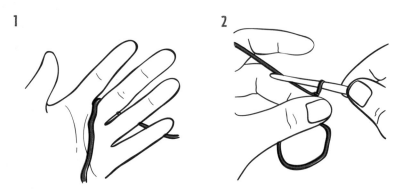

1   2

Here's how to chain (see illustrations on next page):

1. Rotate the hook so it faces away from you and push up against the working yarn. See figure 1.

2. With the hook pressed against the working yarn, rotate the hook toward you, clockwise. This will wrap the yarn around the shaft of the hook.

3. Continue to rotate the hook another quarter-turn until the hook points down. Pull the hook to the right, and the yarn will catch in the hook. See figure 2.

4. Once the yarn is caught in the hook, continue pulling the hook to the right and through the loop. See figure 3.

You now have one chain stitch completed and a new loop on the hook. Pull a little on the hook to loosen this loop. In the beginning, the looser the loops, the easier it'll be to work the next row.

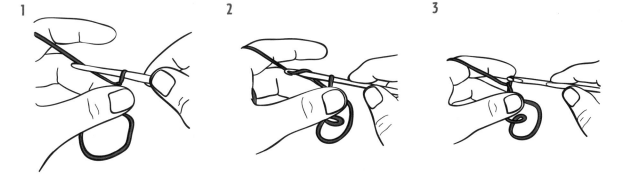

1 **2** **3**

To continue working in chain stitch, just repeat the same process of rotating the hook and pulling through the loop to create a new loop. Do this 10 or 20 (or 50) times, until the motion becomes more natural.

Your first chains will be uneven and lumpy. Don't worry; with a little practice, your chain stitches will soon be nearly identical in size and shape.

Go ahead and make a really long chain if you want. It's just practice, after all. Remember how, as a kid, your mittens were attached by a bit of yarn that went up one sleeve, across your back, and down the other? In all likelihood, that may have been a crochet chain such as the one you're making now.

Let's say you want one of those chains for your now-grown-up mittens. Here's how:

1. Keep chaining until the chain is long enough to reach from one wrist, up your arm, across your shoulders and down to the other wrist. To tie off, cut the yarn, leaving about six or seven inches.

2. Pull on the hook to make the final loop a bit bigger, and with your fingers, thread the end of the cut yarn through this loop.

Macra-What?

For whatever reason, folks tend to confuse crochet and macramé. Macramé is the art of tying decorative knots. In some cases, it can resemble the dense fabric created by basic crochet stitches. But in crochet, you only ever tie two knots: the initial slipknot when beginning to chain stitch and the final knot after cutting the yarn. If you don't believe me, remove the hook from your crochet-in-progress and pull on the yarn attached to the ball. See it unravel, stitch by stitch? I bet you *wish* you had a knot now!

3. Remove the hook and set aside. Pull the end of the yarn tight to make the final knot. And now you have a lovely crochet chain, ready to be sewn onto any store-bought (or hand made) mittens!

Chaining is great and all, but there's only so much you can do with what's essentially a knotted rope. You need the chain for the foundation row, but after that, you'll need a little something more substantial to actually create the fabric.

Let Them Single Crochet!

Single crochet (sc) is the most basic of these stitches. Although other variations exist, they all rely on the fundamental steps of creating a sc stitch.

To get started, you'll need a row made of chain stitches. Similar to a house's foundation, this is the groundwork that needs to be done upon which to build the rest of the project. Not surprisingly, it's called the *foundation row*. So, go ahead and chain 11 stitches. (In patterns, this will be abbreviated as ch 11.) Set up by holding the yarn and hook as if you are planning on continuing in chain stitch. However, you're now going to work back toward the initial slipknot to create the first row.

Working into the Foundation Chain

When working *even* (without adding or removing any stitches in each), one or more of the initial chain stitches becomes what's referred to as the *turning chain,* and simply works to create the height needed to match the rest of the row. In the case of single crochet, the turning chain is only 1 ch. You'll see later on how taller stitches require additional turning chains to make a nice even row.

A common question when beginning this first row is, where do you put your hook? The initial crochet chain has two sides: one that's made of ridges, like camel humps (see figure 1), and one that's made of Vs (see figure 2).

1

2

To work any stitches in the first row, you should place your hook under a single ridge. The hook should not split the yarn, but should be inserted into the small hole between the single ridge and the bottom Vs. Let's try it, by inserting the hook under the second ridge from the hook (see figure 3). This allows 1 chain stitch for a turning chain (you'll learn about turning chains in just a minute).

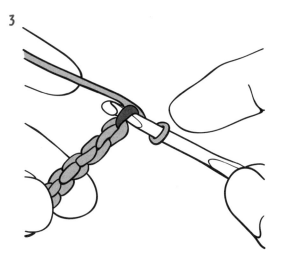

There are many different schools of thought as to the best way of working this first row. Working into the ridges is the way I feel looks best. Whatever way you do it, just be consistent for the best results.

The first row of stitches that you build on the foundation chain is always going to be a bit tough to work. Many problems can be alleviated by ensuring the initial chain stitches are worked loosely.

We'll now work a single crochet stitch into this ridge. Here's how:

1. Rotate the hook to grab the yarn (see figure 1), as you did for the initial chain.

2. Now, pull the yarn through the ridge on the foundation chain, pulling up a loop that's more or less the same size as the loop on your hook. Your hook now has two loops (see figure 2).

3. Rotate the hook to again grab the yarn, but this time, pull it through both loops (see figure 3).

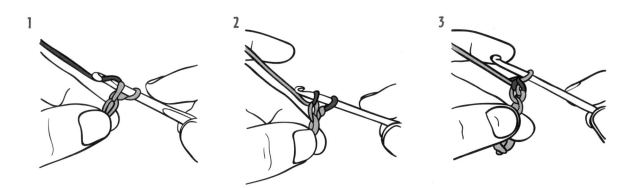

You've just completed a sc stitch. Go ahead and continue to work nine more of these stitches. Assuming you chained 11 stitches in the beginning, this will bring you to the end of the chain (see the top figure to the right). You're now ready to work the second row.

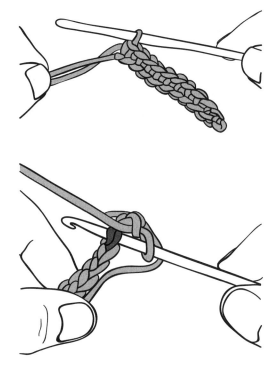

Working into a Previous Row

Crochet is typically worked from right to left. So, when working back and forth in rows, you'll need to flip the work over at the end of each row to be set up for the next row. Remember the bit about the "turning chain" earlier on in this chapter? Well, you'll need a turning chain for every row. Since we're working in sc, go ahead and ch 1 stitch to turn the row.

Unlike the initial foundation chain, a row of any crochet stitch is made up only of the Vs that you see on the bottom of the initial chain. To work a standard sc, insert your hook underneath both pieces of yarn that make up one of these Vs (see the second figure to the right). This is called working in both loops of the stitch. Again, you should skip the chain stitch that's closest to the hook. You'll work the first stitch of your new row into the last stitch of your previous row.

Work a sc in the stitch as before. Continue across the row in this way, working one sc into each stitch of the previous row, until you reach the end. Again, you should have just worked 9 sc stitches. To practice, work a few more rows of sc (see bottom figure). Remember to chain 1 at the beginning of each row to add height, and skip the chain stitch next to the hook on every row to prevent increasing. Single crochet is a fairly dense and compact stitch that creates a firm fabric. For a pattern that uses only sc, check out the "It's a Toque, Eh?" hat in chapter 7. Alternatively, check out the stitch patterns that use sc (or variations of sc) in the following chapter.

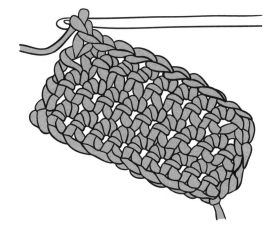

Curly Whirly

Let's pretend you're happily crocheting rows upon rows of single crochet to make a simple scarf. You get a few inches into the scarf and notice that the edges are curling up rather unattractively. What have you done wrong?

Nothing!

Single crochet, due to its compact shape, will almost always cause the corners and edges of the work to curl and twist. The other basic stitches, half double, double, and triple, are loose enough to prevent this natural curling.

If you really want to work in straight rows of single crochet, try going up a few hook sizes to crochet more loosely. This will alleviate some of the curl. You can also wet-block the piece to temporarily prevent curl-age. To do this, check out the instructions on page 24, "Blocking."

Seeing Double; Double Crochet

Double crochet (dc) is aptly named. It takes twice as long to work as sc but results in a stitch that's twice as tall. Consequently, the turning chain for a dc is taller—3 chains rather than 1. You'll do some double crochet now:

1. Assuming you're ready to work your next row, chain 3.
2. Rotate the hook to grab the yarn. This is also called a *yarn over*. See figure 1.
3. Unlike single crochet, when you are working in double crochet, you will skip the first stitch in the row (the last stitch of the previous row) and begin working into the second stitch of the row. *The turning chain counts as the first stitch of the row.* Insert the hook into the second stitch. Be sure to keep the loop of yarn from the yarn over on your hook! Rotate the hook to grab the yarn.
4. Pull up a loop, so that you now have three loops of yarn on your hook. See figure 2.
5. Rotate the hook again, doing a yarn over.
6. Pull this yarn through the first two loops on your hook, so that only two loops remain. See figure 3.

1

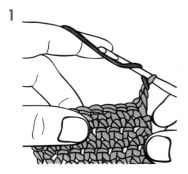

2

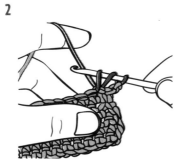

3

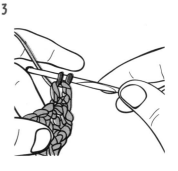

7. Do another yarn over.

8. Again, pull the yarn through the two remaining loops on the hook. Only one loop remains, and you're now ready to work another dc.

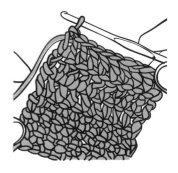

As with the sc, work across the row in dc. You'll see that the dc stitches are much higher than the sc rows (see the figure to your right). They also have larger gaps between the stitches.

When you work your next row in dc, you'll work your last stitch into the *last ch stitch of the turning chain from the previous row.* Remember that this turning chain counted as the first stitch of the row. Now, go ahead and practice a few more rows of dc, remembering to ch 3 at the beginning of each row and to work into the top of the turning chain of the previous row when you reach the end of a new row.

Triple and Beyond!

As when working the dc, you can make an even taller stitch: *triple crochet* (tc), also referred to as *treble crochet.* Because tc is taller than dc, you'll want to chain 4 for your turning chain. This time, bring the yarn over the hook two times before inserting the hook into the second stitch of the row. At this point, it'll look just like the beginning of a double crochet, with one extra loopy thing on the hook in the middle.

1. Insert the hook into the stitch, rotate to grab the yarn, and pull up a loop. You now have four loops on your hook. See figure 1.

2. Yarn over and bring through the first two loops on the hook. Three loops remain.

3. Yarn over again and bring through the first two loops on the hook. Two loops remain.

4. Yarn over again and bring through the final two loops on the hook. One loop remains, and you're set to work the next stitch. See figure 2.

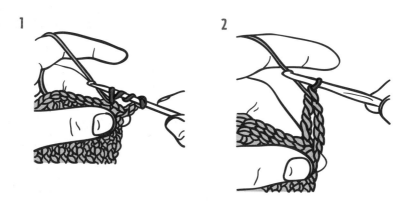

As when working dc, the turning chain will count as the first stitch of the row, and the last stitch of the row will be worked into the last ch of the turning chain of the previous row. After completing one row of tc, you'll see the stitches are quite a bit taller than the dc and have even larger spaces between the individual stitches. With tc, you'll make a lot of progress quickly, but the trade-off (because there's always a trade-off) is a less firm fabric.

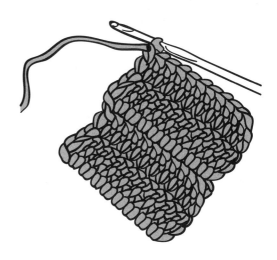

In the same way, you could work taller and taller stitches by working additional yarn overs before inserting the hook through the base stitch. However, these stitches are far less common and are usually explained within any pattern that uses them.

And Everything Else under the Sun

Crochet, of course, is not only these four stitches. But, the basic actions you've just performed form the basis of every other stitch in crochet. Entire volumes are dedicated to detailing and describing the endless possible variations. In chapter 2 is a selection of the most common and a few of my personal favorites.

Don't worry; you're not expected to learn and memorize them all. Because of the immense amount of possible patterns, it's not unusual to run into something you've never done, even after years and decades of experience. You'll be relieved to know that almost any pattern will give you stitch-specific instructions for anything other than the basics that are covered in "Crochet 101."

What's in a Name?

By now, you may have noticed a pattern between the three most common stitches: single, double, and triple. All of these stitches follow one pattern: yarn over, draw through two loops, and repeat until only one loop remains. The only things that vary are the number of loops initially created by the yarn over, before the hook is inserted into the work, and the number of times the pattern is repeated.

In single crochet, you repeat the pattern just once. In double, twice. And in triple? Big surprise, you do it three times. Sometimes, thinking about these repetitions really helps in remembering which stitch is which.

You Spin Me Right 'Round Baby!

So far, we've been only working back and forth in rows, from right to left. But in crochet, it's also possible to move in a circular direction, or as crochet-geeks call it, *in the round*.

Working in the round allows you to do a few things that flat crochet just can't handle. First, it lets you create seamless garments, such as the "It's a Toque, eh?" ski hat pattern in chapter 7. Although you could do the same hat, almost exactly, by crocheting back and forth in rows, at the very end you would need to sew the two sides together with a yarn needle. The seam would also be visible—not necessarily a good thing when wearing something meant to be seen from all sides, like a hat.

Secondly, circular crocheting allows you to create complex designs that lay flat but radiate from a central point. Think of those intricate lace doilies from your grandmother's house. Although you may not ever have "crochet doily" on your list of lifetime things to do, circular motifs can be fashionable, stunning, and fun to make. Just take a look at chapter 8's "Ramblin' Rosie Cardie" or "Uber Femme Capelet" for an example of some current, and stylish, possibilities.

Slipping n' Sliding

Before getting into anything too fancy-shmancy, however, we'll start with a simple crocheted tube.

With your same yarn and hook, ch 6.

At this point, you could just start working stitches into the back loops of the foundation chain as you did before. But then, you wouldn't be working in a circle. So, before you do anything else, you need to join both ends of the chain together to make a ring. To do this, you'll work a slip stitch. Slip stitches tend to be used anywhere you need to move the yarn or join pieces without adding any significant height to the work.

1. Being careful to keep the chain from twisting, insert the hook into the very first chain after your initial slipknot. See figure 1.
2. As with the previous stitches, rotate the hook to bring the yarn over.
3. Draw through both loops on the hook to create one loop. It helps to use your thumb and index finger to hold the ring open while you do this. Otherwise, the ring tends to twist and make it difficult to join. See figure 2.

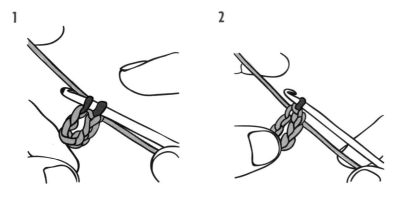

1   2

Totally Tubular

Although it's acceptable to crochet into the back ridges of your initial foundation chain, just as you did when working back and forth, for circular crochet, it's actually more common to crochet *around* those chain stitches. Although this allows your first round to slide a bit, the circular structure keeps it in place enough to prevent any issues. Try this on a row worked back and forth, and all your stitches may bunch up unattractively, or even slide off the end of the foundation chain!

1. We'll now work a round of single crochet around this base chain. So, as before, you'll chain 1 to increase the height.
2. This time, no need to worry about inserting your hook through a specific stitch. Instead, put the hook through the center of the ring from front to back. See figure 1.
3. As before, yarn over and pull up a loop, wrapping the foundation chain in the process.
4. Finish your sc by again working a yarn over and pulling through both loops.
5. Continue to work sc into the ring until 6 sc are completed. Use your fingers to evenly distribute them around the ring. Your final sc should be fairly close to the initial ch 1 of the round. Insert your hook into the top V of this initial ch 1. Any guesses what you're doing? Right! You're getting set to work a slip stitch to join both ends of the round without adding any height. See figure 2.
6. As before, wrap the yarn around the hook.
7. Draw through the Vs and the loop on the hook to join together. *Et voila!* One round completed. See figure 3.

> ### Rounds versus Rows
>
> If you're not sure whether a pattern is worked back and forth or circularly, check out the terminology the designer uses. If she calls the first bit of stitching after the initial foundation chain a "round," you know you'll be working around a circle. If she calls it a "row," you'll be working back and forth.

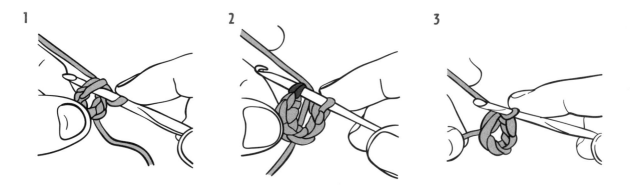

Work several more rounds in this way to see your tube take shape. Remember to begin each round with a turning chain (ch 1) and to end each round with a slip stitch, joining the first and last stitches of the round. As with back-and-forth crochet, after the initial round you can continue to work each sc in the top of the sc on the round below.

In this way, you can create a tube of any length or circumference. Although this finger-sized tube may not seem practical, it could form part of a fitted glove. Likewise, other tubular shapes can make turtlenecks, hats, or legwarmers.

Be Square

Perhaps the best known crochet motif is called the *Granny Square*. These square-shaped motifs have endless variations. But, even at its simplest form, the Granny Square can be seen in everything from dishcloths, to tacky afghans, to the Fashion Week catwalk. Again, the "Ramblin' Rose Cardie" builds upon a basic Granny Square to create a bohemian look.

A Simple Square

To make the simplest of Granny Squares, ch 4 and slip stitch to join, as before.

1. Since you'll be working in double crochet, ch 3 for height. This will take the place of the first dc.
2. You'll now work a dc into the center of the ring. Yarn over and insert the hook from front to back in the center of the ring, just like you did with the tube. See figure 1.
3. Draw up a loop and complete the dc as described in the previous section.
4. Work one more dc in the center of the ring. Including the initial ch 3, you now have 3 dc.
5. Chain 3. This will make one corner of the square. See figure 2.

6. Bring the yarn over the needle and work three more dc into the center of the ring. Chain 3 for the next corner. Repeat the [3 dc, ch 3] sequence twice more, completing the four sides and four corners of a square.

7. Join with a slip stitch to the last stitch of the initial ch 3. See figure 3.

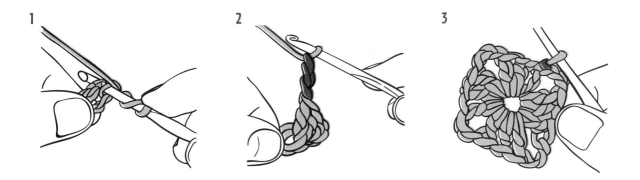

This is the simplest and least complicated of all the motifs. Typically, Granny Squares will have more than one round, following this basic format. I'm guessing this looks pretty familiar. For more motifs, see the stitch guide in the next chapter.

What Goes Up Must Come Down

Making squares and rectangles and tubes is all well and fine, but they only get you so far. To create more complex shapes, you may need to change the number of stitches worked on each row or round. In the Granny Square example, you already did this by working more than the initial 4 stitches into the center of the ring. If you still have your sample, count 'em.

Did you come up with 12 stitches? Close, but no cigar. Because of the corners, you actually worked 24 sts around: 12 dc and 12 ch. This dramatic increase in stitches allowed you to avoid the tube syndrome and create a perfectly flat square.

Of course, this is a simple example. In reality, there are as many ways to increase—or decrease—stitches as there are patterns that use them. 99.9 percent of the time, your pattern will specify how to increase or decrease, whether at the beginning of the pattern in a stitch key, or as part of the instructions. For example, chapter 7's "Getting Dizzy" scarf creates its spiral shape by increasing on every row.

Increases

Increasing, in needlework terminology at least, means the practice of augmenting the fabric's size by adding one or more stitches. In crochet, this is typically done by working multiple stitches into a single base stitch. In that "Getting Dizzy" scarf, the first increase row is made

Crochet Terms Across the Pond

Hamburgers versus Fish 'n Chips. Dollars versus pounds. American versus British crochet terminology. You may not be surprised to hear there are two major English-language systems for naming crochet stitches. The stitches are the same, but the names are significantly, and sometimes confusingly, different. This book, like most produced in North America, uses the American system.

American	British
Slip stitch	Single crochet
Single crochet	Double crochet
Half double	Half treble
Double	Treble
Triple/treble	Double treble

Not sure where your pattern was produced? Check the stitch key first. Many times, patterns will explicitly explain how each stitch is made. If the pattern has no stitch key or only covers more complex stitches, check to see whether the pattern specifies "Slip stitch" anywhere. The British system has no stitch by this name, so you know you're safe proceeding with the American definitions.

by working 2 dc into each sc from the first row. In further rows, the extra stitches are included less frequently.

Try it out on a new sample. Ch 10 or so and then work a few rows in sc without increasing or decreasing. On the next row, work 2 sc into each sc on the row. You'll have doubled your stitches and created the beginning of a ruffle.

Increases are good for more than just spirally scarves and ruffles. Think of your favorite sweater. Is the sleeve all one size from armpit to wrist? Probably not. Most sleeves gradually increase in width as they approach the body of the sweater. This is done, not surprisingly, through carefully placed increases.

Decreases

Conversely, *decreasing* in crochet means reducing the number of stitches present on a given row or round. There are several methods for accomplishing this, but again, most are specified and in fact, created, for the pattern that uses them. One more common means of decreasing is to simply skip a stitch without working it, and work into the next stitch.

You may remember, when working back and forth in double or triple crochet, how we skip the very first stitch on each row? This doesn't decrease because the chain that lends height to the row actually takes the place of the stitch that would normally be worked into that stitch. But, if you're crocheting along and you skip a stitch in the middle of the row, you'll have to work two stitches into one later on to maintain the same number of stitches.

Try this out on your sample swatch. On the next row, sc into the first stitch in the row, skip the next stitch, and sc into the next stitch after that. Continue this way, working an sc into every other stitch from the row before. If you only worked one row of increases before, you're probably back to the same number of stitches you started with.

Putting It All Together

If you're making anything with more than one piece, you're probably wondering what to do next. You have several pieces of crochet and little ends of yarn dangling. Or, maybe you've run out of yarn and need to join in a new ball. Have no fear, none of this is as hard as it might seem.

Joining a New Ball of Yarn

Stripes are one of the most magical aspects of crochet. You can create a beautiful garment, scarf, or blanket in a hundred different colors if you like. What's magical about that? Stripes are deceptively easy, making the finished project a total mystery to anyone who doesn't crochet or knit.

The process of switching yarn for stripes is actually the same as when you finish one ball of yarn and need to start a new one. All you do is drop the old yarn and start using the new yarn, making sure to leave a tail of at least six inches of each so you have enough to sew in the ends later.

Let's say you're crocheting a simple scarf in single crochet, but you want to add in a few rows of a different color. For clarity, I'll call the dark color A and the lighter one B. To switch from A to B, at the end of a row, work until 2 loops remain on the hook. Drop A, yarnover with B, and draw through the last 2 loops of the stitch. Continue, as normal, with B. It may help to hold the dropped A together with the new tail of B to keep some tension on the new yarn.

Work the turning chains using B, continue to work across the row as set. It's that easy!

For a great project using stripes, check out the "Preppy/Hippy Scarf" in chapter 7.

Seaming

If you're making a project with multiple pieces, you'll have to find some way of joining them together. Seaming doesn't have to be a dreaded task. Although it typically comes at the end of the project when you're itching to see the whole thing done, it doesn't actually take as long as it may sometimes seem.

Different types of crochet and different projects require different types of seaming. Typically, your pattern will specify how to seam the pieces together, if a specific method is required. Otherwise, experiment with the following options to see which one works the best for you.

Generally speaking, when seaming, you have the choice of using a crochet stitch to attach two pieces, or sewing two pieces together with yarn and a yarn needle.

With any technique, it's sometimes possible to use the tail end of your yarn, rather than using a new piece of yarn. Just remember when tying off to leave a long enough tail to sew your seam. The length required will vary depending on the size of the piece. To be on the safe side, plan on at least four times the total seam length. This, however, doesn't work with every yarn—sometimes you will crochet a project with a yarn that is not suitable for sewing up, either because it is not strong enough to be used in this way, or because it is too textured. If this is the case, seam with a smooth, lighter-weight, stronger yarn in a suitable color. If you have worked your project in a machine-washable yarn, be sure to seam in a yarn that is also safe for the machine.

Slip Stitch Crochet Seam

Perhaps the quickest and easiest seam is accomplished by slip stitching the two pieces together using the project's crochet hook and yarn. However, a crocheted seam adds bulk to the project and will never be completely invisible.

In the three example figures that follow, contrasting yarn is used for clarity. In reality, you'd want to use yarn that matches the project.

1. To work a slip stitch seam, first line up the edges of the two pieces, with right sides together. Insert the hook through the top right stitch on both pieces, being careful to go through both halves of the V on the top of each stitch. See figure 1.
2. Draw up a loop.
3. With one loop on the hook, insert the hook through the next pair of stitches.
4. Yarn over and pull a loop through the stitches and right through the loop already on the hook.

Continue to work in this way until the seam is finished. From the wrong side, the surface meant to be worn on the inside, you'll see the ridge created by the seam. See figure 2.

On the right side, the outside of the garment, the seam will be much more flat. Keep in mind that, since you'll be working the seam in matching yarn, the seam will be much less visible than it is here. See figure 3.

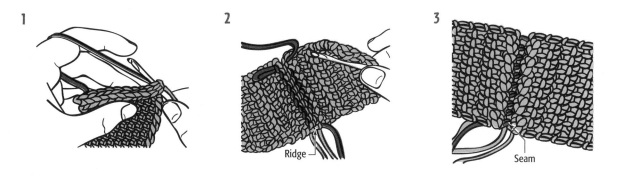

Whipstitch Sewn Seam

For the whipstitch seam, you'll need a yarn needle. These are typically sold everywhere you can buy yarn and can be made out of plastic or metal. Again, place the right sides of the pieces together.

So far, we've only worked through both loops (both sides of the V) of any stitch. For the whipstitch seam, however, we're going to only work with half of the V.

1. Beginning at the top right corner, insert the sewing needle through the two halves of the stitch that are pressed together. Your needle should be going under one loop from the front piece and one loop from the back piece, as shown. See figure 1.

2. Pull the yarn through, being conscious of your tension. If you pull too tightly, the seam will pucker; too loosely, and you'll be left with gaps. See figure 2.

3. Continue to work in this way across the seam until finished. Both sides of the seam are nearly identical. As an additional bonus, the whipstitch seam lies almost perfectly flat. See figure 3.

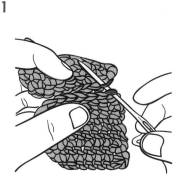

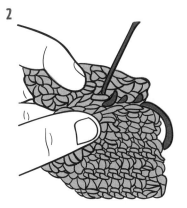

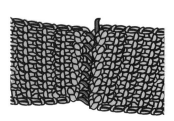

Other Seaming Techniques

As previously mentioned, there are boatloads of other techniques for attaching crochet pieces. Especially when working with motifs, such as Granny Squares, the means of attaching two motifs together can effectively be a part of the overall design. In these cases, the seaming process will be specified by the pattern.

Sewing in Ends

No one . . . and I mean *no one* enjoys weaving or sewing in all those little ends of yarn inevitably left at the end of a project.

1. If your project will have seams, work the seams first; they make great places to hide the sewn ends. If it has no seams, instead weave the yarn in and out of the edge of the piece for an inch or two in one direction.
2. Next, double back and sew in the opposite direction, toward where you started.
3. Cut the yarn, making sure that the piece isn't puckering from being pulled too tightly.

Yarn, depending on what it's made of, can either be quite slippery, quite sticky, or somewhere in between. The slipperier the yarn, the more careful you should be when sewing ends to prevent them from coming loose. For the slickest cottons, you may want to insert the needle not only into the stitches but right through the yarn the stitches are made of, to provide the largest amount of security. As always, be sure to sew at least a few inches in one direction and then back the other way.

Blocking

In crochet and knitting, *blocking* is a technique for helping the fabric to lay flat, or in the case of lacey patterns, helping stretch the lace to most effectively showcase the beautiful stitch work. Two main methods exist for blocking your work; wet blocking and steam blocking.

Wet Blocking

To wet block, you'll need a tub for water, plus a large towel and someplace flat to lay the project while it dries. When blocking lace, you'll also need some rust-proof pins or, alternatively, a blocking wire set.

1. First, submerge the project in room temperature water and squeeze it gently to fully soak the fibers. Allow the piece to soak for 15–30 minutes, especially if you are using a fiber like wool, which is slow to absorb water.
2. Remove the project from the bath and roll in a towel, pressing to sop up any extra water. You're not trying to fully dry the piece, only to remove enough water so the project doesn't drip excessively. Don't be tempted to wring out the excess water;

wringing, even gently, can seriously distort your project and in some cases, cause the fibers to mat, pill, or shrink.

3. Lay a dry towel down on the surface you've selected for drying. If you'll need to pin the piece to stretch it, a spare bed or large carpet can work nicely for this. Otherwise, if just blocking to relax the stitches and make the piece more flat, anywhere will do.

4. Lay the project on the towel and pin, if desired. If you're in a hurry, it's okay to set a fan to blow on the project to speed up the drying process. Depending on the project, climate, and type of yarn, it can take 24–48 hours to fully dry.

Steam Blocking

Steam blocking is the quick and easy alternative to the wet block method. However, steam blocking is really only effective for flattening or smoothing the fabric, and not for any serious stretching.

As its name implies, you'll need an iron capable of producing steam and something to iron on. I prefer to layer a towel or two on a flat work surface if steaming something garment-sized. For smaller projects, such as a hat or scarf, my ironing board works fine.

1. Lay the project on the towels or an ironing board and cover with a dishtowel or other not-too-thick fabric.

2. With the steam set to medium, hover the iron over the protective cloth. If this seems to be ineffective, you can press lightly on the protective cloth.

Not all fibers take well to steam. In addition, pressing too hard with the iron will overly flatten out the cushy crochet stitches, dramatically impacting the size, shape, drape, and density of the finished product. Generally, steam blocking works well for hardy wools and less well for anything synthetic like 100 percent acrylic. If you're not sure whether it'll steam block, consider testing with the same yarn by making a small 10 or 15 stitch square.

When to Block?

How do you know when blocking is necessary, or even how to block? Your pattern should tell you what to do and how. If the pattern doesn't specify whether or not to block, it's optional. You may choose to lightly steam iron the edges of a piece before you sew them if the edges are curling. Or, if your finished sweater is just a smidgen too small, wet blocking and pinning can help it stretch just enough to fit properly.

When Good Crochet Goes Bad: Troubleshooting

Let's face it, problems happen. You make a mistake. You lose your place. The finished product turns out somehow different than expected. Even the most accomplished crocheters run into problems from time to time. The good news is that crochet can be less difficult to troubleshoot than knitting or other crafts. Although problems can be as varied as the types of yarn in your local yarn shop, here are a few quick-and-easy tips to fixing some of the more common issues.

Your Edges Aren't Even

If you're trying to crochet without increasing or decreasing, and your edges don't appear straight, most likely you're not maintaining a consistent number of stitches in each row. Remember to skip the first stitch next to the turning chain if working in double or triple crochet, and to work the first stitch if working in single crochet. Work across to the turning chain from the previous row, working into the last stitch of the turning chain if you are working double or triple crochet, and skipping the turning chain if you are working in single crochet. Sometimes it helps to count each stitch on every row to make sure that you end up with the right number every time. Remember also, if you are working in double crochet or triple crochet, to count the turning chain as a single stitch, no matter how many chains you worked to turn. For example, if you had to chain 3 to obtain the height of a dc, it still counts as one stitch.

It's Tough to Get the Hook in the Stitch

Crochet should never feel like a fight. If you have to push, pull, or otherwise manipulate the hook and yarn to work a stitch, your tension is probably too tight. Tension is a way to measure how tight or loose your stitches are. In chapter 3, we'll discuss tension in depth. In general, the thickness of the crochet hook changes the size of the stitches. A bigger hook makes bigger stitches; a smaller one makes them tighter. If your stitches are too small, try switching to a larger hook, even if you were originally using the size recommended.

Some yarns are also more flexible than others. Pure cotton is fairly inelastic. Although often used in crochet patterns, cotton can be harder for beginning hookers than a wool or acrylic. More elastic yarns help compensate for any tension problems.

The Surface of the Crochet Has Loose Threads

Another common issue for novice crocheters occurs when the hook splits the yarn, either while inserting into the next stitch or while completing a stitch in progress. Although this is sometimes not a big deal, most times split yarn will result in a messy looking stitch. Even worse, these loose threads can unravel over time and cause holes.

The best way to fix this problem is to avoid it in the first place. When working each stitch, be aware of what you're doing. You should be grabbing the entire piece of yarn, not just a strand or two, when completing the stitch. If a snag happens, remove your hook from the loop and gently pull on the yarn until the stitch is frogged. (See the "Rippit, Rippit" sidebar.) Now, rework the stitch, being careful to catch the entire strand of yarn.

Rippit, Rippit: The Joys of Frogging

Hang around any obsessed yarn freaks for long enough, and you're likely to hear the term *frogging*. In crochet-speak, this means unraveling your project to fix a mistake. The term *frog* likely developed from the phrase "ripping back," as in to rip back to where you were before the problem occurred.

Don't be afraid of frogging. In most cases, taking the time to unwind and re-crochet to fix an error is well spent. In crochet, the process of frogging or ripping back is straightforward and can actually be fun. To frog, just remove your hook from the crochet and gently pull on the yarn that's attached to the ball so that each stitch is unworked. (Typically, you'll want to pull the yarn away from the crocheted piece, not towards it.) One by one, each stitch will be pulled out. If you're frogging a fair bit of work, stop every once in a while to wind the yarn around the ball to prevent tangles. When you get past the offending stitch (or rows of stitches, in my case), put the single loop back on the hook and keep on working.

The Crochet Curls Unattractively

Most crochet should lie flat, without curling edges. If your crochet is twisting or biasing, you may be working the stitches too tightly. However, if your tension is correct, it may just be the twist of the yarn. Try wet blocking or steam blocking the project to fix any curly edges.

The exception to this is single crochet. A fabric composed of mostly single crochet stitches will curl, almost invariably. Count on blocking your single-crochet fabric and choose fibers like wool, which respond well to blocking.

You Don't Remember Where You Are

This one happens to all of us. You start a project and, at first, are super excited about each and every stitch. Then, time passes, and like many unfulfilling relationships, you put the project aside in favor of something shiny and new. Months pass, and one day, you find that abandoned project and want to start it up, once again. But where are you? What pattern is it from? What hook do you use?

The best remedy for this is prevention. When you start a project, use a tote or empty shopping bag to hold all the yarn, the work in progress, and the pattern book. Mark the pattern with a sticky note or bookmark and make a note of what size hook you'd been using. You may prefer to make a single photocopy of the pattern, for your own use only, and keep these notes on the copy of the pattern rather than marking up the book. This is what works for me. Other crafters keep project notebooks or online blogs to catalog project information.

But, if you haven't already done this, sit down with the project and the pattern and read both from the beginning to see where you left off. If you're mid-row, it may be easier to rip back to the beginning of a row, rather than guess which stitch should come next for a complex pattern.

When All Else Fails. . .

Don't ever be surprised at the problems you can run into. There's not a book on the planet that can give you the answer to every single issue with crochet. When everything else fails, ask someone who knows. This may be a friend or relative with more crochet experience. This may be doing online research or joining a community such as the ones listed in chapter 12. Or, if you're really in a sticky situation, seek out a quality yarn store in your community. Although yarn stores these days tend to be more geared to knitting, I'd be surprised to run into a yarn store that couldn't at least refer you to a local crochet expert.

What's Next?

Oh, come on. You know you're itching to get started. And it's true that everyone cheats from time to time. So, go ahead and check out chapter 7's delightful newbie patterns. You know you want to. But after that bug wears off, do come back and read the next four chapters. You'll learn crazy stuff about yarn. You'll explore different stitch combinations. You'll read tips on how to make your garments fit properly. It's all good stuff.

But I guess I'll forgive you if you just can't wait to start your first official project. Maybe.

Chapter Two

◆◆◆

Stitches to Make Your Knees Weak

Although most patterns will provide directions for all but the most basic stitches, when you want to experiment, it's great to have a stitch guide for reference. In this chapter, you'll find 12 of my favorite stitch combinations. This is by no means comprehensive. Every year, volumes and volumes of stitch variations hit the shelves. But, it's a place to start.

How to Use This Chapter

Just next to the stitch photo, you'll see a line that indicates how many stitches are required to work the pattern as written. This varies significantly by pattern. The "multiple of X stitches" number can be repeated as many times as you'd like to make a longer row or round. Occasionally, a pattern will require an additional stitch or stitches to allow the pattern to have a neat border. This is indicated by "plus X stitches." For example, the seed stitch is worked over a multiple of **2** stitches plus **1**.

If the stitch pattern introduces a technique or stitch not before seen, it will be described—along with the abbreviation—in the guide. If you see an abbreviation you don't understand, be sure to check out the abbreviation guide in the appendix.

Any stitch directions presented within brackets should be repeated as indicated by the pattern. For example, let's look at the instructions for Row 1 of the Single Seed Stitch pattern:

Turn work, ch 1, sc in 2nd ch from hook, [skip next ch, ch 1, sc in next ch] to end.

The directions specify that you begin by chaining 1, then working a single crochet in the second chain from hook. You'll then repeat only the part within the brackets until you reach the end of the row. Assuming you initially chained the right multiple of stitches, you will end with the final instructions within the bracket. In this case, by working a single crochet in the final chain.

The stitches in this chapter are presented in both written and charted form. Called Symbolcraft, the charts use symbols to stand for each type of stitch. It may all look like Greek to you at first, but eventually the diagrams may make more sense to you than the written directions. See chapter 6 for a more thorough discussion of Symbolcraft and for the symbol definitions.

The Basics and Beyond

These stitches are essentially the same on each and every row and use a simple combination of the basic stitches covered in chapter 1. All of the stitch patterns can be modified through substitution. For example, if the pattern uses double crochet, try it with triple crochet instead. Just remember to use the appropriate number of turning chains. Need a refresher? Don't hesitate to look back in chapter 1.

Single Crochet (sc)

Worked over any number of stitches.
Simple rows of single crochet make a dense and even fabric.
Abbreviation: sc: Insert hook in stitch and pull up a loop. Yarn over and bring through both loops on hook.

Ch the desired number of stitches, +1.
Row 1: Sc in 2nd ch from hook and in each ch to end.
Row 2: Turn. Ch 1, sc in 1st sc and in each sc to end.
Repeat Row 2 until work is desired length.

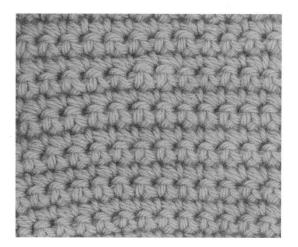

Half Double Crochet (hdc)

Worked over any number of stitches.
Half double crochet is a nice compromise between speed and density. Half double crochet stitches are a little taller than single crochet stitches, and the fabric they form will curl less than single crochet fabric.
Abbreviation: hdc: Yarn over, insert hook into next stitch, and pull up a loop. Yarn over and bring through all three loops on hook.

Ch the desired number of stitches, +2.
Row 1: Hdc in 3rd ch from hook, and in each ch to end.
Row 2: Turn. Ch 2, hdc in 1st hdc and in each ch to end.
Repeat Row 2 until work is desired length.

Double Crochet (dc)

Worked over any number of stitches.

Double crochet is quick and tall. . .great for when speed matters. It forms a fabric that doesn't curl.

Abbreviation: dc: Yarn over, insert hook into next stitch, and pull up a loop. Yarn over and bring through two loops on hook. Yarn over again and bring through remaining two loops on hook.

Ch the desired number of stitches +2.

Row 1: Dc in 4th ch from hook and in each ch to end.

Important Note: The 3 chain stitches at the beginning of this row count as the turning chain which is worked at the beginning of every dc row. Remember that this turning chain counts as the first dc stitch of the row!

Row 2: Ch 3 in 2nd dc and in each dc to end.

Repeat Row 2 until work is desired length.

Triple (Treble) Crochet (tr)

Worked over any number of stitches.

Triple crochet is the tallest of the basic stitches. Incredibly quick, it leaves large gaps between the stitches.

Abbreviation: tr: Yarn over twice, insert hook into next stitch, and bring up a loop. Yarn over and bring through two loops on hook. Yarn over again and bring through two more loops. Yarn over and bring through two remaining loops on hook.

Ch the desired number of stitches, +3.

Row 1: Tr in 5th ch from hook and in each ch to end.

Important Note: The 4 chain stitches at the beginning of this row count as the turning chain which is worked at the beginning of every tr row. Remember that this turning chain counts as the first tr stitch of the row!

Row 2: Ch 4, tr in 2nd tr and in each tr to end.

Repeat Row 2 until work is desired length.

Single Crochet Rib

Worked over any number of stitches.

As seen in the Weekend Vest in chapter 7, rib stitches are frequently worked in a strip and then turned sideways to mimic a knit rib stitch, as on sweater hems and cuffs.

Abbreviation: bl: Back loops. Instead of inserting hook under both loops of stitch, insert hook only through the loop farthest from you on the back side of the fabric. Work stitch into this loop only.

Ch the desired number of stitches, +1

Row 1: Sc in 2nd ch from hook and in each ch to end.

Row 2: Ch 1, sc in bl of 1st sc and in bl of each sc to end.

Repeat Row 2 until work is desired length.

Single Seed Stitch

Worked over a multiple of **2** stitches plus **1** stitch.

Try a variation on this single crochet stitch by sub-stituting hdc or dc for each sc. Just remember to work additional turning chains to make up the additional height.

Abbreviation: Ch1-sp: Chain 1-space. This is the space formed beneath the ch1 which was worked on the previous row.

Ch a multiple of 2 stitches plus 2 (desired number of stitches + 1).

Row 1: Sc in 2nd ch from hook, [skip next ch, ch 1, sc in next ch] across.

Row 2: Ch 1, sc in 1st sc, sc in next ch1-sp, [ch 1, sc in next ch1-sp] to last ch1-sp, sc in last sc.

Row 3: Ch 1, sc in 1st sc, [ch1, sc in next ch1-sp] to last ch1-sp, ch1, sc in last sc.

Repeat rows 2 and 3 until work is desired length.

Double Mesh Stitch

Worked over a multiple of **2** stitches plus **1** stitch. This stitch can also be worked with sc, hdc, or tr instead of dc. You'll just need to alter your turning chains.

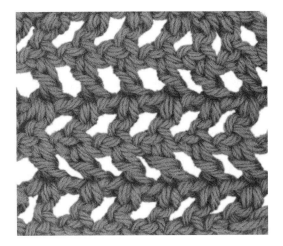

Ch a multiple of 2 stitches plus 4 (desired number of stitches + 3).

Row 1: Dc in 6th ch from hook, [skip next ch, ch 1, dc in next ch] across.

Row 2: Ch 4, skip 1st dc, dc in next dc, [skip next ch-sp, ch 1, dc in next dc] to end. Important: When working last dc of each row, be sure to skip 1 ch1-sp; work into the 3rd ch of the turning chain, not the 4th! (The first time you work Row 2, you will work into the 4th ch of the "turning chain," not the 5th.)

Repeat Row 2 until work is desired length.

Bud Stitch in HDC

Worked over a multiple of **3** stitches plus **2** stitches.

Again, switching to a taller stitch here will give a more lacy appearance.

Ch a multiple of 3 stitches plus 4 stitches (desired number of sts + 2).

Row 1: (Hdc, ch 1, hdc) in 3rd ch from hook, ch 1, hdc in same ch, [skip 2 ch, (hdc, ch 1, hdc) in next ch] to end.

Row 2: Ch 2, skip 1st hdc and ch, (hdc, ch 1, hdc) in next hdc, [skip next hdc and ch, (hdc, ch 1, hdc) in next hdc] to end. Repeat Row 2 until work is desired length.

Basic DC Ripple

Worked over a multiple of **9** stitches plus **1** stitch. Endless variations of ripples are possible with crochet. Here is one of the simplest. For another example, see the Granny's Been In The Bourbon Again throw in Chapter 9.

Ch a multiple of 9 stitches plus 3 (desired number of sts + 2)

Row 1: Dc in 3rd ch from hook, [dc in next 3 ch, skip 2 ch, dc in next 3 ch, 3 dc in next ch] to last 9 ch, dc in next 3 ch, skip 2 ch, dc in next 3 ch, 2 dc in final ch.

Row 2: Ch 3, dc in 1st dc, [dc in next 3 dc, skip 2 dc, dc in next 3 dc, 3 dc in next dc] to last 9 sts, dc in next 3 dc, skip 2 dc, dc in next 3 dc, 2 dc in turning ch of previous row.

Repeat Row 2 until work is desired length.

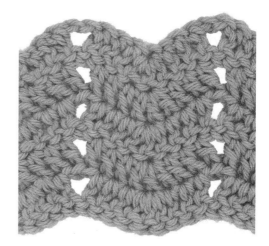

Around-the-post Rib

Worked over a multiple of **1** stitch.

Any stitch can be worked around the *post* of a stitch in the previous row, but double crochet is one of the most popular stitches to work in this way, because of its length. In this stitch pattern, Front Post Double Crochets are used. It's also possible to work a Back Post Double Crochet (BPdc) by inserting the hook from the back to the front, then around the post to the back of the work, on the previous row. See Jennifer Hansen's cool pageboy cap in chapter 8 for a stunning example.

Abbreviations: FPdc: (Front Post Double Crochet): Yarn over, insert hook into row below from front to back, then around the post of the next dc in the previous row, to the front of the work. Pull up a loop and continue to work dc as normal.

Important Note: Unlike other stitch patterns based on double crochet, the turning chain is NOT counted as a stitch when working this stitch pattern. Do not work into the turning chain of the previous row when ending a row of this stitch pattern.

Ch any number of sts (desired number of sts + 3).
Row 1: Dc in 3rd ch from hook and into each ch to end.
Row 2: Turn work. Ch 2 FPdc around 1st dc and around each dc to end.
Repeat Row 2 until work is desired length.

Round Peg in a Square Hole

Sometimes you can fit a round peg in a square hole. This circular motif is proof! Starting with a circle and ending with a square makes these guys easy to sew together for a larger project.
Abbreviation: sc: Insert hook into stitch and pull up a loop. Yarn over and bring through both loops.

Ch 6, sl st in 1st ch to form a ring.
Rnd 1: Ch 1, 13 sc in center of ring, sl st in 1st sc to join. 12 sts.
Rnd 2: Ch 4 (counts as 1 dc and 1 ch1-space), skip the 1st sc, dc in next sc, [ch 1, dc in next sc] to last sc, ch 1, sl st into 3rd ch of initial ch-4 to join. 26 sts.
Rnd 3: Ch 1, sc in 1st ch, sc in 1st ch-sp, [sc in next dc, 2 sc in next ch-sp, sc in next dc, sc in next ch-sp] 5 times, to end, sl st t in 1st sc to join. 32 sts.
Rnd 4: Ch 7 (counts as 1tr and 3ch), tr in first sc, [ch 4, skip 3 sc, dc in next sc, ch 4, skip 3 sc, (tr, ch 3, tr) in next sc] 3 times, ch 4, skip 3 sc, dc in next sc, ch 4, sl st to 4th of initial ch-7 to join. 56 sts.
Rnd 5: Ch 3 (counts as dc), (2 dc, ch 3, 3 dc) in first ch3-sp, * [ch 1, 4 dc in next ch4-sp] twice, ch 1(3 dc, ch 3, 3dc) in next corner ch-sp **; repeat from * to ** twice more, [ch 1, 4 dc in next ch-sp] twice, ch 1 sl st to last ch of initial ch-3 to join. Break yarn, draw tail through last st, and pull tight.

Lacy Flower

Circular shapes are fun for experimenting. For example, you can easily adapt this flower shape by substituting taller stitches for the single crochet and half double crochet or by changing the size of the petals.

Ch 6, sl st to join.

Rnd 1: Ch 2 (counts as 1 hdc), work 11 hdc into center of ring, sl st in 2nd ch of initial ch-2 to join. 12 sts.

Rnd 2: Ch 1, sc in 1st ch, [ch 5, skip 1 hdc, sc in next hdc] 54 times, ch 5, sl st in initial sc to join. —6 ch5-sp.

Rnd 3: Ch 1, 6 sc in each ch5-sp to end, sl st in 1st sc to join. 36 sc.

Rnd 4: Ch 2, [hdc into the back loops of next 6 sc, ch 3] 6 times, sl st in 1st hdc. Break yarn, draw through last st and pull tight.

What's Next?

These basic stitch patterns give a good overview of the possibilities, but it is by no means a comprehensive guide. Do a Web search for "free crochet stitch pattern," and you'll find a vast collection of stitches, most designed by crocheters like yourself! Or, pick up one of the many stitch libraries. Some are formatted like calendars and feature a different crochet stitch every day of the year. Others are more like reference books, with patterns indexed and cross-referenced, and can provide a solid foundation for design work of your own.

Have no fear! You don't need to know every possible stitch combination to work a pattern. Most crochet patterns publish any stitch combination instructions right in the same volume. Dig in . . . you'll be just fine!

Not Your Granny's Squares

The basic Granny Square pattern shown in chapter 1 is just the beginning to modular crochet. Working circularly lets you create lovely and inspired designs not constrained by side-to-side rows. By crocheting in rounds, you can make circles, squares, triangles, flowers, and more.

Motifs are fun to make and even more fun to design for yourself. Start with a simple ring by chaining 3 or 4 and joining with a slip stitch. Then, see where the hook takes you! Using only chain, single crochet, double crochet, and treble crochet, you can develop intricate and intriguing designs.

For square motifs, a little blocking can help you create those hospital corners. Just dampen the square and using four rust-proof pins, pin into shape over a towel. A small bulletin board works well for a few squares. For many, consider using the carpet in a rarely used room, or a mattress. For more blocking tips, see page 24. When sewing multiple square motifs together, the process of seaming helps straighten out your edges so that blocking isn't always necessary.

Chapter Three

♦◆♦

All about Yarn

If life is not worth living without chocolate, crochet is not worth doing without the spectacular yarns available in today's shops. Yarns can be found in all colors, thicknesses, and textures. You can buy glitter yarn, fake (and real) fur yarn, nubbly yarn, or smooth yarn. You can buy yarn barely thicker than a bit of sewing thread, or yarn so thick you need broomstick-sized hooks to work with.

Yarns can be made of sheep wool, cotton thread, acrylic, or nearly any fiber under the sun. They can be dyed with natural plant matter, such as indigo, or chemical-dyed in glow-in-the-dark colors.

Walk into your friendly neighborhood yarn store, or take a few moments to yarn shop online and you'll be amazed at what you find.

A Yarn for All Seasons

From traditional yarns your mother would recognize to new and spectacular novelties, today's crocheters have an amazing variety from which to choose. Whatever your style, you're likely to find a yarn that's perfect for whatever project you choose.

Traditional Yarns

Traditional yarns are smooth and even and most closely resemble the stuff your mother (and her mother, and her grandmother) worked with. They can be spun of any type of fiber and dyed any color. They can be made of a single thread or of several threads wound together. This is called the *ply* of the yarn. While any number of plies are possible, some of the most common are single ply, and 2, 3, and 4 ply.

Traditional yarns are ideal for any type of crochet in which your stitch work is important. After all, why spend all those hours on those complicated crossovers if your work is obscured by a furry yarn?

- **Single Ply:** Single-ply yarn is soft and tends to show wear by forming balls on the surface (called *pills*), but it can be lighter in weight than its equivalent in a plied yarn. In general, the higher the ply, the tougher the yarn is and the more resilient it is to pilling.

- **Multiple Ply:** Multiple-plied yarns are made of single-ply strands twisted together. These individual strands can be identical in color and thickness or can be unique colors for a tweedy look. The number of plies typically varies between 2 and 8, although it's possible to ply as many individual strands as you'd like.

- **Cabled Yarn:** When two or more strands of 2-ply yarn are twisted together, it's called a cabled yarn. Cabled yarns are extremely strong and resistant to shedding or pilling. Because of their crisp spin, they are ideal for highlighting the individual stitch definition.

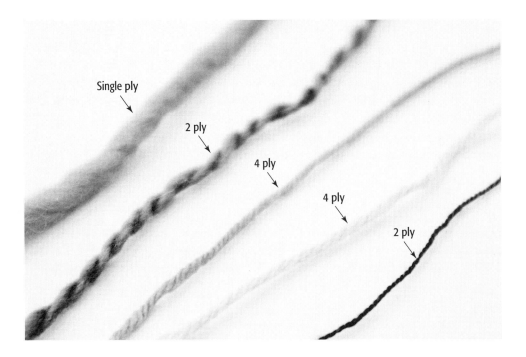

Novelty Yarns

Novelty yarns started appearing on the market in the 1960s. Sometimes plush and furry like chenille, sometimes hairy like fun fur, and sometimes sparkly like the numerous glitter yarns on the market, novelty yarns provide an added bit of texture or interest to even the plainest stitches.

Novelty yarns today can be found in just about every color, texture, or fiber type and can be used for any type of pattern. But since the texture can change the look of your crochet, it's important to think about how the yarn will work with your chosen pattern.

Although some patterns use novelty yarns for the main part of a garment or accessory, it's more common to see them added as trim or detail pieces. However, for simple scarves, novelty yarns are ideal.

- **Bouclé:** These yarns are spun with little loops of fiber that stick out from the surface. When crocheted or knit, they become a plush, terry-cloth-like texture.
- **Fur:** Usually made with nylon or acrylic, these furry yarns come in a rainbow of colors and textures.
- **Glitter:** Glitter or sequins can be added to even the plainest of yarns to create drama. Many glitter yarns are extremely thin and should be crocheted with a thicker yarn.
- **Thick and Thin:** Pure wool can be spun into a single-ply strand that varies in thickness from super bulky to super fine. Called "Thick and Thin" yarn, this knits or crochets into a nubbly texture.

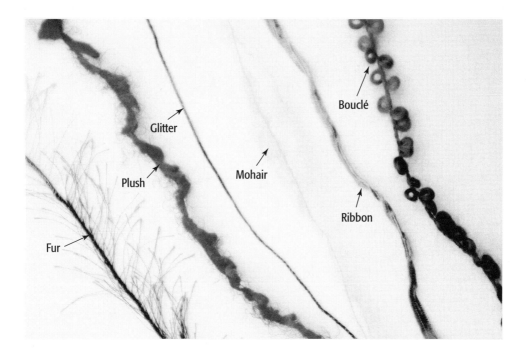

- **Bubble or Pompom:** These yarns feature small poofs attached to a thin thread.
- **Plush:** Like fur yarn, but with shorter and more poofy fibers, plush yarns are used to mimic a fleece-like texture. Typically, these yarns are made from nylon or microfiber.
- **Railroad:** As the name implies, railroad yarn mimics railway tracks. Two thin threads are separated at even intervals by a thicker horizontal bar, like a railway tie. Like most novelty yarns, it's unusual to see these made from nonsynthetic materials.
- **Ribbon:** Like Railroad yarn, ribbon yarns are essentially flat strips of fiber. Usually made from rayon or silk, these yarns twist while you crochet, creating a bumpy fabric.
- **Mohair:** Mohair and acrylic lookalike yarns can be identified by the halo of fuzz around a solid center.

Hanks, Balls, and Skeins, oh my!

In cartoons, yarn always comes in perfect huge balls that kittens love to chase. In reality, yarn can come in many forms.

Many yarn brands are sold in little cake or donut-shaped balls in 50g sizes. These balls, when the labels are removed, are easy to crochet from. Simply pull out the yarn end from the center and keep pulling; the ball will empty from the center out and will sit nicely in your bag or on the table while you work.

Balls

Pull-skeins

Hanks/skeins

A Tangled Mess: How to Wind a Ball of Yarn

It happens to everyone at the beginning. That lovely bit of yarn that came all twisted in a nice perfect hank becomes quickly tangled when you begin to crochet. Avoid this newbie trap by winding the yarn into a ball before you begin!

To wind a perfect ball of yarn from a skein, do the following:

1. Remove the label. Untwist the skein until you have a ring of yarn. The yarn may be tied at one or two places. If so, carefully untie these knots without disturbing the yarn ring.

2. Ideally, get a friend or willing relative to help at this point. He or she should hold the ring open with two hands. If you're on your own, put the ring over the back of an armless chair, or around two chairs if the skein is quite large. (If really desperate, use your knees.)

3. Find one end of the yarn and begin to wind around three of your fingers. After winding a few yards, you can pull this off your fingers and wind in the opposite direction, cinching the small ring you've made in the middle. Then just keep winding at different angles every few yards to create a solid ball. Don't wind the ball tightly or you'll stretch out your yarn, which can wreak havoc on the size and elasticity of your crocheting. You're going for a ball with a comfortable squoosh, not a baseball.

Not every skein is perfect; you may have to stop from time to time to untangle the yarn before winding it. It's also possible to buy a *swift;* a wood or metal contraption that holds the skein open and allows it to rotate for easier winding. Mechanical ball winders create perfect center-pull balls, but they can be pricey. You'll probably want to crochet a few things before you invest in this equipment.

Pull-skeins are similar to balls but shaped more like a log—long rather than round. As with balls, you can crochet directly from a pull-skein; the yarn pulls from the center. Pull-skeins are typically found in standard sizes of 50g and 100g. Less expensive yarns (the type your grandma used to make ripple afghans back in the '70s) come in larger sizes and are often measured in ounces rather than grams. You can find these beasts up to one-pounder sizes.

For both balls and pull-skeins, although the yarn ideally is supposed to come out neatly from the center, in many cases you'll run into some tangles (this is particularly an issue with rougher yarns). Have patience—these are seldom actual knots. Using your fingers to gently jostle and loosen the fibers will help straighten out the yarn.

Not to be confused with pull-skeins, the general terms *hank* and *skein* refer to the same packaging: a large ring of yarn that's been twisted on itself. It's not uncommon, especially when buying fine yarns, or yarns from independent mills, to get yarn in skeins. With skeins, the producer has wound the yarn into a large ring, approximately 24 inches from side to side, and tied it at several points. The skein is then folded in half, or twisted and wound into itself, and secured with a label. To use a skein of yarn, you need to untwist it and wind a ball from the yarn ring. There are special instruments for this task—swifts to hold the ring and ball winders with cranks that make the ball of yarn—but draping the ring over your knees and using your hands to make a ball also works. These skeins are usually found in standard sizes; 50g, 100g, and 250g are common.

One important fact to note: different regions and stores label yarn differently. Whether it comes in a round ball, a log, or a twisted oblong, and whatever it's called, it's all just yarn.

Animal, Vegetable, or Mineral?

When your mother (or her mother) learned to crochet, the fiber choices were fairly limited. The choice, for the majority of folks, was between 100 percent acrylic, 100 percent wool, or 100 percent cotton. And in generations before, most crochet projects were geared to super-fine, super-thin cotton thread and teeny tiny hooks.

Thanks largely to the recent renaissance of yarn crafts, today's variety is unparalleled. From novelty fur yarns to the traditional classics, updated in luxury fibers like cashmere and silk . . . if you can dream it, you can crochet it!

The source material of the yarn, whether it's cotton, wool, nylon, or silk, is called the *fiber content*. Every ball of yarn is labeled to indicate the fiber content as well as the percentage of each content type. One of my favorite yarns is 70 percent alpaca and 30 percent silk.

While it's not essential to understand the specifics of every fiber type, understanding some general characteristics can really help when choosing a yarn for a specific crochet project. For example, a hat crocheted in a stiff cotton will have a completely different character from the same hat crocheted in buttery-soft alpaca.

Everyone Needs Protein

Protein-based fibers—those derived from animal hair, fur, or insect cocoons—are perhaps the most common. These fibers greatly vary in characteristics, but share certain qualities. They are absorbent, naturally elastic, and crease resistant. Can you remember the last time you had to iron your favorite wool sweater? This elasticity is well-suited to garments where fit is a priority; no one wants socks that slip down or a sweater that bags with wear.

Many protein fibers will also shrink and matte with agitation and hot water. This process, called *felting* or *fulling*, can be accidental; just think of the time you (or your partner) shrunk

The Magic Properties of Felt

Since Mongolia's nomadic families move several times a year to follow their herds, their houses must be light, portable, and easy to assemble. Although a sturdy brick construction would be handy for the harsh Mongolian climate, it's out of the question.

Instead, the families live in round tent-like structures called *gers*. For insulation, the walls of the ger are lined with sheep and goat fleece that has been felted into inch-thick blankets. In addition to keeping the tent warm in the sub-zero winter temperatures, the felt also keeps the interior cool during the heat of summer.

your favorite wool sweater in the washing machine. It can also be purposeful; felting creates a dense, warm, water-repellent fabric. Many wools are actually treated with chemicals to prevent this shrinking. Called *superwash* wool, items made from the treated wool can be safely washed in the machine without worrying about shrinkage. (Keep in mind, though, that if you're ever felting intentionally, you need to steer clear of superwash wool!)

Protein fibers are typically very lightweight due to the hollow core that provides similar insulation as your coffee thermos. The space in the center of the fiber traps in the air and keeps it warm or cool, depending on the climate. This combination of warmth and lightness makes protein fibers ideal for all thickness of yarn. Even a superbulky merino sweater, although warm, will be relatively lightweight, dry, and easy to wear.

Wool

Wool is the most common of the protein fibers. In many parts of North America, the words *wool* and *yarn* are actually interchangeable. Wool is the final product of sheep fleece, shorn from the adult sheep, typically once a year. Hundreds of breeds of sheep can be found around the world, with each breed possessing different lengths and colors of fleece. Merino is one of the softest and finest breeds of sheep, providing one of the softest types of wool yarn. Shetland is another popular sheep breed. Originally hailing from the Shetland Islands off the coast of Britain, Shetland wool is coarser and tougher than merino; ideal for hardy outerwear. As the most common of the animal proteins, wool can be quite inexpensive, especially when locally produced.

Cashmere

Cashmere comes from a special breed of goats that originally hailed from Central Asia. Mongolia and the Inner Mongolia region of China are today the leaders in cashmere production, and are known for some of the world's finest cashmere. Cashmere, as we know it, is the soft and plush undercoat that the goats grow for warmth during the harsh winter months. As the weather grows warmer in the spring, the undercoats are plucked or shed. In the past decade, the term "Pashmina" has been occasionally used to describe a type of yarn. Pashmina isn't a type of fiber. Instead, it's a derivative of the Persian word "pashm," which means the softest wool. So, it's most often used to describe either pure cashmere or a wool and cashmere blend. In other words, don't go looking for a Pashmina animal.

Mohair

Mohair also comes from goat hair. Kid mohair is typically the softest, shorn from goats younger than 18 months. Adult mohair can vary from fine and lustrous to coarse and hairy. Most commercial mohair is blended with wool to provide the halo and shine of mohair combined with the thickness and elasticity of wool. Alternatively, pure mohair is often spun quite thin for fine lace knitting and crochet work.

But Wool Is So Itchy!

The word "wool" may conjure up painful and itchy memories of your least-favorite childhood sweaters. However, not all wool itches. While a fair percentage of folks are indeed allergic to any animal fiber–including wool–many types of wool are non-itch to the majority of the population. Take a look in your local yarn shop; you may be surprised! Look for *merino* or *extra-fine merino* on the yarn label. If you're not sure whether or not the final piece will itch, try rubbing the yarn against your throat. On most people, this is the most sensitive part of your skin, and will be the most prone to irritation from a scarf or sweater collar.

Why are some fibers itchy while others are not? Among many other factors, the length of the original protein fiber has something to do with the fiber's itchiness quotient. The longer fibers are less itchy, because they have fewer ends that, when spun, stick out and agitate. The shorter fiber breeds, such as Shetland, are often more itchy because they have more ends that refuse to lie flat and, hence, will irritate sensitive skin. The softness of the wool also depends on many factors in addition to heritage, but–in general–look for merino or corriedale for softness. Blends are also a great way to soften a tough wool. Wools with some silk, angora, tencel, or cashmere will have the softest feel.

In addition, many commercially-produced wool garments are made using wool that has been treated with harsh chemicals, which can cause the wool to irritate the wearer. Wool used for hand-knitting and crochet yarn doesn't usually receive the same sort of treatment, leaving it free of these irritants.

Angora

Angora, not surprisingly, is shorn or plucked from Angora rabbits. The long fur is quite soft and silky, and tends to shed unless spun with a more resilient fiber like silk, wool, or nylon. Angora is quite warm and can make lovely and delicate mittens and scarves and other luxury goods. Because of its shedding tendencies, angora will pill quickly and isn't well suited to hard wear. One important note: avoid using angora for baby items! Although it looks cute, bits of the fine fur can easily be inhaled by babies. Also, angora is much warmer than wool, and may overheat babies.

Silk

Many folks are surprised to learn that silk comes from moth cocoons. Several processes are used to harvest these fibers. One of the most common is by boiling the cocoons to kill the developing moth, though some silk is harvested after the moth has emerged from the cocoon. Silk, on its own, is an incredibly versatile but inelastic fiber. For this reason, many yarn companies blend it with a more stretchy fiber such as wool, alpaca, or even elastic nylon.

And Everything Else

Scores of other, more exotic protein fibers are available, from alpaca to llama to musk ox and camel. It's even possible to spin your own pet's fur into an exotic blend.

Most protein fibers are shorn or plucked in humane ways, without harm to the animal. However, if you make animal rights a priority, read your labels carefully: It's now possible to find actual fur pelts that have been spun into luxury yarn.

Cellulose Fibers

Either natural or synthetic, fibers from plant origin are sometimes called *cellulose*. These plant-based yarns are hollow and absorb water readily, making them cool to the touch and pleasant for warm-weather wear. High-tech clothing stores describe this sweat-reducing property as *moisture-wicking*, which means that some fabrics made of these fibers will draw moisture (i.e. sweat) away from the skin of the wearer. Like protein fibers, they can be spun into many textures and thicknesses.

Cotton

Cotton originated in India but soon spread to every warm climate. Egypt is especially famous for its soft and shiny cottons. Because the fibers are very short, they must be tightly spun to hold together. However, these fine threads are crisp and bright, and will showcase the detail of

---

I'll Pack-a My Alpaca

In the 1980s, the get-rich scheme *du jour* was to begin an alpaca farm. These intelligent and sweet animals were seen as the ticket to big money in the textiles trade in North America. Today, although several alpaca companies are based in the United States, most alpacas are raised and cared for in Peru and other South American countries.

Why is alpaca worth checking out? Alpaca is often softer than the finest merino, and at a considerably lower price point. Still considered an exotic fiber, even 100 percent alpaca can be inexpensive enough to consider for just about any project. Even better, buttery-soft pure alpaca is extremely warm. My thin fingerless mittens, made of 100 percent alpaca, are actually warmer and softer than the bulky wool ones I purchased one desperate spring in Canada. Any time I travel, I make sure to tuck them into a corner of my bag, just in case.

Just be aware—if using alpaca in a project that calls for wool—that alpaca makes a more drapey fabric than wool does. Many fiber artists will say that alpaca has a poorer stitch "memory" than wool. In laygirls' terms, this means that while a wool sweater will stay in relatively the same shape and size over the years, one crocheted from alpaca will tend to droop and stretch. This can be a lovely effect in a softly-flowing cardigan but isn't what you're looking for in a structured jacket.

every stitch. Crochet was traditionally a cotton art. Think of the fine lace doilies and table-cloths that many people associate with crochet; these were done in 100 percent cotton to show the artisanship of the craftswoman.

Like yarns made of protein fibers, cotton yarns comes in all constructions. You're likely to see both softly-spun 2-ply yarns and tightly twisted, shiny yarns labeled as *mercerized*. For the fiber geeks out there, *mercerization* is a finishing process applied to the fiber that results in a smoother, shinier, and stronger yarn.

Cotton is rarely itchy, and is used frequently for baby goods. However, cotton can be quite heavy and has little "memory"; for crochet, it's best suited for tiny hooks and fine gauge work.

Note: Some people think that they need greater yardage of cotton yarn than they would if they used wool yarn because cotton isn't as stretchy as wool. Whatever your fiber choice, it will not have any effect on yardage. You can substitute wool or cotton for each other and—as long as you're knitting or crocheting at an identical gauge—use the same amount of yarn.

Linen

Produced from flax plants, linen is a smooth and crisp yarn that becomes shinier and softer with wear. Pure linen is rarely found in commercially produced yarns. Rather, it's often blended with other cellulose fibers like cotton or rayon, to provide a softer yarn. Unlike linen in cloth form, spun linen yarn tends to withstand wrinkling when knit or crocheted.

New Age Fibers

In the past few years, it's been possible to find yarns made from hemp, corn, bamboo, banana, or even soy! South West Trading Company produces a broad range of soy-based yarns that are nearly indistinguishable from cotton or fine silk. These fibers can take on many qualities, but should be treated as other cellulose fibers.

Synthetic Cellulose Fibers

Plant matter, frequently in the form of wood chips, can be regenerated into fibers such as vis-cose, rayon, or tencel. These fibers are usually blended with natural cellulose or protein fibers for commercial yarn. When blended with cotton or linen, the synthetics provide a lighter and softer feel than pure cotton or linen. Because these fibers have a natural origin, they are still considered natural fibers, as opposed to man-made.

Synthetic Fibers

Long the staple of superstore craft aisles, 100 percent synthetic yarn has received a bad reputation over the years. Although synthetics are usually inexpensive, some crocheters feel that synthetics feel plastic and artificial. Like the Twinkie, which has a reputation for being indestructible, synthetic yarns are tough to damage. They stand up to abrasion and abuse and are typically machine wash- and dry-able.

Acrylic

These fibers are a spun form of vinyl and are the most common of the synthetic blends. While 100 percent acrylic yarn used to be more prevalent, today you're more likely to find acrylic blended with superwash wool or cotton. In a good blend, the strength of the acrylic will nicely complement the soft elasticity of the wool. Acrylic yarns also provide a good and inexpensive substitute for those who are allergic to animal protein fibers.

Nylon and Polyester

These synthetics are used predominately in novelty yarns to provide glitter or texture. A bit of nylon is typically added to yarns that need strength, such as yarns intended for socks.

Microfiber and Microfiber Blends

Microfiber isn't so much a unique type of fiber as a generic term that describes a super-fine and super-soft synthetic material. While you can find 100 percent microfiber yarns, the latest thing on the yarn market are natural fibers blended with microfiber. Meant to blend seamlessly with the natural content, the microfiber enhances the softness and lightness of the wool or cotton. Some of the best microfiber blends are priced as true luxury yarns.

How to Choose?

In most cases, your pattern will give specific yarn requirements, including fiber content. As you've seen, the choice of fiber can dramatically impact the finished fabric. Not all yarns are interchangeable.

However, don't be afraid to experiment! You'll soon be able to envision how a yarn will look and feel when crocheted. Do you think that plain hat would look spectacular with a fake-fur trim? Try it! Is your sister allergic to wool? Try substituting a cotton/microfiber blend in a similar weight. Later in this chapter, I talk about some hints for more effective yarn substitution.

A Weight Problem

Don't be surprised if you hear one crocheter ask another, "What weight yarn are you using?" She'll likely answer in terms such as *worsted, bulky,* or *fingering,* rather than in ounces, grams, or pounds. While it's true that yarn is sold in balls or skeins that weigh 50g, 2oz, or some other standard amount, the term *weight* generally refers to the thickness of the yarn.

The yarn world has developed a few systems of labels for yarn weight. Most commonly, these are based on the gauge or tension of the yarn.

Tense? Who, me?

The number of stitches per inch is called your *gauge*, or alternatively, *tension*. Every crocheter will have a different gauge or tension, depending on the way she holds her yarn or the method he uses for tightening each stitch. For example, if you and I were given the same yarn and the same hook, I may end up with 4 single crochet stitches per inch. With the same materials, you may have 4 and a half.

As much as I hate to admit it, crochet and math go hand in hand, especially when discussing gauge. A half a stitch per inch may not seem like a lot, but if you're crocheting a scarf that's 28 single crochet stitches wide, my scarf will be 7 inches wide and yours will be just over 6.

For the math geeks out there, this is determined by a simple formula:

$$\text{Final size} = (\text{number of stitches}) / (\text{gauge in stitches per inch})$$

In this case:

$$7 = 28/4$$

For a scarf, 1 inch isn't a huge deal. But if you're making a time-intensive fitted sweater and are a half stitch off in gauge, your sweater will not fit the way you'd hoped. If I'm working on a sweater that has 160 stitches around, at my gauge of 4 sts per inch, I'll end up with a 40 inch circumference. With your 4.5 stitches per inch, yours will be less than 36 inches around.

Although gauge can and should be measured prior to starting a new project, the general concept of gauge is fairly straightforward. The thicker the yarn, the larger the hook, the larger your stitches will be, and you'll have fewer stitches per inch.

Swatch It!

Find some yarn and a hook. If you don't have a pattern in mind, check the yarn's label to see the recommended hook size. This is a good place to start.

To create a gauge swatch, begin by chaining a few stitches more than the label or pattern's recommended gauge. For example, if the pattern specifies a gauge of 20 single crochets (sc) to 4 inches on a US G/4.5mm hook, chain 22 or 23. (Refer back to chapter 1 for information on how to chain.)

♦ Row 1: Beginning in the second ch from hook, sc across to the end of the row. Ch 1, turn.

♦ Repeat row 1 until the gauge swatch is 4 inches long. Cut yarn and pull it through the last loop to tie it off.

♦ Next block the swatch. This is an important step. Your tension can change a surprising amount after blocking, and it's definitely better to know this before you begin your project, than after you've applied the final touches, and realize that your sweater is suddenly too large! Check out the blocking instructions in Chapter 1, and block your swatch as you would block your garment.

♦ Lay your blocked swatch on a table or other flat surface (not your lap!). Take a hard ruler and lay it across the swatch. Be sure to place the ruler even and parallel to the initial chain edge. Now, count how many single crochets are in 4 inches. If you have the 20 specified in the pattern, bonus! You're right on gauge! If you have more than 20, you'll need to increase your hook size to make larger stitches and get closer to that ideal 20. If you have fewer than 20, you'll need to select a smaller hook size to tighten up your stitches.

If you need to change hook size, be sure to repeat the swatching process until you *get gauge*. This will ensure the finished product turns out the correct size and texture.

So, What Weight Is it?

Unfortunately for crocheters, the yarn world is rather knit-centric, and has developed standard weight terms based on the gauge or tension of the yarn when knitted in stockinette stitch. Even if you never plan on holding a pair of knitting needles, it's helpful to understand these terms. Although crochet patterns give the gauge over the crochet stitch specified, most commercially-produced yarn labels will only include the gauge in these knitted terms.

- **Super fine (fingering or lace):** This weight of yarn typically knits anywhere from 7 to 8 stitches per inch and crochets from 6 to 8 stitches per inch. It's most commonly used for teensy tiny work like lace, socks, or baby items. In crochet, fingering or lace-weight cotton has been traditionally used for open-work lace.
- **Fine (sport or baby):** In knitting, you'll see a gauge of 6 to 6.5 stitches per inch, and 4 to 5 in crochet. Sport-weight yarn is still considered fine gauge, and is often used for garments with multiple colors, as well as for baby items.
- **Light (double knitting [DK]):** At one point in time, DK weight yarn was the most common. Today, it offers a good balance between speed and a wearable weight of fabric. Light weight fabrics provide a good drape that flatters most body types. (You'll read more about drape in chapter 5.) With knitting, the gauge is 5.5 to 6 stitches per inch. With crochet, you'll see 3 to 4 stitches.
- **Medium (worsted or Aran):** Worsted and Aran weight yarns are perhaps the most popular today. Knit with a gauge of 4.5 to 5 stitches per inch or crocheted to 2.5 to 3.5 stitches per inch, these yarns are quick to use without offering excess bulk.
- **Bulky (chunky):** Although not new, the bulkier gauges are becoming increasingly popular. New crafters love the concept of being able to create a garment in a few evenings, and bulky yarns provide this instant gratification. But, there is a trade-off. Chunky yarns can be quite heavy and warm, making them uncomfortable for indoor-wear. These yarns are knit with a gauge of 3 to 4 stitches per inch or crocheted with 2 to 3 stitches per inch. Check out the "Weekend Vest" in chapter 7 for one example.
- **Super bulky (bulky or roving):** These intense yarns are often thicker than an adult's finger and should be knit or crocheted with implements resembling broomsticks. A typical knit gauge is 1.5 to 2 stitches per inch. With crochet, you'll see 1 to 2 stitches per inch.

Dame Fashion Says "Dye It!"

Of course, yarn and color go hand in hand. Rarely does a crocheter decide she wants to make a chunky ski cap without first thinking color. Red! Green! Purple! Everything's an option.

Why Dye Lots Matter

Most commercial yarn is batch-dyed a single color that's consistent through the ball or skein. When crocheted, this will produce a solid-colored fabric without dye variations. Even when switching balls, the color will be identical. However, there's one catch. You must make sure each ball is from the same batch, or *dye lot*.

Since commercial yarn is dyed in batches, different batches may have subtle variations in color. The companies will label the yarn with a dye lot code or number so you can easily tell which yarn has been dyed at the same time. Many times the differences, if any, will be so subtle only your anal-retentive neighbor would be able to tell. But why take the risk of inadvertent stripes? When choosing yarn, try to make sure the dye lots match by comparing the numbers on the labels. Most importantly, buy enough yarn ahead of time! When in doubt, err on the side of caution and grab an extra ball or two. Even if you don't need it for your project, chances are you'll be able to do something with it. In any case, it's far better than being one ball short of a full sweater.

Some yarn claims to have no dye lot. In most cases these yarns are still batch-dyed, but under such strict controls that little color variation is possible. Of course, one obvious example is yarn that has never been dyed, such as natural wool. But, don't think you can buy one ball now and another a year later and be guaranteed the same results. Just as with any yarn, buy enough for your entire project at the same time. With any dyed yarn, some variation is possible. With undyed yarn, different batches may vary in "natural" color just enough to be obvious.

It's a Wonderful, Colorful World

Single colors are great, but sometimes a gal needs more color. Luckily, yarns are available in variegated or hand-painted colors. Yarns can even be found that produce stripes or faux Fair-Isle patterns with even the simplest of stitches.

Hand-painting and Hand-dyeng

One of the latest trends in yarn are *hand-painted* colors. A master dyer will line the skeins of yarn on a table, squeezing the dye into the yarn in various colors. Sometimes this is done by gloved hands, other times it's performed with a plastic baster or syringe. After the dye sets, the skeins are steamed for 45 minutes to an hour to set the color. The skeins can then be rinsed, either by hand or in the washing machine, to remove any excess dye.

Even single-colored yarns are less than solid when dyed with this technique. Because the dye is hand worked, subtle variations in color will appear on the yarn. For example, a mostly denim blue yarn may vary in intensity from pale to deep blue. Such hand-painted *solids* can provide spectacular depth to even the simplest stitch work.

Because of the variation introduced by human dyeing techniques, dye lots are never more important than with hand painted yarns. Even so, these multi-color beauties will create a spotted or variegated pattern that can change from skein to skein. If working a large project, you should blend the dye pattern by working from one skein for two rows, and another skein for the next two rows, for the length of the project.

For some examples of hand-dyed yarns at work, see the Chunky Monkey Scarf in chapter 7, Granny's Been in the Bourbon Again Throw in chapter 9, and the Ramblin' Rosie Cardie in chapter 8.

Self-Patterning Yarns

Some yarns are commercially dyed to produce a specific pattern when knit. Mostly prevalent in fine weight yarns for sock knitting, some of the more spectacular self-patterning yarns create complex designs that mimic the finest Scandinavian fair-isle patterns. While designed for knit fabrics, these yarns can look equally interesting while crocheted—although the pattern created will be different from the pattern created when knit.

Perhaps more versatile are the yarns that are dyed to produce broad stripes of color when knit or crocheted. The first major yarn company to adopt this technique is Eisaku Noro, from Japan. Noro's Kureyon yarn is 100 percent wool that cycles through more than six or seven colors in a single 50g ball. Although it's straightforward to work your own stripes by alternating colors of yarn, self-striping yarns like Kureyon make easy work of it; no pesky ends to sew! Check out the Too Good for your Boyfriend sweater in chapter 8 or the Deliberate Shrinkage Sack in chapter 10 for examples of self-striping yarns.

Dye Your Own

Dyeing your own yarn can be extremely satisfying. You have total control over the color (or colors). You can dye it a solid color, or use your hands or paintbrushes to incorporate multiple colors. Protein fibers take on color the best, but it's possible to dye cellulose or synthetic fibers with the correct materials. Some dye materials can be toxic or dangerous to work with. If you're interested in experimenting with dye techniques, consult one of the many excellent books, magazines, and online references that are devoted to this art, or take a class at your local art school. For a good place to start, check out the online resources in chapter 12. Many can point you on to dye-specific sites.

Just the Facts, Ma'am

Luckily, buying yarn is not a guessing game. Every yarn should come with a detailed label. While the content of these labels can vary based on company and country of origin, ideally every label has a consistent set of information to help your yarn purchase.

For the purpose of discussion, let's look at this fictional yarn label from *Amy's Yarns*.

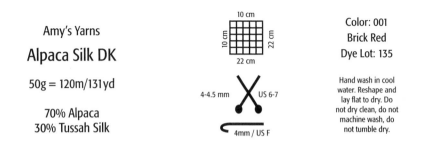

Kool-Aid: Not Just for Cults and Kids

For an easy and safe introduction to common dye techniques, consider dyeing wool with Kool-Aid or other powdered drink mixes. This technique is great for stitch n' bitch parties or for kids. The wool gets a little stinky, but it's fun to see what develops!

What you'll need:

- ◆ Protein-based yarn, such as pure wool, tied into skeins. (If the yarn is balled, wind into a skein by wrapping around the back of a chair.)
- ◆ Several packages of unsweetened Kool-Aid or other unsweetened drink mix. If the mix contains any sugar or artificial sweetener, you'll end up with a sticky undyed mess. Look for mixes that contain instructions for adding sugar and you'll be fine. You'll need approximately one package per ounce of yarn. Dye all the yarn a single color, or pick multiple colors for a hand-painted look.
- ◆ One large pot and steamer basket, with lid
- ◆ Turkey baster or wide paintbrush for applying Kool-Aid
- ◆ Large plastic bag
- ◆ Cups or mugs, one for each color
- ◆ Plastic or latex gloves for each participant

Steps to dyeing wool with Kool-Aid:

1. Before beginning to dye, place your yarn in the sink and wash it lightly with a bit of mild soap (the soap helps set the color).
2. Lay the skeins on top of the plastic bag on a hard surface, such as a kitchen counter. Put each color of Kool-Aid into a separate cup and add water, two tablespoons for each packet. Mix well.
3. Use the turkey baster to suck up some of the mix and squirt it carefully over the yarn. Be sure to rinse the baster between colors. If using a paintbrush instead, use the brush to liberally apply the mix. If your skeins are quite large, you may need to use your hands to work the dye through the entire skein.

   Be careful when adding multiple colors; the dye will bleed slightly at any areas that overlap, and may turn the wool muddy.
4. After the skeins are fully dyed, add water to the large pot and heat until boiling. Turn the burner off. Place the yarn in the steamer basket and cover, steaming for 45–60 minutes. Remove the basket and let cool in an empty sink.
5. When the yarn is room temperature, wash it gently in room-temperature water using mild soap. (Note: Using water that's too cold or too hot could cause the wool to felt.) Rinse the last of the soap and dye out of the yarn, squeeze to remove as much water as possible, and hang to dry.

On this yarn label is just about any bit of information you could ask for, except for how it actually looks when crocheted.

- **Brand, variety, and color:** From this label, you can see that this is a yarn called *Alpaca Silk DK*, produced by Amy's Yarns. On the right side of the label, it specifies a color. In this case, the color is coded *001*, and named *Brick Red*. Not every yarn has a color name. Some only have color codes. But some, as in this example, have both. The dye lot here is *135*. So, if I were going to purchase six balls of *Alpaca Silk DK*, I'd want to make sure all the dye lots are consistent.
- **Fiber content:** This yarn, as its name implies, is made of alpaca and silk. This sample indicates 70 percent of the yarn is alpaca and the remaining 30 percent is silk.
- **Weight and length:** This is one of the two most essential bits of information on the yarn label. The weight, or size, of the skein will be given in grams. Sometimes the size is instead given in ounces, although this is getting less and less common. More important than the physical weight of the skein is the length of the yarn in that skein. In this case, the 50g skein contains 120m or 131 yards.

A Word about Metric

Ah, the metric system. You know, kilometers instead of miles, meters instead of yards, grams instead of ounces. You may be surprised to see that most yarns and patterns either wholly use the metric system or include metric measurements. Still, some companies, particularly from the US, still use only yards and ounces instead of meters and grams. The Craft Yarn Council of America is encouraging metric as the standard for yarn crafts.

In the following examples, only metric examples are given. In addition to following the standard, metric makes prettier numbers and math more clear. For example, 50g is a much nicer number than 1.74 oz when doing math.

While you don't need to know the calculations by heart—that's what a computer is for—just be sure to be consistent. If your pattern asks for a certain number of meters of yarn, make sure to buy enough. One yarn is about .9m, so if you need 1000m and buy 1000 yards instead, you'll be short by 100m or so. Watch this especially when substituting yarns.

Compare the Weight and Yardage!

Here's where you have to be especially careful when substituting yarns. Let's say your pattern calls for four 50g balls of DK weight yarn. The brand called for contains 140m of yarn per ball.

Can you just buy four balls of Amy's *Alpaca Silk DK* instead? After all, the pattern calls for 200g and you'll be buying 200g?

Nope. Not a chance. If you do this, you'll run out of yarn and be running back to the store to pick up a fifth ball.

When yarns were mostly the same length per weight, it was common to provide only the physical ball weight in the yarn requirements section of the pattern. But now, the length of yarn to 50g can vary dramatically based on the fiber content and number of plys.

In this case, four balls of *Alpaca Silk DK* will give 480m of yarn and the pattern requires 560m of yarn. So, you'll need to buy a fifth ball of the *Alpaca Silk DK*.

Comparing the size or weight of the ball and the length of the yarn is also helpful for finding the closest substitution of yarn. In the example we've just discussed, the new yarn, the *Alpaca Silk DK*, is a bit heavier in physical weight than the yarn called for in the pattern. While the extra 30 or so grams probably won't be noticeable, this is something to watch for when substituting yarns of differing fiber contents.

I'll give a rather extreme example. Let's say your sweater pattern calls for 100g of super-fine mohair, knit to a gauge of 20 stiches to 4 inches. The mohair called for comes in 25g balls of 250m each. So, multiply 250 by 4 and you'll need 1000m of mohair. But, your aunt can't wear mohair. So you decide to substitute a nice shiny cotton that knits to the same gauge. You check the cotton ball label and see that each 50g ball has 50m. So you'll need 20 balls of cotton.

All of a sudden, your sweater weighs 1k instead of 100g! That's ten times as heavy! While it may still work out and fit beautifully, it certainly won't feel or look as the pattern designer intended. Aside from the weight factor, the drape of cotton and the loft of mohair are so different, your sweater will be an entirely different animal from the original.

Vintage Patterns and Yarn Substitution

What if you stumble across a killer vintage pattern in your grandmother's attic or the neighborhood antique store? By all means, use it! Some terms may be different than what we use today, but you'll be able to figure that out just fine. Most vintage crochet patterns were more specific and relied less on symbols and abbreviations than those we have today.

Yarn substitution is the main tricky point. Most vintage patterns give the yarn requirement in ounces. For example, an afghan may require 24 ounces of worsted-weight yarn.

To convert this to a more useful measurement of yards or meters, you'll first need to find a likely equivalent of yarn. In most cases, this will be a standard 100 percent acrylic yarn such as Red Heart Super Saver. Look up this yarn online or in your superstore and you'll see 145 1 yards to 3 ounces of yarn. So, if the pattern requires 24 ounces, that means you'll need approximately 1160 yards or nearly 1100m.

Of course, this is just an estimate. Err on the side of caution and buy an extra ball or two. Most yarn shops will let you return or exchange unused balls of yarn within a reasonable time frame. And if not? You can always crochet a hat or scarf for a gift. Having too much is far better than running out and being unable to find the same dye lot.

For the best substitutions, you want to look for the yarn that's not only the right thickness, but that has the same weight and yardage of the yarn specified in the pattern. In the example of your aunt's sweater, you'd be better off checking out a mohair-like nylon yarn that has a lighter weight closer to the mohair specified in the pattern.

Gauge and Needle/Hook Sizes

If the yarn manufacturer is following standards, a small gauge chart will be printed on the label. As shown above, this is usually a square grid that represents 10cm (4 inches). The chart shows both the number of stitches as well as the number of rows of knitted stockinette stitch (1 row knit, 1 row purl), that fit into the 10cm square. I have yet to run into a yarn brand that also gives the equivalent crochet gauge. However, many crochet patterns are now specifying the target weight of yarn in terms of its knitted gauge. You can use this chart to determine if the yarn has a good likelihood of also crocheting to gauge.

In addition to the gauge, a suggested needle and hook size is given, both in US sizes and in mm. On some European brands, only the mm size is given. Most hooks come labeled with both size schemes, but you can also use the chart found in appendix A.

Keep in mind that these are just suggestions to obtain the gauge specified on the label. Many patterns will require you to work more tightly or more loosely than the standard, in which case, you'll need to use smaller or larger hooks.

Care Instructions

Finally, the label should include any specific washing instructions that apply. If this portion is absent, use care when washing. It's always safe to hand wash in cool water with gentle detergent, then lay flat to dry. Wools that are labeled *superwash* are treated to prevent shrinkage and are considered safe for the gentle machine cycle. When in doubt, test wash with a small swatch of the same yarn.

Staying Organized

Many yarn crafters choose to keep a small notebook, almost like a diary, in which to log completed projects. Saving the yarn labels–one from each type of yarn–and attaching them to the project notes can be a handy way of keeping a record of not only what yarn was used, but how to care for it.

Including a yarn label and a few spare yards with a gift is also a nice way to help the recipient care for the garment. The spare yarn can come in handy for fixing snags or making other repairs.

For an example of a page from a project log, see appendix B.

Yarn Shops: Not Just For Knitting Anymore

With the recent resurgence in yarn crafts, dedicated yarn shops can be found in nearly all towns and cities across North America. At first glance, these shops may be seen as knit-centric. Most of the patterns may be geared towards knitting. Most of the classes and shop owners may know more about knitting than crocheting. But any yarn can be crocheted, and increasingly, crochet is receiving the recognition it deserves as a functional and beautiful craft.

Your local yarn shop is often your best resource and your first line of defense against unnecessary pitfalls. Crocheters also have a bit of an advantage over knitters. Due to the smaller number of crochet patterns that are produced, it's likely the shop owners will be more familiar with the crochet offerings than the wide range of knit patterns.

Increasingly, yarn shops are becoming more like community centers. Like-minded crafters can pop in for questions, or stay for hours while working on their latest obsession. Classes and workshops and lectures are available, and many shops sponsor stitch n' bitch knitting or crochet circles.

Even if you're the most introverted gal out there, consider joining one of these circles. The inspiration and information you'll get from the other members is invaluable. And, as a new crochet fanatic, you'll likely inspire someone else to take up the hook.

The Hooker's Secret Stash

No, we're not talking about anything overtly illegal. For the uninitiated of you, a stash is a hoarding of crafting supplies. In crochet's case, this will be yarn, patterns, and hooks. Maybe you are a dedicated quilter or scrapbooker and well understand the concept of a stash. Or maybe, in the best of intentions, you vow to only work one project at a time and buy only the yarn you need. When I started crocheting and knitting, this was how I operated. As soon as I'd finish a project, I'd diligently choose the next one. Once I had made a decision, I'd run out to the store and pick up the necessary supplies.

Several years later, my technique changed. I've learned that sometimes a yarn deal is too good to pass up. And sometimes, I buy supplies for a project and later decide it's not really what I want to work on. And so, the yarn goes into my stash. In my case, my stash takes up a large portion of my office bookshelves. At times, it threatens to take over my living room as well.

I'm sure there are many well-thought arguments *against* the practice of stashing. The issue of space comes to mind immediately. But there is also the philosophy of starting what you finish, an admirable trait for sure.

I love my stash for many reasons. It provides a yarn shop–like atmosphere that I can browse when I'm itching to start something new. It allows me to be surrounded in color and texture. But most of all, it allows for spontaneity.

If I get frustrated with a project that's just not working, or if I get struck with a brilliant design idea, I can spend a few minutes in my stash and find the right yarn for whatever idea I have. I don't have to wait for the next morning to run out to the store or the next week for my Internet purchase to arrive at my door. Maybe the yarn I find isn't completely perfect, but I'm likely to find something that will work just fine.

This may sound a lot like justification. After all, my stash is a bit of an insurance policy. What if I can't afford to buy yarn someday? Well, I have about 20 projects' worth on my shelves. That'll keep me busy for awhile. What if my favorite yarn goes out of production? Well, I've stocked up when it was on sale and won't be completely heartbroken.

But, I do support responsible stashing. I don't stash for the purpose of just increasing my stash. If I really love a yarn and can afford it, I may buy it to put into my stash and let the ideas percolate for awhile. But at the same time, if I fall out of love with something, I'm quick to trade with another crocheter for something more thrilling. Perhaps most importantly, I do use my stash. After all, that's what it's there for.

Stash Enhancing Online

Some of my favorite yarn resources can be found on the Internet. A great place to browse for bargains or to check out exotic yarns that aren't in your neck of the woods, the Internet can be a great time-saver and inspiration-builder.

Chapter 13 of this book contains a list of my favorite sites, both for information and for shopping. Many of these, like your local shop, may be more focused on knitting. However, sites like Knitter's Review (www.knittersreview.com) feature weekly yarn reviews, including detailed photographs, that apply to any yarn craft. The forums at Knitter's Review also have areas with crochet-focus, where you can post questions and discuss crochet-specific techniques.

Because I'm a huge yarn-a-holic, I subscribe to a few online shops mainly to receive the weekly newsletters that highlight new patterns and yarns. Elann.com (www.elann.com) is a bargain-hunter's dream site. In addition to their own line of quality fibers, Elann features closeout and discontinued brand-name yarns, often at 40 percent off the original prices. Such impulse buys—I mean *bargains*—have become a large part of my stash, and allow me to work with yarns that I ordinarily wouldn't be able to afford.

Just like any other online purchase, buying yarn over the Internet does have risks. Without the hands-on appeal of shopping in your local store, you may find your bargain yarn not as soft, not as colorful, or not as pretty as you'd hoped. Many sites will sell you shade cards so you can compare the actual colors in person. This does slow things down a bit. If you just can't wait, do some research on the store you're considering. Have other crocheters or knitters enjoyed their purchases? Do they report the online colors being fairly accurate? If you really hate the yarn, how is the store's return policy? Sometimes just getting your expectations in line in the beginning helps keep your online shopping happy!

Hooked on Spinning

Just like crochet and dyeing, the process of spinning yarn is undergoing a modern renaissance. Spinning, although time intensive, provides the ultimate control. You choose the fiber or blend of fiber, you pick the colors, you choose the thickness, twist, and ply. In addition, although a quality spinning wheel can cost upwards of $500, a simple drop spindle and bag of raw wool will set you back less than the cost of a few balls of basic yarn.

While many yarn shops, both in your town and online, sell the raw wool and spinning supplies, an excursion to one of the many Sheep and Wool Festivals can be an exciting introduction to the possibilities. Not only can you meet the sheep who provided that lovely fleece, you can often try out spinning with a drop spindle, learn how sheep are sheared, and see how the raw fleece is washed, combed, and carded into spinnable wool. For a list of major wool festivals, see *Sheep and Wool Festivals* in chapter 13.

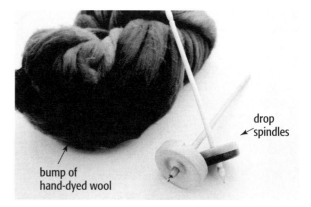

drop
spindles

bump of
hand-dyed wool

Recycled Yarn

Knitting supplies, especially quality yarns, can be quite pricey. If your tastes run farther than your budget, you can save big bucks by recycling yarn from old thrift-store sweaters. When shopping for good candidates, look for worsted or bulky weight sweaters in good condition, without holes or snags. Since you'll be unraveling the sweater, be sure to check the seams, if any, to see if they're machine sewn or hand sewn with yarn. The easiest sweaters to unravel are knit in one piece, without seams. Solid-color sweaters are also easier and quicker to unravel, but stripes work well.

1. The first step in recycling yarn is to unwork the sweater by picking apart the seams. Once you end up with the separate pieces, you can begin to unravel the sweater and wind the yarn into balls.

2. Once all the balls are completely wound, take a large piece of cardboard or a phone book and wrap the yarn around it to create hanks.

3. You'll now want to wash the yarn to remove many of the kinks now set in the yarn by months or years of living in knitted form.

4. Tie each hank separately to keep from tangling and hand wash in a bit of gentle detergent and cool water. Hang the hanks to dry.

   If the hanks seem especially *kinky*, you may wish to hang weights on the bottom so they straighten as they dry.

5. Once the hanks are dry, you're ready to rewind into balls to start crocheting!

This technique is also great for once-loved but now unfashionable sweaters. Just make sure to inspect the fabric for damage before starting. One hole isn't a huge deal; you'll just create separate balls. But, many tears, snags, or frays will be tough to work with down the road.

Chapter **Four**

◆◆◆

One Hook or Two?

crochet hook is essentially just a stick with a hook at one end. The earliest hooks were probably just whittled out of a short piece of wood. Today, the variety is endless. You can get plastic hooks, steel hooks, hand-carved wood hooks, even hooks made from glass or precious metals. But, all of these varieties boil down to the same three pieces.

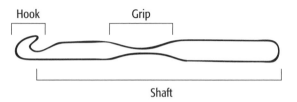

A Study of the Crochet Hook in Its Natural Habitat

- ◆ **Hook:** This is where it all happens. This little curved piece at the end is what grabs the yarn to make the stitch.

- ◆ **Grip:** Many crochet hooks have a slight indention or nonslip surface that creates a bit of a grip, similar to the handle on a golf club or high-end cooking tool. Although you don't have to hold the hook at this point, it's often the most comfortable, especially if settling in for a marathon hooking session.

- ◆ **Shaft:** The crochet hook is measured and labeled by the circumference of the *shaft*, or handle. Since the yarn makes a loop around this shaft, the physical size of the shaft directly influences the size of the stitches.

- ◆ **Sizing conventions:** As with stitch names, hooks are labeled differently in different parts of the world. When looking at hooks meant to be used with yarn, U.S. hook sizes tend to use letters, while elsewhere in the world, millimeters are the norm (see the table that follows). For wire or thread crochet, teeny tiny steel hooks are numbered in the U.S., but remain in millimeters elsewhere.

U.S. Size	mm Size	U.S. Size	mm Size
B	2.25mm	I	5.5mm
C	2.75mm or 3.0mm	J	6.0mm
D	3.25mm	K	6.5mm
E	3.5mm	L	8.0mm
F	3.75mm	M	9.0mm
G	4.0mm	N	10.0mm
G7	4.5mm	P	11.5mm
H	5.0mm		

No matter where you live, don't count on every hook and pattern you buy to be labeled with the same sizing conventions. Depending on where the hook was made or the pattern was written, it's common to have a pattern listing millimeters and a hook that only has the lettered size. Vintage hooks may be named entirely differently.

Fortunately, for a few bucks, you can buy a hook sizing tool such as this one by Susan Bates.

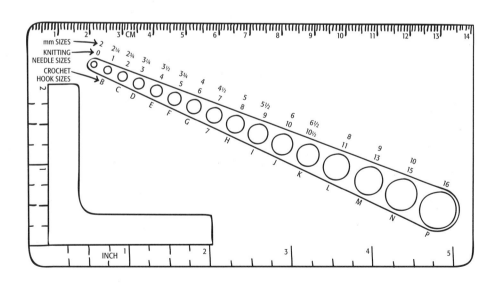

These little guys also work great for sizing knitting needles and are labeled with both the U.S. sizes and the metric sizes. This version also includes a handy ruler in both metric and imperial; great for measuring gauge.

Other Doodads that Make Life Worth Living

While, technically, you need only a hook and some yarn, the vast variety of crochet accessories and notions can make projects easier, more clear, and more fun.

Hook Sizer and Gauge Check

As seen previously, hook sizers are almost invaluable when you can't remember whether a U.S. G hook is a 4mm or a 4.5mm. Just insert the shaft of the hook through the hole and see what size fits just right.

Retractable Tape Measure

My dad always carries an industrial strength aluminum tape measure on his belt buckle. So, it shouldn't be a surprise that I recommend keeping a retractable fabric tape measure in your project bag. Good for checking gauge, taking your measurements, cutting fringe, or keeping track of how much you have left to do, these guys are useful much more often than you'd probably think. As a bonus, a basic fabric tape measure will set you back only a few dollars. You can also buy pricier (but cuter) ones shaped like fuzzy sheep or Pinocchio.

Scissors or Yarn Snips

Some yarn snaps easily with a tug, but most of the time, you'll need a small pair of scissors or a yarn cutter. Although most crochet goods are airline-safe, scissors are still not. If planning to crochet on your next cross-country journey, consider packing a box of dental floss in your carryon instead. The same metal notch that cuts the floss will also cut through most types of yarn with minimal fuss.

Notebook and Pencil or Pen

If you're like me, you're constantly losing pens. My cats tend to think they're handy paw-sized toys to be batted down the stairs or under the furniture. So, I always keep two or three pens or pencils in my bag, along with a small notebook for making design notes, or keeping track of which row I'm on in a complex pattern. My notebook also serves as a history of my crochet projects—inspirational and humbling at the same time.

Stitch Markers

Knitters have this one easy. When using stitch markers for knitting, they typically just stay on the needle, keeping place between sets of stitches. In crochet, the few times markers are used, they are usually placed around the stitch. So, if you need a stitch marker, make sure to buy ones, like the one pictured here, that have an opening along one side so you can slide it off the stitch after you're finished. A safety pin or bobby pin works as well. In a pinch, you can also use a bit of yarn in a contrasting color.

Something to Keep It All in

From pocketbook-like cases hand-sewn to keep your hooks organized, to neat handbags specially designed for yarn crafts, hundreds of styles are available to keep you coordinating while crocheting! For a list of companies who specialize in hook cases and knitting or crochet bags, see the list in appendix A.

Of course, you don't need a fancy bag to crochet. But it does help to keep your projects separated and organized, with all the yarn, patterns, and necessary hooks in one place. I have one hand-sewn bag I use for my favorite project. The other projects go into the zippered vinyl pouches that bed sheets are packaged in, or hard-sided shopping bags from my last trip to the mall.

Chapter Five

◆◆◆

Be a Fashion Designer (Or Just Look Like One!)

One of the not-so-secret benefits of learning a needle craft is the ability to custom-tailor garments to fit your body shape. Crochet or knitting allows you to take your wardrobe by the neck and shake it into fitting the way you've always wanted. Want a frilly little bolero cardigan? No problem. Do store-bought sweaters hit you at the elbows? No problem! Have you always wanted a hat with a hole for your off-center ponytail? I could question why this is a priority in your life, but instead, I'll say, no problem!

Whether or not you begin to design your own patterns, keeping in mind the principles of fit and flattery will greatly increase your satisfaction with your finished projects.

Measure Up

Do you sew? If so, you are probably already aware of the importance of proper measurements. After all, our bodies are rarely as simple as S, M, or L.

Measure Yourself

For this exercise, you'll need a flexible fabric tape measure. These can be purchased at most general or craft stores for a few bucks. Look for a retractable one, and you'll never regret it. Don't spend a lot of money on it and do replace it often, as tape measures stretch over time.

In appendix B, you'll find a Measurement Worksheet. Use this or make a photo-copy for your reference. If writing in this book, you may want to use a pencil.

Although I can hope my hips stay the same size until I'm 90, you and I both know this isn't likely.

Even though you'll only need a few of these measurements for any one project, it's handy to have the full picture of your body shape. However, since you're unlikely to crochet pants, we'll be skipping the legs this time.

Head Circumference Wrap the measuring tape around your head as if it's a close-fitting hat.

Head Height Take the tape from the top of one ear to the top of the other ear, over the top of the head. Divide this by two.

Neck Circumference Wrap the tape around your neck comfortably, at the base of your neck, below your throat.

Shoulder Width Measuring across your back, stretch the tape from the tip of one shoulder to the tip of the other.

Arm Circumference Wrap the tape around your bicep at its widest point. You may want to take the measurement of each arm separately and choose the larger of the two to ensure a comfortable fit.

Wrist Circumference Wrap the tape around your wrist at its smallest point.

Arm Length With the tape positioned in your underarm, measure to the smallest point on your wrist. This measurement will be compared to your desired sleeve length. For example, if you like your sleeves to hit mid-hand, add 2 inches to your sleeve length when working the pattern.

Chest Circumference Wrap the tape around the widest part of your chest. This is also known as your bust measurement. This is important to note, as many people make the mistake, in choosing a size, of using the number portion of their bra size as their bust size. Your chest measurement will almost certainly be a different number from your bra size.

Waist Circumference Wrap the tape around the smallest part of your waist.

Torso Height Measure down your back, from the top of your shoulders to the smallest part of your waist.

Hip Circumference Wrap the tape around the widest part of your hips. No, it's not okay to fudge this one!

Ankle Circumference For socks, wrap the tape around the top of your ankle, above your ankle bone.

Foot Length Measure your foot sole from end of heel to tip of longest toe.

Garment Construction Basics

For better or for worse, the best fitting garments are often the ones that most accurately mimic your body's natural shape.

Shaped Body with Set In Sleeves

Since most women have an hourglass shape, many women's sweaters or tops are shaped at the waist for a smoother fit. The body will also include the neck shaping. For a crew-neck sweater, such as the one pictured below, the circular dip is usually lower in the front than across the back shoulders. Each sleeve has a cuff at one end and what's called cap shaping at the portion that is sewn to the body. There are many types of sleeves. The one pictured above is called a *set in sleeve* and is widely considered to be the best fitting on most body shapes for both men and women.

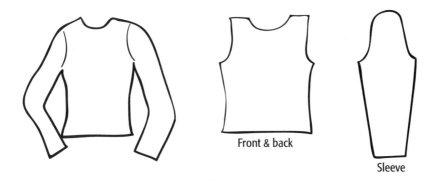

Front & back

Sleeve

Plain Body with Raglan Sleeves

For a man's sweater, or any loosely fitting sweater, it's common to omit the curvy-girl waist shaping and work the body straight from the hem to the underarms. The sleeves shown here are set into the body with a diagonal shaping called *raglan*. These sleeves are looser fitting and have more fabric in the underarms.

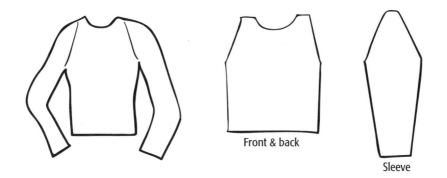

Front & back

Sleeve

Ease In: Fit Matters!

Every garment you wear has a certain amount of ease built in. This is the space allowed between your body and the garment. For a heavy outdoor sweater, you may have 5 or 6 inches of ease in the chest to allow for additional layers of clothing. A sexy crocheted T-shirt meant to show off your every curve may have only an inch of ease. For a hat that should be worn snugly, you may actually have negative ease and will be instructed to crochet the hat smaller than your actual head measurement.

Figure Out the Intended Ease to Find the Right Size

Many patterns will provide information about the intended ease of the garment. For example, a pattern may list the size small to fit a 32-inch bust, with a finished chest measurement of 35 inches. This means 3 inches of ease are built into the pattern.

Sometimes the finished measurement is listed in the pattern sizing. In many cases, these measurements are only drawn on a schematic diagram near the end of the pattern. For our hypothetical pattern, to select the proper fit for your body, add 3 inches to your chest measurement and select the size with the finished measurement closest to this number.

In my case, my chest is 41 inches around. I'd want to select the size closest to 44 inches.

Sometimes a pattern will not provide information about the measurements each size is intended for and will only give the finished measurements for each size. When this happens, a little informed guesswork is necessary.

In general, you'll want 1-2 inches of ease for a close-fitting garment, 3-4 inches for a more loose-fitting garment, and 5-6 inches or more for a very loose garment, or for a garment meant to be worn as an outer later. If you are using a bulky yarn, more ease is necessary. If you are using a very fine yarn, you may wish to make a size with less ease.

If you have a well-fitting garment in your wardrobe which is a similar style and weight to the garment you wish to make, you will hardly need to guess at all! Lay your garment flat and measure it across the chest below the underarms. Multiply the measurement by 2 to get the bust measurement of the garment, and choose a size from the pattern which is as close as possible to the measurement of your tried-and-true garment.

Assess the Schematic for Alterations

After the target size has been selected, you may want to review the schematic to make sure that no additional alterations are required. Although changing the chest measurement or neckline or building in additional room for a full bust are fairly time-intensive and advanced techniques, some changes are simple to make on almost any garment pattern.

Adjusting Sleeve Length

Almost any sweater is designed for basic sleeve-length adjustments. Compare the finished sleeve length on the schematic to your desired sleeve length. If you need to add (or subtract) an inch or two, try to do it in the middle of the sleeve, after any edging or hem but before the sleeve cap shaping.

If the sweater will have large armholes, your sleeves won't need to be as long as if it has small, close-fitting armholes. It's often a good idea to crochet your sweater body before your sleeves, so you can see how the armholes will fit. If you do this, you can take a new sleeve length measurement especially for sweater, by measuring from the underarm edge of the armhole, to the desired point where the end of your sleeve will fall.

Alter-natives

Just as in sewing, any other amount of alterations can be performed on any garment to create a customized tailored fit. These techniques are beyond the scope of this book. Perhaps the best reference is Sandra Bettina's *Fast Fit*, a book geared toward sewing techniques but with advice applicable to any garment craft.

Because sewing allows you to work with traceable pattern shapes, many crafters more quickly pick up the basics of fit and alteration when working with fabric. If this is of interest, call your local fabric or quilting stores about pattern drafting, alteration, or basic sewing classes.

Adjusting Body Length

It's also straightforward to add or subtract length from the body of the garment. In most cases, these adjustments should be done after the hem but before any waist shaping.

Flattery Gets You Everywhere

Even if you never intend to design or alter a previously written crochet pattern, simply paying attention to the styles and shapes that flatter your form can help make every garment a success. Perhaps by this point in your life, you have a good idea which colors highlight your eyes, which shapes draw attention to your most-loved body parts and flatter those other not-so-loved areas.

Surprisingly, even though I considered myself a fashion hound, I rarely spent any time thinking about why I liked what I liked. Instead, I'd plow ahead on one beautiful sweater pattern after another, simply because I liked the photograph. Time and time again, I would be disappointed with the final fit, even if I'd crocheted the garment to the exact specifications.

And then one of my closest friends made a comment that the store-bought clothes I wore bore little resemblance to the things I'd make for myself. I'd never thought of it before, but she was right! I would spend months working on complicated sweaters that I'd never think of buying in the store, simply because I loved the design idea.

Many of these sweaters have found better homes with family members. That beautiful ripple-edged cardigan looks lovely on my mother. On me, it looked more like a dumpy rag.

Here is where the cardinal rule of fashion applies. No garment universally flatters. This goes for old standards as well as new trends. Wear what you love and what loves you back, and life will be good.

Inspiration: Finally! An Excuse to Window Shop!

Maybe you've been stung a time or two by that sweater you thought would be perfect or that catalog item with hidden shoulder pads that over-emphasized your buff arms. One of the best ways to predict what's going to work with your style and body is to go shopping.

I use shopping as an excuse to try on as many trendy and unusual styles as I can. Aside from the fun of playing dress-up, it allows me to assess whether or not that bulky shrug would really look nice on my frame, before I spend weeks crocheting. Doing a trial run of a new trend allows me to separate my emotion (That's amazing! Look at those tucked seams!) from reality (Hmm. Tucks don't really make my belly look any smaller.). It also gives me a concrete garment to pin, pull, and hold in a place that looks good. All these things just give me more information from which to choose a pattern that will work for me.

Bring along a notebook and tape measure, and if possible, a dear but honest friend. Make notes on the shapes, sizes, and details that flatter you best (and least). If the neckline of a sweater looks great on you but the body is too short, note both the length of the body (to be avoided in the future) and the type of neckline (a detail to be sought out in future).

Be sure to try on sizes both larger and smaller than what you expect to wear. It's easy to get in a rut when it comes to garment sizing, and trying on sizes outside of your norm, especially when you are not planning to buy, can be very informative. Don't be afraid to stealthily measure garments that fit you well!

Crochet Pret-a-Porter

Only a few years back, crochet was rarely found on the clothes racks of local shopping malls. Relegated instead to secondhand shops and the dowdy department, it was tough to find crocheted garments that the fashion-conscious female would be likely to wear.

Today, it's a different story. Stores such as Anthropologie (www.anthropologie.com) have reinvented vintage chic and feature crochet goodies for all seasons. It's probably no secret that Anthropologie has become one of my favorite window-shopping destinations, both in person and online. But as more and more fashion designers get hip to the hook, expect to see more and more interesting crochet in your local stores.

Whether trying on or just looking at a photo in a magazine, try to look beyond the color of the yarn and the styling of the photograph. Instead, take a look at the garment. How do the sleeves fit? What about the neckline? A high neckline can emphasize a full bust but is flattering on other body shapes. Deep v-necks may flatter busty gals, but if they are too deep, they may require another layer beneath. What about the hem? Is it belly-baring or belt-skimming?

It may seem silly, but one of my favorite crochet scarf patterns was published and photographed in a tacky sparkly acrylic yarn. Because of the yarn, it was easy to skim past the pattern. I'm not sure why I stopped to consider the possibilities, but after I substituted a lovely heathered alpaca yarn and did a swatch, I was hooked, so to speak. The pattern itself was lovely and just my style. What was photographed was decidedly not.

For the Men in Your Life

A lot of this chapter has been focused on fit for women's bodies. I don't mean to say that men have it easier. Color and fit are still important. However, in terms of sweaters, very few designers in recent years have been creating flattering and appropriate male garments in crochet. Crochet is well suited to lacy and frilly stitches, neither of which are traditionally found in menswear.

Does this mean men shouldn't crochet or be the recipient of crocheted goods? Absolutely not. In my store, I run a class just for snowboarders and skiers, mostly male, to crochet close-fitting hats to match their gear. The It's Called a Toque, eh? pattern in chapter 7 is a great start if this is of interest.

Simple crocheted sweaters or jackets are also ideal. Remember, crochet is an incredibly sturdy and structured stitch that lends itself well to outerwear, for men as well as women.

Without making any excuses for the state of the craft, I would like to encourage any crochet dudes out there to pick up the hook and paper and begin designing. Knitting has undergone a huge transformation on both sides of the gender spectrum. I would love to see guys and crochet do the same thing.

A Little Light Color Theory

The best color theory comes, not from a book or manual, but from what you love. If you love orange and green together, go with it! One of my favorite color combinations is deep brown with baby blue, something that's rarely seen in nature, but a combination I love. Especially as fashion trends change, don't be surprised to see that one season you are nearly obsessed with a color you hated just a season before.

Inspiration for color combinations can come from anywhere: your favorite striped sweater, your cat's fur, paint chips at the hardware store, and so on. Even Domestic Goddess Martha Stewart claims to have gotten color karma from her pets. If stumped for what to put with that

---

Computerize Your Color Wheel

Your personal computer comes built-in with a number of tools to help in color combinations. Even a basic spreadsheet program such as Microsoft Excel can go a long way in helping plan out your colors. For the Preppy/Hippy Scarf pattern in chapter 7, you need to select five colors.

To use Excel to help plan, start a new spreadsheet file and then adjust your columns to be a bit wider. Excel, by default, includes a set palette of only a few colors. In most cases, you'll want to customize these before continuing. Select Preferences... and then Color to establish a custom color palette. Maybe you have a few colors already in mind. Use the slider bars and color wheel to pick the range of colors you'd like to play with. When satisfied, save your preferences and return to the worksheet.

Select the first cell or row and set the background color as desired. Repeat this with as many cells or rows as you need to mimic the pattern. For the Throw pattern, you'll want a repeat of 6 colors across 12 rows of pattern. For the most accurate picture of your final project, try to make the thicker bands of color in the pattern thicker in the worksheet.

Excel-less? Any photo editing or paint program can be used in a similar way.

lovely mint green and chocolate brown, maybe your box of Mini Mint Milanos will show that ivory is a nice contrast.

Just look around you. I'd bet that you already surround yourself with color combinations you love, whether you realize it or not. Look at favorite photographs and jewelry; even take a peek in your closet. It's all there. One of the best things about color is that it's already everywhere, just waiting.

When Good Projects Go Bad

It happens to everyone, even the most die-hard obsessed crafter. You see a pattern; you fall in love. Tenderly, you select the right yarn, find the right hook to get gauge, and even select the right size based on your carefully taken measurements. Painstakingly, you put in a few alterations. The sleeves could be shortened. The hem is a bit too belly-baring for winter. And finally, you devote hours, weeks, or months with hook to yarn, creating the *tour de force* that is your perfect sweater. But then, when all the ends are carefully darned, you put it on, close your eyes, and walk to the closest (or most flattering) mirror.

Eyes still closed, you imagine yourself as the picture of perfection—the most beautiful of the beautiful. Your friends will sigh in awe of this, the fruit of your creative labor.

But then, you open your eyes. You see something much less than your every imagining. Sure, your alterations worked out. But the neckline is too tight. The waist clings like sausage casing instead of the lovely drape you'd expected.

What now? The answer varies from crocheter to crocheter and from project to project. Chances are, at this point you've thoroughly assessed the situation, noting every detail that's even a millimeter out of place. Some of them, such as a neckline that's too low or sleeves that are too long, are easy to fix after the fact. Others, like a clingy waistline, are more problematic and may require the dreaded rip.

The sad fact is, there's no surefire way to guarantee you'll adore the finished project. But there are a few preventative measures that will greatly increase your chance of falling in love.

Make the Right Size

Did I stress this enough earlier in the chapter? Well, it bears repeating. Take the time to compare the pattern's size recommendations with the actual finished measurements of the various sizes. Pick the right size based on the finished measurement, not based on what you think you are. It's the same as jean shopping. You don't just blindly buy size 8s from every store without trying them on first, do you?

Check Your Gauge

This one deserves to be on the list three or four times. For anything where size matters, if you're not on the recommended gauge, your finished product will be a different size than expected. If it's a scarf, it may not matter. If it's a sexy tank, you may end up with either a bikini top or a loose hippy dress.

Checking gauge takes only a few minutes, but it can save your project long before you start. For more information about gauge and how to check it, see chapter 3.

Block It

Make sure you block your finished garment before you judge the fit. The fit and drape can change dramatically, and can really make the difference between "too tight" and "just right." In fact, careful blocking can help make up for bad choices in both width and length. You can find more information on blocking in chapter 1.

Choose the Right Yarn

Ninety-nine percent of all crochet patterns specify a specific yarn by a specific company. Does this mean you can only use that one type of yarn? Not a chance. Yarn substitution can be one of the most rewarding and creative ways to ensure that the project really fits what you want to do. Chapter 3 is chock full of ideas for effective yarn substitution.

The CliffsNotes version of that advice is to substitute with a yarn that has a similar look and feel to the yarn recommended. Compare thickness, fiber content, and weight of the yarn for the most predictable results. Although you could crochet a bulky oversized sweater in a thick cotton instead of the lofty mohair recommended, it would probably be saggy, floppy, and too heavy to wear.

Fix Mistakes When They Happen

I am guilty of this one a lot. I mess up one row or one stitch and, at the time, rationalize myself into believing it's not going to show. And then, without fail, it's the only thing I can see on the finished garment. When a student comes to me asking whether or not it's worth fixing one tiny issue, I always put the question back to her. If you know the problem is there, will it keep you from absolutely loving this thing you're creating? If the answer is even a weak "Maybe," I'll advise her to take the time to rip back and fix the problem. It's much easier—and quicker—to fix problems when you've only crocheted the first half of the blanket rather than after the fact.

When All Else Fails . . .

Say you've done everything right and you still hate it? It's time to let go. For some projects, this means giving it away to a friend or a loved one whom it will flatter. Remember that rippled sweater? My mom just called and told me again how much she loves it. For other projects, you may want to undo the seams and rewind the yarn into balls to be used for some future, much improved, project. Other projects may be permanently doomed to the back of your closet.

Use your gut. Or your wallet. One of the two will tell you the right option for any disappointment. I would certainly never promote any single option. But then, I don't want to show you what's in the back of my closet, either.

Chapter Six

◆◆◆

Ready, Set, Crochet!

Last minute advice for those of you who skipped ahead from Crochet 101: The best way to learn is usually by *doing*. Of course, you know that, or you wouldn't have skipped ahead from chapter 1. Plus, this is the fun part. Tiny little squares of different stitches might be your cup of bubble tea . . . but not mine. As much as I enjoy the process of crochet, I'm really in it for the finished product. I suspect you're more like me than you care to admit.

Although the remaining pattern chapters have projects that range from easy to tough to Mt. Everest challenging, the first pattern chapter, chapter 7, focuses on projects that will make you smile, make you learn, and make you proud to say, "I made this!" Even better, with the exception of the Weekend Vest, all projects in this chapter can be started and finished in a single evening while still letting you get your beauty sleep.

The Anatomy of a Crochet Pattern

Crochet patterns are like recipes. A well-written pattern will tell you not only the materials you need and the *serving size* (a.k.a., finished measurements) of the project, but will also give you hints and tips for making the work as enjoyable as possible. After all, if it wasn't fun, who would do it?

Although every pattern publication has a slightly unique pattern format, most share a few elements in common.

Introduction and Sizing

Along with the pattern's name and designer(s), you should see a brief written introduction to the pattern. Sometimes, this gives you an idea of the design's inspiration. Sometimes, this can be a place to find hints and information that greatly help the project's success.

Perhaps the most important thing to look at when selecting a project is the sizing. Sweaters and top patterns usually give the chest circumference. Hat patterns provide the circumference around the forehead area, generally where the lower edge of the hat will sit. Socks and glove patterns usually list the ankle or wrist circumference. Additionally, it's common to find length or height measurements for each size, such as the crown to brim measurement on a hat.

Unfortunately, sizing information is far from standard. Some companies publish garments in one-size-fits-all format. Others publish the finished measurements for generic sizing labels such as small, medium, and large. Still others provide only generic information, such as, "fits size medium."

As you saw in chapter 5, size really *does* matter. Simply crocheting a sweater that's labeled "medium" may or may not fit you the way you'd like. For that reason, in this book, the actual finished measurements are provided along with the generic sizing labels we all know and love. When multiple sizes appear, choose the right one by comparing your actual measurements with the finished measurements of the garment.

For projects other than shaped garments, the finished dimensions are given. It's less common to see multiple sizes of a throw blanket, pillow, or even a scarf. For these, even though fit is less important, it's still good to check out the measurements before you start. Otherwise, you may discover that what you thought would be a bed-sized blanket is really more of a lap throw.

Cost

Unlike most other yarn craft books, the books in the *Not Your Mama's* series highlight the approximate cost to crochet the project as photographed. This means that we've taken an estimate cost of the yarn used for the size photographed. All prices are listed in U.S. dollars and will naturally vary depending on the source.

With some projects, especially those that use a variety of colors, the prices will be higher. However, you'll most always be able to get a few finished products out of the single set of yarn. Where this is possible, it's clearly noted. Some projects are also well suited to using up leftovers from your stash. This is also noted in the pattern introduction.

Finally, please do use the yarn substitution notes for a guideline as well. For example, the cost to knit the Uber-femme Capelet in chapter 8 is well over $100 in the pure cashmere yarn we suggest. However, substitute a stunning pure alpaca and you're looking at a drapey and slinky soft $40 wrap.

If you're in love with a project out of your price range in the original yarn, take this book to your nearest yarn shop and ask for some advice. In most cases, you'll be able to find a yarn you love at a price that suits your budget.

Materials and Gauge

The materials section lists the yarn you need, along with the hook sizes recommended and any other notions or supplies necessary to complete the project as pictured. For crochet patterns, the gauge is typically given in the project's main stitch pattern as the number of stitches to 4 inches (10cm) on a specific hook size. Occasionally, you'll see the gauge in single crochet instead. Remember, the hook size the designer uses to get gauge will likely be different than the hook size you will need. Do take the time to check your gauge before starting, and change hooks if necessary.

In this book, you'll notice we've given the gauge in knitted stockinette stitch as well as in the crochet stitch (it's listed in "Materials", under the yarn substitution notes). Most crochet patterns don't do this. However, since yarn ball bands tend to give gauge only for knitting, the crochet gauge isn't helpful when substituting yarns. In case your yarn store doesn't have (or hasn't heard of) the yarn we used, you can use this information to find a suitable yarn from a different brand.

Stitch Patterns

Any unique stitch patterns specifically developed for the pattern may be listed and described at the beginning of the pattern for clarity. Similar to the approach we took in chapter 2's stitch guide, stitch patterns such as these are typically described, row by row, and occasionally diagramed for clarity.

Not Your Mama's Crochet also lists the skills and techniques required along with the page numbers on which you can get a refresher.

Instructions

In this part of the pattern you'll find, not surprisingly, the instructions for how to make the thing exactly as pictured. If the project is a more complicated garment, the instructions may be broken down into pieces to be assembled later. For smaller projects, don't be surprised to see all the instructions in one block. It's a good habit to read through the instructions at least once before starting. This way you have an idea about what's coming up.

Finishing

Any sewing or other finishing instructions will be located in a separate section of the pattern. This could be as simple as "sew in all ends," or something more complex that includes sewing instructions, edgings or hems, embroidery, or the like.

Schematics

Somewhere in the pattern should appear a simplified drawing of the project with all relevant measurements specified. Called a *schematic diagram*, this is where you should go to see how long the sweater sleeves are or how deep the V-neck is. In chapter 5, if you've read it yet, we chatted about how to assess a pattern to see if any alterations are needed. The schematic is your most detailed source for that information.

Unless you're crocheting a scarf, blanket, or other regularly shaped item, beware of any complex patterns that do not include schematics. Any garment that needs to fit in a particular way, such as a sweater or tank, should have a schematic that illustrates the length and width of all major pieces. In general, you should expect to see schematics for non-rectangle or circular shaped items.

Symbolcraft: The Illustration of Crochet

You've heard the overused cliché, "A picture is worth a thousand words." But rarely is it more true than in crochet patterns. Especially for more complicated motifs and lacework, after a few rows, all those dc, sc, and ch blend together into a big pot of alphabet soup.

Enter what many refer to as *symbolcraft*, a visual language for graphing crochet stitches. Each basic stitch has a corresponding illustration; the illustrations are then combined to effectively graph the entire design, as you see here.

When an entire motif is charted, these basic illustrations will be combined to show the motif. For example, the following chart illustrates the basic Granny Square motif from chapter 1, page 18.

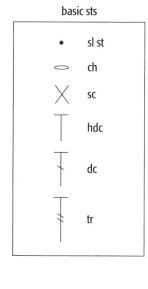

basic sts

•	sl st
◠	ch
✕	sc
⊤	hdc
⟊	dc
⟊⟋	tr

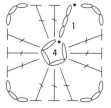

Granny Square, chapter 1

Working in Rows

For an example of a symbolcraft chart worked back and forth, check out the stitch guide in chapter 2. When working in rows, diagrams are read from bottom to top. The rows are read from right to left and then left to right in the order that the stitches are worked. Just as you crochet back and forth, diagrams are read back and forth. Usually, row numbers are placed next to the first stitch on each row to show which direction the row is worked.

The foundation chain is not marked with a row number and is always read from left to right. When a turning chain is required, any turning chains are illustrated vertically rather than horizontally.

Working in Rounds

As shown on the Granny Square Motif diagram, motifs are usually diagramed from the inside out, working in a counter-clockwise motion. In other words, exactly in the same direction you crochet.

Practice Perfect

Try it out with some spare yarn and the Granny Square Motif shown previously. Can you read what needs to be done from the illustration and stitch key?

A good thing to note is that, while not all patterns will include the symbolcraft chart, all will include the stitch pattern written out with abbreviations. So, you always have that to fall back on. With a little practice, however, you may find you relate better to the illustrations!

In this book, only the more complex stitches are charted for the pattern chapters. For example, the It's Called a Toque, Eh? pattern in chapter 7 only uses single crochet. So, no chart is provided.

Symbolcraft: Good or Evil?

Talk to any group of crocheters and you're likely to find several who hate-hate-hate symbolcraft diagrams and half who couldn't live without 'em. This rift is simply another extension of the verbal versus visual debate. Just as some folks learn better from reading or hearing a fact, others retain the knowledge only through seeing a photo or diagram. The same goes for crochet. What makes the most sense for me maybe won't work for you.

In patterns, just as in education, it's best to target both groups by providing the written instructions as well as the diagrams. If you don't get symbolcraft, ignore it and use only the written instructions. Conversely, if the written instructions drive you batty, give the diagram a chance. With a tiny bit of time, you'll figure out which way works best for you. However, since not every pattern provides both options, do make sure that you understand both the symbols and the written abbreviations, even if one is more natural for you than the other.

Get Hooking or Go Home!

Now you're more than ready for your first crochet. Enter Part II of this book; the patterns and projects. Whether you've tried a few of the stitches in chapter 2 or not, chapter 7's stylish designs are easy enough for even the newest crochet-a-holic. Chapter 8's fashion-forward patterns will have you looking picture-perfect in no time. Looking for the perfect gift? Check on chapter 9 for neat things to crochet for others (or even yourself). Chapter 10 closes the series of projects with a set of non-traditional crochet. From plastic bags to cut-up jeans, you can use crochet!

Each of the patterns in this book includes some suggested variations. While these suggestions may range from yarn substitution to sizing, don't be shy about applying your own creativity! Chances are, when looking at the photos, you'll probably want to change a thing or two to make the project reflect your own true style. Go for it!

Now, grab a hook, some yarn, and get moving!

• Part Two •

Projects

Chapter Seven

◆◆◆

Jump Right In, The Water's Fine!

From the Crochet Test Kitchen

Dishcloths may be the cliché of the crochet world, but this bag, made from two easy squares, is a great way to cut your teeth on the craft. Whip this one up as quickly as you can say "you're doing the dishes tonight!"

Preppy/Hippy Scarf

Let two sides of your fashion personality shine with this conservative scarf with kicky hippy fringe.

It's Called a Toque, Eh?

Keep your guy warm on the slopes while looking cool at the same time. And if you want to borrow it or make one for yourself, no problem!

Getting Dizzy Scarf

Soft hand-dyed mohair crocheted in a spiral makes a stunning scarf.

Weekend Vest

Start it on Wednesday night and be done in time for the weekend. This vest can be left open or closed with a zipper.

Chunky Monkey Scarf

Perfect for quick gifts, with a little practice one of these babies can be whipped up in a single night.

From the Crochet Test-Kitchen: Market Bag

The crocheted dishcloth is a rite of passage. Your grandmother probably made dozens of these as family gifts. Take this basic pattern and crochet a versatile drawstring bag; perfect for market day.

Project Rating: Flirtation

Cost: Expect to spend $15–$20

Necessary Skills: ch (page 7); sc (page 10); dc (page 13); sewing ends (page 24)

Abbreviations: ch-sp: the space made in the previous row by chaining one or more times between stitches

Finished Size

Length: 14 inches
Width: 14 inches

Materials

- Blue Sky Alpacas Organic Cotton (100g; 100 percent cotton; 192yd/175m); Color: Espresso - 2 balls
- Substitution: Look for approx. 384yd/350m aran weight cotton.
- Ball band will indicate a knitted gauge of 18 sts = 4 inches / 10 cm.
- US G/4.5mm crochet hook
- US L/8mm crochet hook
- Yarn needle

Gauge

16 sc = 4 inches / 10 cm using US G/4.5mm hook

Note: Exact gauge isn't critical for this project. A looser gauge or a bigger yarn will result in a larger bag. A tighter gauge or smaller yarn will create a smaller bag.

Seed Stitch Pattern

Ch an even number of sts (desired number of sts + 1).

Set-up Row: Sc in 2nd ch from hook, [ch 1, skip next ch, sc in next ch] to end.

Row 1: Ch 1, sc in 1st sc, sc in ch1-sp, [ch 1, skip next sc, sc in ch1-sp] to last ch1-sp, sc in last sc.

Row 2: Ch 1, sc in 1st sc, [ch 1, skip next sc, sc in ch1-sp] to last ch1-sp, ch 1, skip next sc, sc in last sc.

Repeat rows 1 and 2 for Seed Stitch.

Instructions

Using smaller hook, ch 42.

Work in Seed Stitch until work measures 14 inches, ending with Row 1.

Break yarn, draw through last st and pull tight.

From the Crochet Test-Kitchen:
Market Bag (see page 86)

Necklace instructions available in Not Your Mama's Beading

Dishcloth (variation of From the Crochet Test-Kitchen; see page 87)

It's Called a Toque, Eh? and Preppy/Hippy Scarf
(hat, see page 90; scarf, see page 88)

Getting Dizzy Scarf (see page 92)

Weekend Vest (see page 94)

Chunky Monkey Scarves (see page 99)

Uber-Femme Capelet (see page 101)

Peek-a-boo Plaid Skirt (see page 104)

Pseudo-Kimono (see page 107)

Ramblin' Rosie Cardie and
S³ Sari Silk Shrug (cardigan, see page 117;
shrug, see page 114)

The "Too Good for Your Boyfriend"
Sweater (see page 123)

Skull motif (variation for The "Too Good
for Your Boyfriend" Sweater; see page 126)

Cozy Peacoat (see page 128)

Granny's Been in the Bourbon Again:
A Drunken Throw (see page 141)

Classic Street Page Boy
(see page 144)

Necklace instructions available in Not Your Mama's Beading

Daisy Chain Neck Warmer
(see page 148)

Daisy Pin (variation of Daisy
Chain Neck Warmer; see page 149)

Lucy-Lou and Tim-Bob, Too
(see page 150)

Bubble Belt and Woven Fringe Scarf
(belt, see page 157; scarf, see page 155)

Who Hat (see page 159)

Straight-Laced Tank and Shrug (see page 163)

The Wowie Zowie Eco-Tote
(see page 167)

Crocheted Bling (see page 169)
Variation: bracelet

When the Jeans Don't Fit:
A Recycled Denim Rug (see page 171)

Deliberate Shrinkage Sack (see page 173)

Felted Trellis Scarf (see page 176)

Creatures of the Wooly Deep
(see page 178)

Finishing Instructions

Holding Front and Back together, work 1 row of sc through both layers to attach side and bottom edges of bag. Work 1 row of sc around top opening edge. Sew in ends.

Make 2 cords as follows:

Holding 3 strands of yarn together and using larger L/8mm hook, ch 70. Sl st in each ch to end. Break yarn, draw through last st and pull tight.

Weave 1 cord through the 2nd row of eyelets on one side of bag as pictured. Sew the ends of the cord together to make a loop. Repeat for the other side of the bag. When pulled tight, cord will cinch up the top of the bag and allow the straps to be long enough to comfortably hang on the shoulder.

Variation

Want a quicker project? Use a smaller yarn and hook and crochet up a dishcloth by completing only one side of the bag.

Preppy/Hippy Scarf

Show off both sides of your personality with this demure striped scarf with kicky bohemian fringe. The best part? The fringe secures all the ends from your single-row stripes; no ends to sew! Since each row uses approximately 20 yards of yarn, this scarf is ideal for using up leftovers from other projects. For best results, choose yarns that are similar in weight and texture. Or, if purchasing new yarn, you'll be able to get two scarves out of one set of balls.

Project Rating: Flirtation

Cost: Expect to spend $40 on the initial supplies. However, yarn will be plenty for at least 2 scarves.

Necessary Skills: ch (page 7); sl st (page 16); hdc (page 31); sewing ends (page 24)

Finished Size

Width: Approx. 3.75 inches
Length: Approx. 60 inches, excluding fringe

Materials

- Debbie Bliss Cashmerino Aran (50g, 98yd/90m, 55 percent Merino Wool, 33 percent Microfibre, 12 percent Cashmere); 1 ball each color
  A: Color 617 (wine)
  B: Color 501(olive)
  C: Color 615 (orange)
  D: Color 201 (teal)
  E: Color 505 (yellow)
- Substitution: For each color, approximately 40yd/37m of aran or heavy worsted weight yarn.
- Ball band will indicate a knitted gauge of 18 sts = 4 inches/10 cm.
- US H / 5.0mm crochet hook, or size needed to obtain correct gauge

Gauge

11hdc = 4 inches/10 cm on 5.0mm hook

Note: Exact gauge isn't critical for this project. A looser gauge or a bigger yarn will result in a larger (and longer) scarf. A tighter gauge or smaller yarn will create a smaller (and shorter) scarf. Since the scarf is worked sideways, just make a longer or shorter chain for the scarf length you want.

Instructions

Using A, make initial slipknot approximately 8-12 inches from end of yarn. This tail will become part of the fringe. When switching colors, make sure to leave the same length of yarn tail at the beginning and end of each row.

Using 5.0mm crochet hook and A, ch 152.

Row 1: Hdc in 3rd ch from hook and in each ch to end across; 150 hdc.

Cut the yarn at the end of each row, leaving an 8-12 inch tail.

Row 2: Using B, ch 2, hdc into 1st hdc and in each hdc to end.

Row 3: Using C, ch 2, hdc into 1st hdc and in each hdc to end.

Row 4: Using D, ch 2, hdc into 1st hdc and in each hdc to end.

Row 5: Using E, ch 2, hdc into 1st hdc and in each hdc to end.

Row 6: Using D, ch 2, hdc into 1st hdc and in each hdc to end.

Row 7: Using C, ch 2, hdc into 1st hdc and in each hdc to end.

Row 8: Using B, ch 2, hdc into 1st hdc and in each hdc to end.

Row 9: Using A, ch 2, hdc into 1st hdc and in each hdc to end. Do not break yarn.

Row 10: Still using A, ch 1, sl st into 2nd hdc and in each hdc to end. Cut A, leaving an 8-12 inch tail; draw yarn tail through remaining stitch and pull tight.

Finishing Instructions

Cut eight 20" lengths of colors A, B, C, and D, and four 20" lengths of color E.

With crochet hook and two strands of color A, attach fringe as follows:

Fold strands in half. Insert hook between last two stitches at end of stripe worked in A (you can start from either end). Use hook to pull the strands about 2 inches through the edge of the scarf, creating a loop. Use your fingers or the crochet hook to pull the ends of the strands, along with the end left from switching colors, through the loop. Pull on the ends to tighten and secure.

Repeat this process for every stripe, using two 20" lengths for each end of each stripe. To mimic the look of the scarf shown here, make sure the fringe lines up with the striped colors.

When finished, the fringe will be quite uneven. Use a scissors to trim the ends for a neater appearance.

Variation

I like the look of hdc for simple stripes. Slightly more substantial than a sc, it adds a bit more height without the space you find between the taller stitches. However, this scarf is great for experimenting with different stitches. Try doing some rows in sc and some in dc. See how the stripes get skinnier and wider based on what type of stitch you use?

It's Called a Toque, Eh?

In Canada, where I live, close-fitting ski hats are called *toques* (tookes) and are worn year-round by guys and gals. Many teen guys crochet these for themselves and their girlfriends. Pick your team colors or just match your coat. One toque takes very little yarn and can be crocheted in a single evening.

Project Rating: Flirtation

Cost: Expect to spend $15-$20, less for a one color hat.

Necessary Skills: ch (page 7); sc (page 10); sl st (page 16); sewing ends (page 24)

Finished Size

Circumference: 20 inches

Height, from crown to brim: 8 inches

Materials

- Elsebeth Lavold Designer's Choice Angora (50g, 91yd/83m, 60 percent Angora, 20 percent Wool, 20 percent Polyamide), 1 skein each color
  MC: Color 011 Robin Red
  CC: Color 012 Cloudberry
- Substitution: Aran or worsted-weight yarn, approx. 88yd/80m of MC and 55yd/50m of CC.
- Ball band will indicate a knitted gauge of 18 sts = 4 inches/10 cm.
- US G / 4.5mm crochet hook, or size needed to obtain correct gauge
- Yarn needle

Gauge

12 sc = 4 inches/10 cm

Note: At the end of each round, you will be instructed to "sl st in 1st sc". This means that you will work a slip stitch into the first single crochet of the round, in order to join the ends of that round. This is how a round is usually finished when crocheting in the round.

Instructions

Using MC, ch 3. Sl st in first ch to form a ring.

Round 1: Ch 1, work 9 sc into ring, sl st into 1st sc.

Round 2: Ch 1, 2 sc in 1st sc and in each sc to end, sl st in 1st sc. 18 sts.

Round 3: Ch 1, [sc in 1 sc, 2 sc in next sc] to end, sl st in 1st sc. 27 sts.

Round 4: Ch 1, [sc in 2 sc, 2 sc in next sc] to end, sl st in 1st sc. 36 sts.

Round 5: Ch 1, [sc in 3 sc, 2 sc in next sc] to end, sl st in 1st sc. 45 sts.

Round 6: Ch 1, [sc in 4 sc, 2 sc in next sc] to end, sl st in 1st sc. 54 sts.

Rounds 7 & 8: Ch 1, sc in each sc, sl st in 1st sc.

Round 9: Ch 1, [sc in 8 sc, 2 sc in next sc] to end, sl st in 1st sc. 60 sts.

Rounds 10–18: Ch 1, sc in each sc, sl st in 1st sc.

Note: CC will be introduced in the next round. Do not break MC.

Rounds 19 & 20: Using CC, ch 1, sc in each sc, sl st in 1st sc.

Break CC, leaving 6-inch tail.

Rounds 21–24: Using MC, ch 1, sc in each sc, sl st in 1st sc.

Break MC, leaving 6-inch tail.

Rounds 25–29: Using CC, ch 1, sc in each sc, sl st in 1st sc.

Break CC, leaving 6-inch tail. Draw tail through last st and pull tight.

Finishing Instructions

Using yarn needle, sew in ends securely.

Variation

Add in additional colors or change the stripe pattern. After you stop increasing and begin to work in even rounds, the sky is the limit! Want a frilly girly hat brim? On the final row, work 2 sc into each sc around for a gentle ruffled edge.

Getting Dizzy Scarf

A spiral scarf adds a bit of drama to the coolest winter nights. Crocheted in a lightweight, hand-dyed mohair, these scarves work up quickly with double crochet and make great gifts! With the yarn specified, the yardage in one hank is enough for three or four scarves. Make a matching set for your friends.

Project Rating: Flirtation

Cost: Expect to spend $70–$80 for yarn as shown. However, yarn is plenty for at least four scarves, bringing the per-project cost down to less than $20.

Necessary Skills: ch (page 7); dc (page 13); sewing ends (page 24)

Finished Size

Length: Approx. 72 inches
Width: Approx. 5 inches

Materials

- Lorna's Laces Heaven (200g, 975yd/890m, 90 percent Kid Mohair, 10 percent nylon), color Daffodil–1 skein
- Substitution: Look for approximately 300yd/270m of a lightweight mohair or mohair-blend yarn. The ball band gauge indicates a knitted gauge ranging from 16–22sts = 4 inches/10cm.
- US I / 6.0mm crochet hook
- Yarn needle

Gauge

12dc = 4 inches/10 cm

Note: With mohair, the ball band gauge sometimes varies dramatically depending on how the yarn manufacturer thinks you will knit the yarn. Consequently, for this project, the ball band gauge is less important. Try the 6.0mm hook and get close to 12 dc to 4 inches, and the scarf will turn out great!

Instructions

Ch 121.

Row 1: Dc in 4th ch from hook, [2 dc in next ch, dc in next 2 ch] to end. 158 sts.

Row 2: Ch 3, dc in 1st dc, [dc in next dc, 2 dc in next dc] to last st, dc in last dc (turning chain from first row). 237 sts.

Row 3: Ch 3, dc in 1st dc, 2 dc in each dc to end. 474 sts.

Row 4: Ch 3, (dc, ch1, dc) in 2nd dc, [skip next dc, (dc, ch1, dc) in next dc] to end. 711 sts (chain spaces are counted as sts). Break yarn and draw through last st; pull tight.

Finishing Instructions

Sew in ends.

Variation

Mohair is a super-lightweight yarn. So, by simply substituting a yarn, for part or all of the scarf, with a different fiber content, you can create a significantly different look. In the color insert photo we used a plain mohair for the first three rows and switched to a hand-dyed silk for the final row to give some weight to the edging. Try using a solid colored mohair for the first three rows and then switch to a furry novelty yarn or contrasting color for the final row.

Weekend Vest

Oversized vests are great for wearing while bumming around on weekends; this one can be crocheted with bulky yarn over the course of a few evenings. A great way to practice seaming and making a garment to fit without the time commitment! Add an optional zipper to keep the front zipped, or wear open.

Project Rating: Summer Fling

Cost: Expect to spend $25–$45 for yarn as shown.

Necessary Skills: ch (page 7); sc (page 10); hdc (page 31); seaming (page 21); single crochet rib (page 33); sewing ends (page 24)

Finished Size

S[M, L, XL]
Finished chest measurement 36[39, 42, 45]

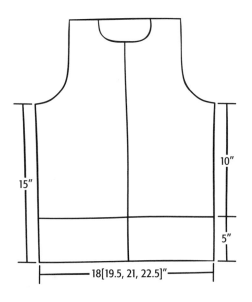

Materials

- MC: Lion Brand Wool-Ease Thick & Quick (170g, 108yd/98m, 80 percent acrylic, 20 percent wool), color Grass (131)–4[5, 6, 7] balls
- Substitution: Look for approximately 432 [540, 648, 756] yd/395 [494, 593, 692]m of a super-bulky wool-blend yarn.
- Ball band will indicate a knitted gauge of 8-9 sts = 4 inches/10 cm.
- US N / 9.0mm crochet hook, or size needed to obtain correct gauge
- Yarn needle
- Optional: 20" heavy-duty separating zipper, sewing needle, and matching thread

Gauge

6.5sc to 4 inches/10 cm

Note: When crocheting a garment, gauge really matters, especially with super chunky yarn. If you're even off a half stitch, it will dramatically impact the size of the finished garment. Use a different size hook if necessary to acheive the correct gauge. Fortunately, crochet hooks are cheap, and it doesn't hurt to have a wide variety of sizes; you'll use them all eventually!

Instructions

Back

Ch 10.

Sc in 2nd ch from hook and in each ch to end. 9sc.

Work in single crochet rib as follows:

Next Row: Ch1, sc in back loop of each sc to end.

Repeat this row 28 [30, 32, 34] times more. At the end of the last row, rotate your work 90 degrees clockwise. You will be working the next row along the edge of the strip you have just crocheted.

Next Row: Ch 1, sc into edge of last sc from previous row, sc in edge of each row to end. 29 [31, 33, 35] sts.

Begin Stitch Pattern:

Row 1: Ch 1, sc in each sc to end.

Row 2: Ch 2, hdc in each sc to end.

Row 3: Ch 1, sc in each hdc to end.

Repeat these 3 rows until work measures 14 inches from bottom of rib, ending with Row 2 of pattern.

Shape Armholes:

Next Row: Sl st in first 4 hdc, ch 1, sc in next hdc and following 20 [22, 24, 26] hdc, leaving remaining 4 hdc unworked. 21 [23, 25, 27] sts.

Next Row: Sl st in 1st sc, ch 1, sc in next sc and in following 18 [20, 22, 24] sc. 19 [21, 23, 25] sts.

Next Row: Sl st in 1st sc, ch 2, hdc in next sc and in following 16 [18, 20, 22] sc. 17 [19, 21, 23] sts.

Work 8 more rows in Stitch Pattern as set. Break yarn, draw yarn tail through last st and pull tight.

Left Front:

To start, *Ch 10.

Sc in 2nd ch from hook and in each ch to end. 9sc.

Work in single crochet rib as follows:

Next Row: Ch1, sc in back loop of each sc to end.

Repeat this row 14 [15, 16, 17] times more. At the end of the last row, rotate your work 90 degrees clockwise. You will be working the next row along the edge of the strip you have just crocheted.

Next Row: Ch 1, sc into edge if last sc of previous row, sc in edge of each row to end. 15[16, 17, 18] sts.

Work in Stitch Pattern as for Back, until work measures 14 inches, ending with Row 2 of pattern.*

Shape Armhole:

Next Row: Sl st in first 4 hdc, ch 1, sc in next hdc and in each hdc to end. 11 [12, 13, 14] sts.

Next Row: Ch 1, sc in first sc and next 9 [10, 11, 12] sc. 10 [11, 12, 13] sts.

Next Row: Sl st in 1st sc, ch 2, hdc in next sc and in each sc to end. 9 [10, 11, 12] sts.

Work 4 rows in Stitch Pattern as set.

Shape Neckline:

Next Row: Sl st in first 3 sc, ch 1, sc in next sc and in each sc to end. 6 [7, 8, 9] sts.

Next Row: Ch 2, hdc in 1st sc and in following 4 [5, 6, 7] sc. 5 [6, 7, 8] sts.

Work 2 rows in sc. Break yarn, draw yarn tail through last st and pull tight.

Right Front

Work from * to * as for Left Front.

Shape Armhole:

Next Row: Ch 1, sc in 1st hdc and following 10[11, 12, 13] hdc. 11 [12, 13, 14] sts.

Next Row: Sl st in 1st sc, ch 1, sc in next sc and in each sc to end. 10 [11, 12, 13] sts.

Next Row: Ch 2, hdc in 1st sc and in following 8 [9, 10, 11] sc. 9 [10, 11, 12] sts.

Work 4 rows in Stitch Pattern as set.

Shape Neckline:

Next Row: Ch 1, sc in 1st sc and in next 5 [6, 7, 8] sc. 6 [7, 8, 9] sts.

Next Row: Sl st in 1st sc, ch 2, hdc in next sc and in each sc to end. 5 [6, 7, 8] sts.

Work 2 rows in sc. Break yarn, draw yarn tail through last st and pull tight.

Finishing Instructions

Sew shoulder seams and side seams.

Note: When working edgings, it's important to achieve an even, flat edge. If your edging doesn't look like it will lay flat and look nice, rip it out and try again, working your stitches either closer together or further apart. Make sure to do the same number of stitches on both sides, and on both the front and back.

Armhole Edging:

Beginning at underarm, work 1 row of sc around armhole edge. Sl st in first sc, break yarn, draw through last st and pull tight.

Repeat for other armhole.

Stand-up Collar:

Note: For instructions on how to make the wide collar photographed in tan yarn, see the "Variation" below.

Beginning at right front neck edge, work 1 row of sc around neckline edge, ending at left front neck edge.

Row 1: Ch 1, sc in each sc to end.

Row 2: Ch 2, hdc in each sc to end.

Row 3: Ch 1, sc in each hdc to end.

Break yarn, draw through last st and pull tight.

Front Edging:

Beginning at lower right front edge, work 1 row of sc along right front edge, to top of collar. Break yarn, draw through last st and pull tight.

Beginning at upper left front edge, work 1 row of sc along left front edge, to bottom of ribbing. Break yarn, draw through last st and pull tight.

If using zipper:

Baste zipper to inside front edges of vest. Try on vest to ensure that zipper meets correctly, and will hang smoothly. Do not omit this step; a badly inserted zipper can ruin the look of your vest!

Once you have the zipper positioned correctly, sew in securely and remove basting stitches.

Sew in all ends and enjoy!

Variation

Crave drama? A wide ribbed collar is a cinch to work to fit the neckline. In order to give your vest this look, instead of working the stand-up collar described above, work as follows:

♦ Ch 16.
♦ Sc in 2nd ch from hook and each ch to end. 15 sc.

♦ Work in single crochet rib until work measures approx. 20 inches when slightly stretched. (The collar will be a bit longer than the circumference of the neckline. This will help the collar lay flat once it's sewn in place. Since the ribbing is, by nature, very flexible, it's not a problem to adjust the fit when seaming.)

continued

continued

- ◆ Break yarn, pull through last st and pull tight.
- ◆ Sew the collar to the neckline, making sure to line up the side edges of the collar with the front edges of the vest, and easing the remaining portion to fit the neckline.

Now you're ready to work the front edging as in the instructions above.

Chunky Monkey Scarf

Some yarns just beg to be crocheted. Premium Painter's Palette Merino, by Koigu, is one of them. Holding three strands together and working in a simple double crochet pattern makes the scarf as quick and simple as the colors are stunning.

Project Rating: Summer Fling

Cost: Expect to spend $30-$40 for scarf as shown.

Necessary Skills: ch (page 7); dc (page 13); sewing ends (page 24)

Finished Size
Length: 50 inches
Width: 6 inches

Materials

- Koigu PPPM (50g, 175yd/160m, 100 percent merino wool), Colors: P125, P126 and P419, 1 ball each color
- Substitution: Look for a soft, handpainted fingering or sock weight wool yarn.
- Ball band will indicate a knitted gauge of 26–28 sts = 4 inches
- US J / 6mm crochet hook

Gauge
Exact gauge is unimportant for this project.

Instructions

Using 3 strands (1 strand of each color) held together, ch 23.

Row 1: [Dc, ch 3, dc] in 7th ch from hook, [skip next 3 ch, (dc, ch 3, dc) in next ch] 3 times, skip next 3 ch, dc in last ch.

Row 2: Ch 3, [dc, ch 3, dc] in 1st ch3-sp, [(dc, ch 3, dc) in next ch3-sp] 3 times, dc in top ch of turning ch.

Repeat Row 2 until scarf measures 50 inches (or until you run out of yarn!).

Break yarn, draw through last st and pull tight.

Finishing Instructions

Sew in ends.

Variation

Just changing the colors of the yarn can drastically change the look! In the pictured variation (see color insert), we used one strand of predominantly red, one of mainly gold and green, and one of turquoise and lime. The scarf, as shown, has also been shortened to allow for a dramatic brooch closure.

Chapter Eight

◆ ◆

Fashionistas Unite!

Uber-femme Capelet
Drapey cashmere meets feminine lace for the ultimate cover up.

Peek-a-boo Plaid Skirt
Revel in your inner naughty schoolgirl with this kicky skirt.

Pseudo-Kimono
A stylish lace wrap sweater is great for the office or the office party.

S³: Sari Silk Shrug
Recycled bits of sari fabric make the perfect yarn for this dramatic shrug.

Ramblin' Rosie Cardie
Rose-studded granny squares complete this bohemian look.

The "Too Good for Your Boyfriend" Sweater
Self-striping yarn makes the colors, the shaping is all for you.

Cozy Peacoat
Double strands of yarn make a tweed thick enough to keep out the chill.

Uber-Femme Capelet

This elegant shoulder-hugging capelet evokes a more elegant era. Equally fetching over a summer sundress or an evening gown, it's crocheted in delicious pure cashmere.

Project Rating: Summer Fling

Cost: $100–$140 as shown in pure cashmere. In a substitute yarn, cost can range upwards of $30.

Necessary Skills: ch (page 7); sc (page 10); dc (page 13); sewing ends (page 24)

Abbreviations: ch-sp: the space made in the previous row by chaining one or more times between stitches

Finished Size
Fits most adult women

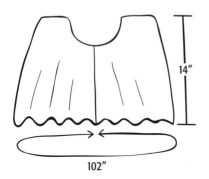

14"

102"

Materials
- Jade Sapphire 4-ply Pure Cashmere (55g, 200yd/183m, 100 percent cashmere), Color Lapis–4 skeins
- Substitution: Approximately 750m sport or DK weight yarn. Stick with cashmere or alpaca blends for the best drape.
- Ball band will indicate a knitted gauge of 23 sts = 4 inches / 10cm.

- US E / 3.5mm crochet hook
- 2 safety pins
- Yarn needle

Gauge
20 sc = 4 inches / 10cm

Instructions
Note: When counting sts, each sc, dc, and each ch in any ch-sp counts as 1 st, **except**: "ch 4" at the beginning of a row counts as 1 dc and 1 ch1-sp (2 sts), and "ch 6" at the beginning of a row counts as 1 dc and 1 ch3-sp (4 sts).

Ch 4, sl st in 1st ch to form a ring.

Row 1: Ch 4, dc in ring, [ch 1, dc in ring] 3 times. 9 sts. Turn work; capelet is worked back and forth.

Row 2: Ch 6, dc in ch1-sp, ([dc, ch 3, dc] in next ch1-sp) twice, dc in ch4-sp, ch 3, dc in 3rd ch of initial ch-4. 20 sts.

Row 3: Ch 1, 6 sc in each ch3-sp. 24 sts.

Row 4: Ch 3 (counts as 1st dc), dc in 2nd sc and in each sc to end.

Row 5: Ch 1, sc in each dc to end.

Row 6: Ch 6, skip 1st 2 sc, dc in 3rd sc, [ch 3, skip next 2 sc, dc in next sc] to end. 33 sts.

Row 7: Ch 6, dc in 1st ch3-sp, [(dc, ch 3, dc) in next ch3-sp] 6 times, dc in ch6-sp, ch 3, dc in 3rd ch of initial ch-6. 40 sts.

Row 8: Ch 1, 6 sc in each ch3-sp. 48 sts.

Row 9: Ch 6, skip 1st 2 sc, dc in 3rd sc, [ch 3, skip next 2 sc, dc in next sc] to end. 65 sts.

Row 10: Ch 6, dc in 1st ch3-sp, [(dc, ch 3, dc) in next ch3-sp] to last ch3-sp, dc in ch6-sp, ch 3, dc in 3rd ch of initial ch-6. 80 sts.

Row 11: Ch 1, 6 sc in each ch3-sp. 96 sts.

Row 12: Ch 3 (counts as 1st dc), dc in 2nd sc and in each sc to end.

Row 13: Ch 1, sc in each dc to end.

Row 14: Ch 6, skip 1st 2 sc, dc in 3rd sc, [ch 3, skip next 2 sc, dc in next sc] to end. 129 sts.

Row 15: Ch 6, dc in 1st ch3-sp, [(dc, ch 3, dc) in next ch3-sp] to last ch3-sp, dc in ch6-sp, ch 3, dc in 3rd ch of initial ch-6. 160 sts.

Row 16: Ch 1, 6 sc in each ch3-sp. 192 sts.

Row 17: Ch 6, skip 1st 2 sc, dc in 3rd sc, [ch 3, skip next 2 sc, dc in next sc] to end. 257 sts.

Row 18: Ch 6, dc in 1st ch3-sp, [(dc, ch 3, dc) in next ch3-sp] to last ch3-sp, dc in ch6-sp, ch 3, dc in 3rd ch of initial ch-6. 320 sts.

Row 19: Ch 1, 6 sc in each ch3-sp. 384 sts.

Row 20: Ch 3 (counts as 1st dc), dc in 2nd sc and in each sc to end.

Row 21: Ch 3 (counts as 1st dc), dc in 2nd dc and in each dc to end.

Row 22: Ch 1, sc in each dc to end.

Row 23: Ch 6, skip 1st 2 sc, dc in 3rd sc, [ch 3, skip next 2 sc, dc in next sc] to end. 513 sts.

Row 24: Ch 6, dc in 1st ch3-sp, [(dc, ch 3, dc) in next ch3-sp] to last ch3-sp, dc in ch6-sp, ch 3, dc in 3rd ch of initial ch-6. 640 sts.

Row 25: Ch 6, skip 1st ch3-sp, dc in next dc, [ch 3, skip next dc and ch3-sp, dc into next dc] to last pair of dcs, ch 3, dc in 3rd ch of initial ch-6. 513 sts.

Row 26: Ch 4, [dc, ch 1, dc] in 1st ch3-sp, [dc, ch 1, dc, ch 1, dc] in each ch-3 sp to last ch3-sp, [dc, ch 1, dc, ch 1] in ch6-sp, dc in 3rd ch of initial ch-6. 640 sts.

Row 27: Ch 6, dc in 3rd dc, [ch 3, skip next 2 dc, dc in next dc] until 2 dc and ch-6 remain, ch 3, skip last 2 dc, dc into 3rd ch of initial ch-6. 513 sts.

Row 28: Ch 6, dc in 1st ch3-sp, [(dc, ch 3, dc) in next ch3-sp] to last ch3-sp, dc in ch6-sp, ch 3, dc in 3rd ch of initial ch-6. 640 sts.

Row 29: Ch 1, 4 sc in each ch3-sp to end. 512 sts.

Row 30: Ch 3, dc in 2nd sc and in each sc to end.

Row 31: Ch 1, sc in each dc to end.

Row 32: Ch 3, dc in 2nd sc and in each sc to end. Do not turn work.

Work 1 row sc along straight edge of capelet. This edge forms the front and neck edge of the piece. Sl st in last st, break yarn and draw through last st, pull tight.

Finishing Instructions

To crochet ties for front, put on capelet and hang evenly across both shoulders. Decide at which point you'd like the ties to attach on either side of front edge. In most cases, this will be somewhere between 8 and 10 inches from each corner. Place a safety pin in the sc at this point on each side.

Use a sl st to attach yarn to this point on 1 side, ch 70.

Sl st into each ch to end; work 1 last sl st in edge of capelet, break yarn and draw through last st, pull tight.

Repeat for other side.

Sew in ends securely and block as desired.

Variation

Circular-shaped capelets are, in many ways, the ideal pattern for experimentation. Selecting a finer (or heavier) weight yarn will just change the finished size. Or, switch up the fiber content for even more dramatic flair. A laceweight mohair on the same hook will be light, airy, and full of romance.

Peek-a-boo Plaid Skirt

by Jodi Green

Worked in the colors of a traditional Black Watch tartan, this sassy skirt is a far cry from the prim private school uniform. The peek-a-boo mesh border is worked sideways, and an optional side slit offers an extra flash of thigh.

Project Rating: Summer Fling

Cost: $45–$75 in yarn as shown.

Necessary Skills: ch (page 7); dc (page 13); hdc [half double crochet] (page 31); tr [treble crochet] (page 14); sewing ends (page 24)

Abbreviations: hdc-dec: Yarn over, insert hook in 1st st and pull up a loop, yarn over, insert hook in 2nd st and pull up a loop, yarn over, draw through all 5 loops on hook. 1 st decreased.
ch-sp: the space made in the previous row by chaining one or more times between stitches.

Materials

- ♦ Lorna's Laces Shepherd Worsted (4oz, 225yd/206m, 100 percent superwash wool), color: Blackwatch; 3 [3, 3, 4, 4, 5] skeins
- ♦ Substitution: Look for an aran weight yarn. 675 [675, 675, 900, 900, 1125] yd/618 [618, 618, 824, 824, 1030]m are required.
- ♦ Ball band will indicate a knitted gauge of 18 sts = 4 inches / 10cm.
- ♦ US F / 4mm crochet hook
- ♦ Yarn needle

Sizes

XS [S, M, L, XL, XXL]

Finished Measurements:

Hip: 37 [39, 41, 43, 45, 47] inches
Waist: 29 [31, 33, 35, 37, 39]

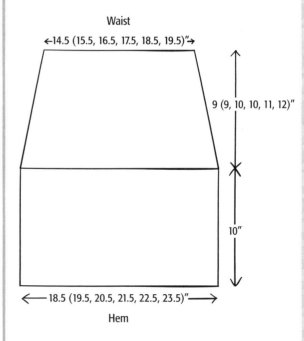

Waist

←14.5 (15.5, 16.5, 17.5, 18.5, 19.5)"→

9 (9, 10, 10, 11, 12)"

10"

←— 18.5 (19.5, 20.5, 21.5, 22.5, 23.5)"——→

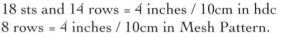

Hem

Gauge

18 sts and 14 rows = 4 inches / 10cm in hdc
8 rows = 4 inches / 10cm in Mesh Pattern.

Stitch Pattern

Mesh Pattern (Worked over an odd number of sts):

Ch an even number of sts (desired number of sts + 1).

Set-up Row [WS]: Hdc in 2nd ch from hook and in each ch to end.

Row 1 [RS]: Ch 5 (counts as 1 tr and 1 ch1-sp), tr in back loop of 3rd hdc, [ch 1, skip next hdc, tr in back loop of next st] to end.

Row 2 [WS]: Ch 2, hdc in 1st tr, [hdc in ch1-sp, hdc in next tr] to last tr, hdc in next ch-sp, hdc in 4th ch of initial ch-5.

Repeat Rows 1 and 2 for Mesh Pattern.

Instructions

Mesh panel:

Ch 40.

Work Set-up Row of Mesh Pattern, then work Rows 1 and 2 19 [20, 21, 22, 23, 24] times. A WS row has just been worked.

Skirt body:

Fold panel so that wrong sides are together. Sl st in 1st ch of foundation chain to join panel in a ring. Skirt will now be worked in the round. The first round will be worked along the long side edge of the mesh panel.

Round 1: Ch 2, [work 1 hdc in the edge of the first hdc row, work 3 hdc in the edge of the first tr row, work 2 hdc in the edge of the next hdc row, work 3 hdc in the edge of the next tr row] 18 [19, 20, 21, 22, 23] times, work 1 hdc in the edge of the next hdc row, work 2 [3, 2, 3, 2, 3] hdc in the edge of the last tr row, work 1 hdc in the edge of the last hdc row, sl st in 1st hdc to join. 166 [176, 184, 194, 202, 212] sts.

Round 2: Ch 2, hdc in 1st hdc and in each hdc to end, sl st in 1st hdc to join.

Repeat this round until work measures 4 inches from top of mesh panel.

Place a safety pin in work after 83 [88, 92, 97, 101, 106] sts to indicate side "seam" of work. This pin will be referred to as the "marker" in the directions which follow.

Shape Waist:

Decrease Round: Ch 2, hdc-dec, hdc in each hdc to 2 hdc before marker, hdc-dec, hdc-dec, hdc to 2 sts before end of round, hdc-dec, sl st in 1st hdc to join. 4 sts decreased.

Work 1 [1, 1, 1, 2, 2] round(s) without shaping.

Repeat these 2 [2, 2, 2, 3, 3] rounds 7 times more, then work Decrease Round once more. 130 [140, 148, 158, 166, 176] sts.

Work without shaping until skirt measures 18[18, 19, 19, 20, 21] inches from lower edge of mesh panel.

Drawstring Waistband:

Next Round: Ch 4 (counts as 1 dc and 1 ch1-sp), skip first 2 hdc, dc in next hdc, [ch 1, skip next hdc, dc in next hdc] to end, sl st in 3rd ch of initial ch-4 to join.

Next Round: Ch 2, hdc in each dc and each ch1-sp to end, sl st in 1st hdc to join. Break yarn, draw through last st and pull tight.

Finishing Instructions

Sew in ends securely.

Drawstring:

Work a chain which is 20 inches longer than your waist measurement. Thread through dc row, with ends emerging at center front of skirt.

Variation

- The slit can be placed in the back of the skirt instead of the side, if desired. Before working the waist shaping, place a marker after 42 [44, 46, 48, 50, 53] sts, then after another 82 [88, 92, 98, 102, 106] sts, and work the decreases on either side of each marker.

- The mesh panel can be shortened or lengthened by a multiple of 2 sts, and the solid section of the skirt can be lengthened as well. If you choose to lengthen the solid section, extra width is needed. Make the mesh panel a little longer, and work extra sts along the edge. Decrease these sts gradually in the first few inches of the solid section of the skirt.

- Try working the mesh and solid sections in two contrasting solid colours, or coordinating a variegated yarn with a solid. Switching colours after every two rows on the mesh section will create vertical stripes when turned sideways.

- If you prefer an elastic waistline to a drawstring, just work an extra inch of hdc instead of the dc drawstring row, then fold this section in half and whipstitch closed to form a casing (leaving a 2 inch opening). Cut a length of 1/2 inch elastic two inches less than your waist measurement, thread into the casing and sew ends together, being careful not to twist elastic. Sew casing closed.

- If you're handy with a sewing needle, you can try adding a fabric lining to the skirt.

Pseudo-Kimono

by Robyn Chachula

Searching for that perfect sweater that you can wear with jeans at the bar or a skirt at the office? Want something modern with just the right amount of funky? Well, stop searching, your sweater is here. This design takes the traditional kimono style and marries it with a ribbed corset, which creates a stunning, waist-flattering sweater with light airy sleeves.

Project Rating: Love o' Your Life

Cost: Approximately $100–$140 with yarn as shown.

Necessary Skills: ch (page 7); sl st (page 16); sc (page 10); dc (page 13); sewing ends (page 24)

Abbreviations: ch-sp: the space made in the previous row by chaining one or more times between stitches.

Finished Size

S[M, L, XL]

Chest (when closed): 33.5[36.5, 40, 43.5] inches

Length: 18.5[19, 22.5, 23] inches

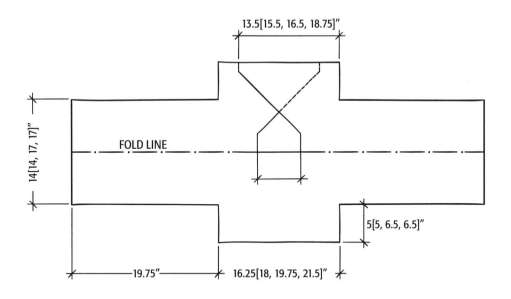

13.5[15.5, 16.5, 18.75]"

14[14, 17, 17]"

FOLD LINE

5[5, 6.5, 6.5]"

19.75"

16.25[18, 19.75, 21.5]"

Materials

- Knit Picks Ambrosia (50g, 110yd / 330m, 80 percent baby alpaca, 20 percent cashmere), Color: Fog—14, [15, 17, 19] balls
- Substitution: Look for approx. 1500 [1600, 1850, 2000] yd/1372 [1463, 1692, 1829]m of a worsted weight, baby alpaca blend yarn. The quality of the yarn is important for this sweater, to achieve the correct drape and feel.
- Ball Band will indicate a knitted gauge of 24 sts = 4 inches / 10cm.
- US H / 5.0mm crochet hook
- Safety pin
- Yarn needle
- 3 x 0.5 inch buttons
- One hook and eye closure
- Sewing thread and needle

Gauge

To measure gauge, ch 18 and work 15 rows in Stitch Pattern according to directions below. Block swatch before measuring.

Width of swatch = 3.5 inches / 8.9cm
Length of swatch = 4 inches / 10cm

Note: It is very important to block this stitch before measuring the gauge, because the gauge may vary greatly during blocking.

Stitch Pattern

Note: Set-up row increases number of sts from a multiple of 8 sts + 1 to a multiple of 10 sts + 1. All subsequent rows are worked over a multiple of 10 sts + 1.

Ch a multiple of 8 sts + 2.

Set-up Row: Sc in 2nd ch from hook, sc in next 2 ch, [ch 5, skip next 3 ch, sc in next 5 ch] to last 6 ch, ch 5, skip next 3 ch, sc in last 3 ch.

Row 1: Ch 1, sc in 1st 2 sc, ch 3, skip next sc, sc in ch5-sp, [ch 3, skip next sc, sc in next 3 sc, ch 3, skip next sc, sc in last ch5-sp] to last ch5-sp, ch 3, skip next sc, sc in last 2 sc.

Row 2: Ch1, sc in 1st sc, [ch 3, skip next sc, sc in ch3-sp, sc in next sc, sc in ch3-sp, ch 3, skip next sc, sc in next sc] to end.

Row 3: Ch 4, sc in 1st ch3-sp, sc in next 3 sc, sc in ch3-sp, [ch 5, sc in next ch3-sp, sc in next 3 sc, sc in ch3-sp] to last ch3-sp, ch 2, dc in last sc.

Row 4: Ch 1, sc in dc, [ch 3, skip next sc, sc in next 3 sc, ch 3, skip next sc, sc in ch5-sp] to last ch5-sp, ch 3, skip next sc, sc in next 3 sc, ch 3, skip next sc, sc in ch4-sp.

Row 5: Ch 1, sc in 1st sc, sc in ch3-sp, [ch 3, skip next sc, sc in next sc, ch 3, skip next sc, sc in ch3-sp, sc in next sc, sc in next ch3-sp] to next-to-last ch3-sp, ch 3, skip next sc, sc in next sc, ch 3, skip next sc, sc in ch3-sp, sc in last sc.

Row 6: Ch 1, sc in 1st 2 sc, sc in ch3-sp, [ch 5, sc in next ch3-sp, sc in next 3 sc, sc in ch3-sp] to next-to-last ch3-sp, ch 5, sc in last ch3-sp, sc in last 2 sc.

Repeat Rows 1–6 for Stitch Pattern.

Instructions

Pattern Notes: The back of this sweater is worked first, then stitches are added for the sleeves. The upper back and the backs of the sleeves are worked at the same time, then the work is divided at the back neck. The upper fronts and the fronts of the sleeves are worked at the same time, then the fronts are continued until they are the same length as the back. The ribbed corset at the bottom of the sweater is worked last.

When counting sts, each sc, dc, and each ch in a ch-sp counts as 1 st. "Ch 4" at the beginning of a row counts as 3 sts.

Back:

Ch 82 (90, 98, 106).

Work Set-up Row of Stitch Pattern. 101 [111, 121, 131] sts.

Work Rows 1-6 of Stitch Pattern 2 [2, 3, 3] times.

Work Rows 1-5 of Stitch Pattern.

Sleeves:

Without turning work or breaking yarn, use a slip stitch to join a new ball of yarn to beginning of last row. Ch 96 using new ball of yarn. Break this yarn, draw tail through last ch.

Turn work; ch 97.

Next row: Continue working in Stitch Pattern, working Set-up Row over new ch sts at beginning and end of row, and Row 6 over center sts. 341 [351, 361, 371] sts.

Work Rows 1-6 of Stitch Pattern 3[3, 4, 4] times.

Work Rows 1-5 of Stitch Pattern.

Last Back Row: Ch 1, sc in 1st 2 sc, sc in ch3-sp, [ch 5, sc in next ch3-sp, sc in next 3 sc, sc in ch3-sp] 15 [16, 16, 16] times, [ch 3, sc in next ch3-sp, sc in next 3 sc, sc in ch3-sp] 4 [3, 4, 5] times, [ch 5, sc in next ch3-sp, sc in next 3 sc, sc in ch3-sp] 14 [15, 15, 15] times, ch 5, sc in last ch3-sp, sc in last 2 sc.

*Divide for Fronts:

(Sizes S and XL Only)

Row 1: Ch 1, sc in 1st 2 sc, [ch 3, skip next sc, sc in ch5-sp, ch 3, skip next sc, sc in next 3 sc] 15 [–,–, 16] times, ch 3, skip next sc, dc in ch3-sp.

Place a safety pin in the post of the dc just worked; this Front panel will be worked over these 156 [–,–, 166] sts only.

Row 2: Ch 1, sc in dc, sc in ch3-sp, ch 3, skip next sc, sc in next sc, [ch 3, skip next sc, sc in ch3-sp, sc in next sc, sc in ch3-sp, ch 3, skip next sc, sc in next sc] to end.

Row 3: Ch 4, sc in 1st ch3-sp, sc in next 3 sc, sc in ch3-sp, [ch 5, sc in next ch3-sp, sc in next 3 sc, sc in ch3-sp] to next-to-last ch3-sp, ch 5, sc in last ch3-sp, sc in last 2 sc.

Row 4: Ch 1, sc in 1st 2 sc, ch 3, skip next sc, sc in ch5-sp, [ch 3, skip next sc, sc in next 3 sc, ch 3, skip next sc, sc in ch5-sp] to last ch5-sp, ch 3, skip next sc, sc in next 3 sc, ch 3, skip last sc, sc in ch4-sp.

Row 5: Ch 1, sc in 1st sc, sc in ch3-sp, [ch 3, skip next sc, sc in next sc, ch 3, skip next sc, sc in ch3-sp, sc in next sc, sc in next ch3-sp] to last ch3-sp, ch 3, skip next sc, sc in last sc.

Work Rows 3-5 1 [–,–, 3] times more.

Work Row 3 once more.

Proceed to Increase Row 4; see directions below, under "Shape Front Neckline."

(Sizes M and L Only)

Next Row: Ch 1, sc in 1st 2 sc, [ch 3, skip next sc, sc in ch5-sp, ch 3, skip next sc, sc in next 3 sc] 15 times, ch 3, skip next sc, sc in ch5-sp, ch 3, skip next sc, sc in next 2 sc.

Place a safety pin in the side of the last sc just worked; this Front panel will be worked over these 161 sts only.

Work Stitch Pattern Rows 2–6.

Work Stitch Pattern Rows 1–6.

Proceed to Increase Row 1; see directions below under, "Shape Front Neckline."

Shape Front Neckline:

Increase Row 1: Ch 1, sc in 1st 2 sc, ch 3, skip next sc, sc in ch5-sp, [ch 3, skip next sc, sc in next 3 sc, ch 3, skip next sc, sc in ch5-sp] to last ch5-sp, ch 3, skip next sc, sc in next sc, 2 sc in last sc.

Increase Row 2: Ch 6, skip 1st sc, sc in 2nd sc, [ch 3, skip next sc, sc in ch3-sp, sc in next sc, sc in ch3-sp, ch 3, skip next sc, sc in next sc] to end.

Increase Row 3: Ch 4, sc in 1st ch3-sp, sc in next 3 sc, sc in ch3-sp, [ch 5, sc in next ch3-sp, sc in next 3 sc, sc in ch3-sp] to last ch3-sp, ch 5, 3 sc in ch6-sp.

Increase Row 4: Ch 1, 2 sc in 1st sc, sc in 2nd sc, ch 3, skip next sc, sc in ch5-sp, [ch 3, skip next sc, sc in next 3 sc, ch 3, skip next sc, sc in ch5-sp] to last ch5-sp, ch 3, skip next sc, sc in next 3 sc, ch 3, skip next sc, sc in ch4-sp.

Increase Row 5: Ch 1, sc in 1st sc, sc in ch3-sp, [ch 3, skip next sc, sc in next sc, ch 3, skip next sc, sc in ch3-sp, sc in next sc, sc in next ch3-sp] to last ch3-sp, ch 3, skip next sc, sc in next sc, ch 3, dc in last sc.

Increase Row 6: Ch 1, 2 sc in dc, sc in ch3-sp, [ch 5, sc in next ch3-sp, sc in next 3 sc, sc in ch3-sp] to next-to-last ch3-sp, ch 5, sc in last ch3-sp, sc in last 2 sc.

10 stitches have been increased.

(Sizes S, XL Only)

Work Increase Rows 4–6 once.

Work Increase Rows 1–6 1 [–,–, 2] times.

Work Increase Rows 1–5 once. 24 [–,–, 34] sts increased. 180 [–,–, 200] sts.

(Sizes M, L Only)

Work Increase Rows 1–6 twice.

Work Increase Rows 1–5 once. 29 sts increased. 190 sts.

(All Sizes)

Last Sleeve Row: Ch 1, 2 sc in dc, sc in ch3-sp, [ch 5, sc in next ch3-sp, sc in next 3 sc, sc in ch3-sp] 6 [7, 7, 8] times. Place safety pin in the center sc of the last 5 sc worked, [ch 3, sc in next ch3-sp, sc in next 3 sc, sc in ch3-sp] 11 times, ch 3, sc in last ch3-sp, sc in last 2 sc. 157 [167, 167, 177] sts.

Break yarn, draw through last st and pull tight. Turn work.

Use a sl st to rejoin yarn to marked sc from previous row. This will be the first st of the next row; the sleeve is complete, the lower fronts will be worked over the remaining 61 [71, 71, 81] sts.

Work Increase Rows 1-6, 3 [3, 4, 4] times more. 91 [101, 111, 121] sts. Break yarn, draw through last st and pull tight.*

Use a sl st to rejoin yarn to 1st st of Last Back Row. Work from * to * as for first front panel.

Block work by pinning to measurements indicated in schematic.

Steam block lightly.

Sew side and sleeve seams. Whip stitch is recommended for sewing these seams.

Corset:

Note: When working the corset, one end of each row is joined to the edge of the kimono body using a slip stitch. Join each row to the next stitch (sc or ch) along the lower edge, *except* omit the 2nd ch of each ch3-sp. This will result in a slightly gathered effect below the bust, and will provide waist shaping.

Use a sl st to join yarn to corner of right front. Ch 36 [36, 41, 41].

Row 1: Sc in 2nd ch from hook and in each ch to end, sl st in end st of lower edge of body.

Row 2: Sl st in next st of lower edge of body (counts as turning ch), sc in back loop of each sc to end.

Row 3: Ch 1, sc in back loop of first 16 [16, 21, 21] sc, [ch 2, skip next 2 sc, sc in back loops of next 5 sc] twice, ch 2, skip next 2 sc, sc in back loops of last 3 sc, sl st in next st of lower edge of body. 3 button-holes formed.

Row 4: Sl st in next st of lower edge of body (counts as turning ch), sc in back loop of each sc to end.

Row 5: Ch 1, sc in back loop of each sc to end, sl st in next st of lower edge of body.

Repeat Rows 4 and 5 until all lower body sts have been joined. Break yarn, draw through last st and pull tight.

Work 1 row sc around front and back neckline edges, and around cuffs.

Finishing Instructions

Sew in ends.

Sew buttons to left front, opposite button-holes.

Sew eye of hook and eye to inside of right front, opposite left front edge.

Sew hook to left front edge.

Charts and Symbols

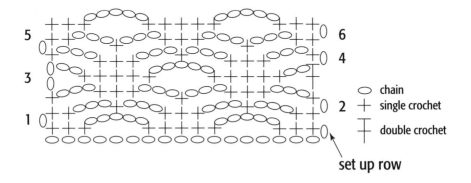

○ chain
+ single crochet
╪ double crochet

set up row

Variation

If a traditional kimono is more your style, then forego the ribbed corset and add extra rows to the back and the front. For a waist-length kimono, add 26 rows prior to joining the sleeves and lengthen the front panels accordingly. Use a frog fastener to close the front.

If a more romantic sweater is your style, forget the buttons and work the corset without the button-holes. Sew a ribbon to the right front edge and to the left front, at the top of the ribbed corset. Use it to close the front with a pretty bow.

Japanese Style

As with many things fashion, knitting and crochet have been hot in Japan for much of the past decade. From crocheted *amigurumi* (plush toys) to cutting-edge (and edgy) wearables, from unusual housewares to innovative hats, it's not hard to find inspiration for your own designs.

Planning a visit to the Land of the Rising Sun? When in Tokyo, make sure to check out the latest in Japanese yarns by visiting Puppy Yarn Company (www.puppyarn.co.jp) as well as the yarn departments of the larger department stores in the fashionable Ginza district.

Don't think you need to learn a new language or cross the Pacific to benefit from this new fashion wave. Simply searching the Web for "Japanese Crochet Patterns" will provide many English-language resources to get you going. Even better, many North American crafters have taken time to provide their translations or interpretations of Japanese-language patterns. Or, check out one of the many online translators, such as Babelfish (babelfish.altavista.com), to get a close enough translation of your new favorite Japanese crochet site. One helpful hint: online translators are far from perfect. On the Puppy Yarn site, what they call a "key needle" is actually a crochet hook.

S³—Sari Silk Shrug

by Catie Berger

Yarn spun from recycled silk saris just begs to be crocheted into something fun and flirty. The surprising weight of the yarn lets the poet sleeve drape beautifully.

Project Rating: Flirtation

Cost: $60-$90

Necessary Skills: ch (page 7); dc (page 13); sl st (page 16); sewing ends (page 24)

Abbreviations: V-st: [Dc, ch 1, dc] in ch or ch-sp, as indicated

Finished Size

Back Width: 16 [20, 24] inches
Sleeve Width: 12 [14.5, 17.25] inches

Materials

- Sari Silk (200g, 200yd/182m, 100 percent silk sari remnants) – 3[3, 4] hanks
- Substitution: Sari Silk yarns are widely available on the Internet, but if you choose another fiber keep in mind that the weight of this yarn is what gives it its drape. The handspun quality of the yarn makes the gauge variable.
- Approx. 600[600, 800]yd/550[550, 730]m are needed.
- Ball band will indicate a knitted gauge of approx. 12 sts = 4 inches / 10cm.
- US K / 6.5mm crochet hook
- Yarn needle
- Hand sewing needle and coordinating thread

Gauge

9 sts (3 V-stitches) = 4 inches / 10cm

Note: Sari Silk is handspun and is variable in size. Gauge is approximate.

V-Stitch Pattern

Ch a multiple of 3 sts + 1 (number of V-sts desired × 3) + 4].

Set-up Row: V-st in 5th ch from hook (first 4 ch form turning ch), [skip next 2 ch, V-st in next ch] until 2 ch remain, skip next ch, dc in last ch.

Pattern Row: Ch 3, V-st in ch1-sp of 1st V-st, [V-st in ch-sp of next V-st] to last V-st, dc in top ch of turning ch.

Repeat Pattern Row for V-Stitch Pattern.

Instructions

Back:

Loosely ch 40 [49, 58].

Work Set-up Row of V-Stitch pattern. 12 [15, 18] V-st.

Work Pattern Row 16 [20, 24] times; 17 [21, 25] rows worked in total.

Sleeves:

Fold work in half so that foundation chain and top edge meet. Sl st in end of foundation chain; sleeves will be worked in rounds, working into the side edges of the back panel.

Next Round: Ch 4 (counts as 1 dc and 1 ch1-sp), dc in sl st (1st V-st formed), [skip 1st row, V-st around post of edge st of 2nd row] 8 [10, 12] times, sl st in 3rd ch of initial ch-4 to join. 9 [11, 13] V-st.

Next Round: Sl st in ch1-sp of 1st V-st, ch 4 (counts as 1 dc and 1 ch1-sp), dc in same ch1-sp (1st V-st formed), V-st in ch1-sp of each V-st to end, sl st in 3rd ch of initial ch-4 to join.

Repeat this round 15 times more; 17 rounds worked in total.

Increase Round: Sl st in ch1-sp of 1st V-st, ch 4 (counts as 1 dc and 1 ch1-sp), dc in same ch1-sp (1st V-st formed), V-st in space between 1st and 2nd V-st, [V-st in next V-st, V-st in space between this and next V-st] to end, sl st in 3rd ch of initial ch-4 to join. 18 [22, 26] V-st.

Work 1 round without shaping.

Repeat these 2 rounds once more. 36 [44, 52] V-st.

Shell Edging: Sl st in ch1-sp of 1st V-st, ch 1, sc in same ch1-sp, 5 dc in ch1-sp of 2nd V-st, [sc in ch1-sp of next V-st, 5 dc in ch1-sp of next V-st] to end, sl st in 1st sc to join. Break yarn, draw through last st and pull tight.

Use sl st to join remaining corners of Back, and work the second sleeve in the same way as the first.

Body Edging:

Use sl st to join yarn to sl st at beginning of first sleeve. Work Shell Edging around body opening. (When you work along the foundation chain, work into each ch2-sp in the same way you worked into the ch1-spaces of the V-sts.)

Finishing Instructions

Sew in ends using yarn needle, then use sewing needle and thread to further secure ends. Steam block.

Note: Due to the humid climate in Nepal, the Sari Silk often smells a bit musty. Steaming the finished piece will set your stitches and remove the musty smell at the same time. If the yarn is still musty, lay it out in the sun.

Variation

Take a cue from my dear friend Debora Lloyd. Turn the shrug into a kicky cardi that dresses up (or down) with ease. You'll need 2 extra balls of yarn at least!

1. Finish the shrug as written.
2. Crochet along the side front edge of shrug. Make a v neck by decreasing a few stitches each row of the neck edge. This panel makes half of the cardigan front. Repeat at other side, reversing shaping.
3. Beginning at left side of front, crochet along front, then across existing back edge of shrug; then along front right edge.
4. Continue to crochet back and forth. Feel free to get creative here! Make the cardi as long and loose as you like. Don't forget to try it on as you go!

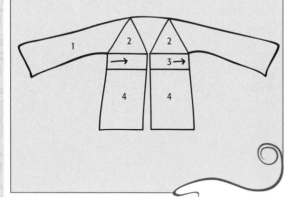

Sustainable Crafting

Back in chapter 3, we looked at different types of yarn. More and more, companies are turning to the 3 Rs for yarn sources: Reduce, Reuse, Recycle.

Sari Silk is just one example. In the past few months, we've seen Banana fiber waste spun into fine yarn and soy byproducts spun into a silk-like texture. In chapter 10, we even look at a few ways to do your own fiber recycling, by cutting up old plastic bags or ill-fitting jeans and making something new.

When working with recycled yarn, don't expect the same evenness of color and texture as with commercial-grade yarn. In fact, a large part of the appeal is the unique texture and color variations that occur.

Ramblin' Rosie Cardie

by Annie Modesitt

This bohemian-style cardigan pairs nifty squares with multi-colored roses for a funky and fresh look. Delicious hand-dyed yarns give the color some depth, but the cardie would be equally stunning in solid shades.

Project Rating: Love o' Your Life

Cost: Approximately $140–$200 as shown. By substituting a smooth lightweight yarn in solid colors, you'll save some dough but lose the hand-dyed appeal.

Necessary Skills: ch (page 7); sc (page 10); dc (page 13); hdc (page 31); sewing ends (page 24)

Abbreviations: ch-sp: the space made in the previous row by chaining one or more times between stitches

Finished Size

S [M, L, XL]
Chest: 36[41, 46, 51] inches
Length: 24[25, 29.25, 33.5] inches

Gauge

18 sc = 4 inches / 10cm
Each rose square should measure 3.75 inches in width and height.

Schematic

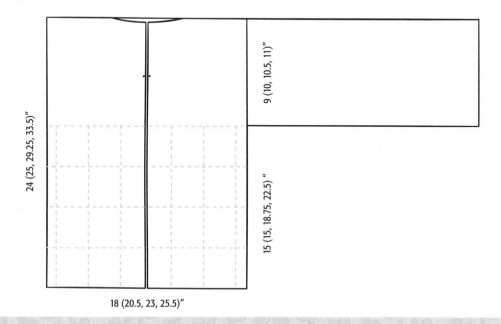

24 (25, 29.25, 33.5)"

9 (10, 10.5, 11)"

15 (15, 18.75, 22.5)"

18 (20.5, 23, 25.5)"

Materials

- ArtYarns Ultramerino4 (50g, 191yd/174m, 100 percent Merino Wool),
- [A] Color: UM115 (Reds) – 1(1, 1, 2) skeins
- [B] Color: UM102 (Yellow/Green/Red) – 1(1, 1, 2) skeins
- [C] Color: UM113 (Brown) – 4(4, 6, 8) skeins
  [D] Color: UM119 (Greens) – 7(7, 8, 9) skeins
- Substitution: Look for a smooth sport-weight yarn. Since ArtYarns Ultramerino4 is hand dyed, you'll most accurately obtain the look of the garment by choosing a similarly hand dyed yarn.
- Ball band will indicate a knitted gauge of 25 sts = 4 inches / 10cm.
- US E / 3.5mm crochet hook
- Yarn needle

Instructions

Rose Squares:

Make 40 [44, 60, 84] Rose Squares, as follows. Use Color A for the roses of half of the squares, and B for the roses of the other half.

Rose

Using A or B, create a slip knot with a fairly open loop; be sure the adjustable loop is formed using the yarn tail, instead of the working yarn (the yarn coming from the ball).

Row 1: Work 9 hdc into the loop, sl st in 1st hdc to join; pull slipknot loop tight.

Note: Each hdc has 3 loops along the top edge. The front 2 loops are formed by the chain which is formed at the top of any crochet stitch, the back loop is formed by the yarn over which begins the formation of an hdc stitch.

When the petals of the flowers in this pattern are formed, different layers of petals are formed by working rows into different loops.

Row 2: Ch 1; working into the center loops only, [(sc, 2dc) in 1st hdc, (3 dc) in next hdc, (2 dc, sc) into next hdc] 3 times, sl st in 1st sc to join.

Row 3: Working into the front loops only, [2 hdc] in each hdc of Row 1, sl st in 1st sc of Row 2. Break yarn, draw through last st and pull tight.

Square

Row 1: Using Color C and working into the back loops of Row 1 of Rose, work 2 sc in each hdc, sl st in 1st sc to join. 18 sts.

Row 2: Ch 1, [sc in 1st sc, 2 sc in next sc] to end, sl st in 1st sc to join. 27 sts.

Row 3: Ch 1, [sc in first 2 sc, 2 sc in next sc] to end, sl st in 1st sc to join. 36 sts.

Row 4: Ch 3 (counts as 1st dc), 2 dc in 1st sc, dc in next 8 sc, [3 dc in next sc, dc in next 8 sc] to end, sl st in 3rd ch of initial ch-3 to join. 44 sts.

Row 5: Ch 3 (counts as 1st dc), 2 dc in 2nd sc, dc in next 10 sc, [3 dc in next sc, dc in next 10 sc] to end, sl st in 3rd ch of initial ch-3 to join. 52 sts.

Row 6: Ch 1, [3 sc in 1st sc, sc in next 12 sc] to end, sl st in 1st sc to join. 60 sts. Break yarn, draw through last st and pull tight.

Join squares into 4 [4, 5, 6] strips of 10 [11, 12, 14] squares each, alternating A squares and B squares, as follows:

Joining Squares

First, *using D, sl st in corner of one square.

Ch 2, sl st in corner of second square.

Ch 4, sl st in 2nd st from last st joined on first square.

Then, [ch 4, sl st in 4th st from last st worked on second square; ch 4, sl st in 4th st from last st joined on first square] 3 times.

Ch 2, sl st in corner of second square. Break yarn, draw through last st and pull tight.*

Arrange the strips so that the A and B squares alternate vertically as well as horizontally, in a checkerboard pattern (see photo). Join the strips as follows:

Work from * to * for the first squares in the strips, [ch 5, work from * to * for the next squares in the strips] until all squares in each strip have been joined. Break yarn, draw through last st and pull tight.

Designate one long edge of the panel you have created, as the top edge of the panel. Using D, sl st in the top right corner of the panel and work along top edge of the panel as follows as follows:

(Size S Only)

For size S, [work 15 sc in edge of 1st square, 1 sc in ch2-sp, 15 sc in edge of next square, 2 sc in ch2-sp, 15 sc in edge of next square, 1 sc in ch2-sp] 3 times, 15 sc in edge of last square. 162 sts.

(Size M Only)

For size M, work 15 sc in edge of each square and 2 sc in each ch2-sp, *except* work only 14 sc in edge of center square. 184 sts.

(Size L Only)

For size L, [work 15 sc in edge of 1st square, 3 sc in ch2-sp, 15 sc in edge of next square, 2 sc in ch2-sp] 5 times, 15 sc in edge of next square, 3 sc in last ch2-sp, 15 sc in last square. 208 sts.

(Size XL Only)

For size XL, [work 15 sc in edge of 1st square, 2 sc in ch2-sp, 15 sc in edge of next square, 1 sc in ch2-sp] 6 times, 15 sc in edge of next square, 2 sc in last ch2-sp, 15 sc in edge of last square. 230 sts.

All Sizes

Continue to work 1 row sc around entire edge of panel, working 15 sc in edge of each square, and 2 sc in each ch2-sp; sl st in 1st sc to join end of round at upper right corner of panel.

Right Front Yoke:

Row 1 [RS]: Ch 2 (counts as 1st dc), dc in 2nd sc, [ch 1, skip next sc, dc in next sc] 19 [22, 25, 28] times. Right Front Yoke will be worked back and forth over these 40 [46, 52, 58] sts.

Row 2 [WS]: Ch 1, sc in each dc and ch1-sp to end, sc in 2nd ch of initial ch-2.

Repeat these 2 rows until work measures 9 [10, 10.5, 11] inches from top of Rose Square panel, ending with a RS row. Break yarn, draw through last st and pull tight.

Back Yoke:

Use sl st to join D to sc adjacent to last st of Row 1 of Right Front Yoke.

Row 1 [RS]: Ch 2 (counts as 1st dc), dc in 2nd sc, [ch 1, skip next sc, dc in next sc] 40 [45, 51, 56] times. Back Yoke will be worked back and forth over these 82 [92, 104, 114] sts.

Row 2 [WS]: Ch 1, sc in each dc and ch1-sp to end, sc in 2nd ch of initial ch-2.

Repeat these 2 rows until work measures same as Right Front Panel, ending with a RS row. Break yarn, draw through last st and pull tight.

Left Front Yoke:

Use sl st to join D to sc adjacent to last st of Row 1 of Back Yoke.

Work as for Right Front Yoke.

Join Shoulders:

With wrong sides facing, fold work so that Fronts meet Back at shoulders. Beginning at armhole edge, sc first 22 [27, 32, 27] sts of each Front panel together with Back panel; center 38 [38, 40, 40] sts of Back and 18 [19, 20, 21] sts of each front are left free.

Collar:

Use sl st to join D to top right front corner. Work along neckline opening as follows:

Row 1 [RS]: Ch 1, sc in each dc and ch1-sp to end. 74 [76, 80, 82] sts.

Row 2 [WS]: Ch 2 (counts as 1st dc), dc in next sc, [ch 1, skip next sc, dc in next sc] to end.

Row 3 [RS]: Ch 1, 2 sc in 1st dc, 1 sc in each dc and ch1-sp to last dc, 2 sc in 2nd ch of initial ch-2. 2 sts increased.

Row 4: Ch 2 (counts as 1st dc), ch 1 (counts as ch-1sp), dc in next sc, [ch 1, skip next sc, dc in next sc] to next-to-last sc, ch 1, dc in last sc. 2 sts increased. 78 [80, 84, 86] sts.

Repeat these 4 rows 4 times more. 94 [96, 100, 102] sts.

Repeat Rows 1 and 2 until collar measures 5 [6, 7, 8.25] inches, ending with Row 1. Break yarn and draw through last st, pull tight.

Sleeves:

Use sl st to join D to work at underarm. Work 1 sc in edge of each sc and 2 sc in edge of each dc or turning chain around armhole edge; sl st in 1st sc to join. Be sure you have an even number of sts; if you do not, then omit the "skip next sc" at end of next row.

Round 1: Ch 3 (counts as 1st dc and 1 ch1-sp), [skip next sc, dc in next sc, ch 1] to end, sl st in 2nd ch of initial ch-3 to join.

Round 2: Ch 1, sc in each dc and ch1-sp to end, sl st in 1st sc to join.

Repeat these 2 rounds until work measures 3 inches longer than desired sleeve length (cuff will be turned back 3 inches), ending with Round 2. Break yarn and draw through last st, pull tight.

Apply Roses to Collar and Cuffs:

Turn cuffs back 3 inches. Fold back collar. Using photo as a guide, decide on placement of flowers on collar and cuffs. Each rose will be centered around one of the holes in the mesh fabric. More or fewer roses may be worked, as desired.

Work each Rose as follows:

Using A or B, work 9 sl st into the sts around the mesh hole. First row of each Rose will be worked into these sl sts.

For Roses on Collar, work Rows 1 – 3 as for Roses at centers of Rose Squares.

For Roses on Cuffs, work Rows 1 and 2 only.

Front Bands:

Use sl st to join C to lower right front corner of jacket.

Row 1: With RS facing, work 1 row sc along right front edge to top of collar, work 3 sc in corner st, work 1 sc in each sc along edge of collar, work 3 sc in corner st, work 1 row sc along left front edge to lower left corner.

Row 2: Ch 1, sc in each sc to 1st corner of collar, 3 sc in corner sc, 1 sc in each sc to 2nd corner of collar, 3 sc in corner sc, 1 sc in each sc to end.

Lay jacket flat and mark placement of 8 buttonholes, evenly spaced, along right front edge.

Row 3: Ch 1, [sc in each sc to 1 sc before center of buttonhole, ch 3, skip next 3 sc, sc in next sc] until all buttonholes have been made, continue as for Row 2.

Row 4: Work as for Row 2, working 1 sc into each ch of each ch3-sp.

Work 4 more rows as for Row 2. Break yarn, draw through last st and pull tight.

Rose Buttons:

Using A or B, create a slip knot with a fairly open loop.

Row 1: Work 9 hdc into the loop, sl st in 1st hdc to join; pull slip knot loop tight.

Row 2: Ch 1, [(sc, 2dc) in 1st st, (3 dc) in next hdc, (2 dc, sc) into next hdc] 3 times, sl st in 1st sc to join. Break yarn, draw through last st and pull tight.

Sew buttons to left front band, opposite buttonholes.

Finishing Instructions

Sew in ends securely. Block as desired.

Variation

Like the Rose Squares? Make a bunch of squares from the motif and sew together to make a long scarf.

The "Too Good for Your Boyfriend" Sweater

by Mandy Moore

A popular theme in knitting and crochet is the "Boyfriend Sweater," which is a basic, often oversized sweater that looks like you may have borrowed it from your boyfriend. This sweater starts with that idea of a basic, versatile sweater in an easy-to-wear (and make!) shape, then adds figure-flattering waist shaping and a sexy wide neckline, worked in a delicious, self-striping yarn. The result is a sweater you'll want all for yourself.

Project Rating: Summer Fling

Cost: Approximately $60–$120 as shown.

Necessary Skills: ch (page 7); sl st (page 16); sc (page 10); dc (page 13); sewing ends (page 24)

Abbreviations: dc-dec: Double Crochet Decrease. Yarn over, insert hook into next stitch and pull up a loop, yarn over and pull through first 2 loops on hook, yarn over, insert hook into following stitch and pull up a loop, yarn over and pull through first 2 loops on hook, yarn over, pull through remaining 3 loops on hook. One stitch decreased.

Finished Size

XS [S, M, L, XL, XXL]
Chest: 30 [34, 38, 42, 46, 50] inches
Length: 24 [25, 25.5, 25.5, 26, 26] inches

Gauge

10.5 dc and 6.5 rows = 4 inches / 10cm after blocking

Schematic

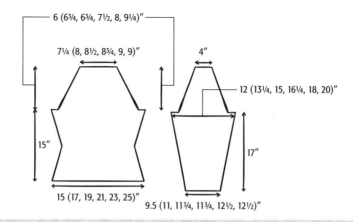

6 (6¾, 6¾, 7½, 8, 9¼)"

7¼ (8, 8½, 8¾, 9, 9)"

4"

12 (13¼, 15, 16¼, 18, 20)"

15"

17"

15 (17, 19, 21, 23, 25)"

9.5 (11, 11¾, 11¾, 12½, 12½)"

Note: Both stitch gauge and row gauge are important for this project. Be sure to block your swatch before measuring the gauge, as the gauge is likely to change considerably upon blocking.

Materials

- Noro Kureyon [50g, 110yd/100m, 100 percent wool]; Color: #147; 6 [7, 8, 9, 11, 12] balls
- Substitution: Look for an aran weight, 100 percent wool yarn. Do not use an acrylic-blend yarn; it will not behave the same way when blocked, and may not yield a sufficiently long row gauge.
- Ball band will indicate a knitted gauge of 18 sts = 4 inches / 10cm.
- 6 mm crochet hook
- Yarn needle

Instructions

Back:

Ch 40[46, 51, 56, 61, 67].

Sc in 2nd ch from hook, sc in each ch to end. 39[45, 50, 55, 60, 66] sts.

Next Row: Ch 3 (counts as 1st dc), dc in 2nd sc and in each sc to end.

Work 5 more rows in dc.

Waist Decrease Row: Ch 3 (counts as 1st dc), dc in 2nd dc, dc in next 3 dc, dc-dec, dc in each dc to last dc to last 7 dc, dc-dec, dc in last 5 dc. 2 sts decreased.

Work 2 rows in dc.

Repeat these 3 rows once more. 35[41, 46, 51, 56, 62] sts.

Waist Increase Row: Ch 3 (counts as 1st dc), dc in 2nd dc, dc in next 3 dc, 2 dc in next dc, dc in each dc to last 6 dc, 2 dc in next dc, dc in last 5 dc. 2 sts increased.

Work 2 rows in dc.

Work Waist Increase Row once more. 39[45, 50, 55, 60, 66] stitches.

Work 8 rows in dc.

Shape Raglan:

Next Row: Sl st in first 3[4, 4, 5, 6, 7] dc, ch 3 (counts as 1st dc), dc-dec, dc in each dc to last 5[6, 6, 7, 8, 9] dc, dc-dec, dc in next dc. Leave remaining 2[3, 3, 4, 5, 6] sts unworked. 33[37, 42, 45, 48, 52] sts.

(Sizes XS and S Only)

Work 1 row in dc.

Raglan Decrease Row: Ch 3 (counts as 1st dc), dc-dec, dc in each dc to last 3 dc, dc-dec, dc in last dc. 2 sts decreased.

Repeat these 2 rows once more. 29[33—, —, —, —] sts.

Work Raglan Decrease Row 5[6, —, —, —, —] times more. 19[21, —, —, —, —] sts.

(Sizes M, L, XL, XXL Only)

Raglan Decrease Row: Ch 3 (counts as 1st dc), dc-dec, dc in each dc to last 3 dc, dc-dec, dc in last dc. 2 sts decreased.

Repeat this row —[—, 9, 10, 11, 13] times more. —[—, 22, 23, 24, 24] sts.

(All Sizes)

Next Row: Ch 1, sc in each dc to end. Break yarn, draw through last st and pull tight.

Front:

Work as for Back.

Sleeve (Make 2 the same):

Ch 26[30, 32, 32, 34, 34].

Sc in 2nd ch from hook, sc in each ch to end. 25[29, 31, 31, 33, 33] sts.

Next Row: Ch 3 (counts as 1st dc), dc in 2nd sc and in each sc to end.

Work 2 more rows in dc.

Sleeve Increase Row: Ch 3 (counts as 1st dc), 2 dc in 2nd dc, dc in each dc to last 2 dc, 2 dc in next dc, dc in last dc. 2 sts increased.

Work 7[7, 5, 3, 2, 1] rows in dc.

Repeat these 8[8, 6, 4, 3, 2] rows 2[2, 3, 5, 6, 9] times more. 31[35, 39, 43, 47, 53] stitches.

Work 0[0, 0, 0, 3, 4] rows in dc.

Note: After blocking, sleeves will measure approx. 17 inches from lower edge to underarm. If extra length is desired, work more rows at this point. 3 rows will add approx. 2 inches.

Shape Raglan:

Next Row: Sl st in first 3[4, 4, 5, 6, 7] dc, ch 3 (counts as 1st dc), dc-dec, dc in each dc to last 5[6, 6, 7, 8, 9] dc, dc-dec, dc in next dc. Leave remaining 2[3, 3, 4, 5, 6] sts unworked. 25[27, 31, 33, 35, 39] sts.

(Sizes XS and S Only)

Work 1 row in dc.

Work Raglan Decrease Row as for Back.

Repeat these 2 rows once more. 21[23, —, —, —, —] stitches remain.

(All Sizes)

Work Raglan Decrease Row as for Back, 5[6, 10, 11, 12, 14] times. 11 sts.

Next Row: Ch 1, sc in each dc to end. Break yarn, draw through rem st and pull tight.

Finishing Instructions

Sew in ends.

Wet block pieces as follows:

♦ Soak all pieces in lukewarm water for at least 20 minutes; pieces must be thoroughly saturated.
♦ Squeeze pieces gently to remove excess water and lay flat, pinning to measurements given in schematic. Let dry completely.

The decorative seams are worked using sc, and are meant to be worn on the outside of the sweater. Work seams as follows:

Hold one body piece and one sleeve together, so that raglan edges are aligned. Work 1 row sc along raglan edge, through edge sts of both pieces. Work all raglan seams in this way.

Work side and sleeve seams in the same way.

Sew in remaining ends. Steam seams lightly if desired

Variation

Alien Skull

by Ande Van der Weken

This basic sweater shape is a great canvas for embellishment; add buttons, embroidery, appliqué, work the decorative seams in a contrasting yarn...anything you can think of! May we suggest making this fantastic "alien skull" appliqué for your sweater?

Project Rating: Flirtation

Finished Measurements:

Height: approx. 7 inches
Width: approx. 6 inches

Materials:

♦ Brown Sheep Lamb's Pride Worsted [100g, 190yd/174m, 85 percent wool, 15 percent mohair]; Color: #M10 Creme; 1 skein (skull uses less than half)
♦ Substitution: Look for an aran weight yarn. Wool is recommended, as it can be shaped and molded during blocking, allowing you to fine-tune the expression on your skull's face!
♦ Ball band will indicate a knitted gauge of 18 sts = 4 inches / 10cm.
♦ 6 mm crochet hook
♦ Yarn needle

Abbreviations:

sc-dec: Single Crochet Decrease. Insert hook into 1st st, pull up a loop, insert hook into second st, pull up a loop, yarn over, pull through all 3 loops on hook. 1 st decreased.

tr: (page 14)

Instructions:

Ch 12, sl st in 1st ch to join in a ring, ch 15, sl st in 12th ch from hook to join in a ring. You will have 2 large rings, joined by a ch3-sp.

Row 1: Ch 3 (counts as 1st dc), work 35 dc in 2nd ring; insert hook into center ch of ch3-sp *and* into 3rd ch of initial ch-3, sl st to join; work 36 dc in 1st ring, sl st in center ch of ch3-sp to join. You will have a figure-8 shape.

Row 2: Ch 1, sc in 1st 6 dc of one ring. Turn work.

Row 3: Ch 1, sc in each sc, sc in sl st at center, sc in 1st 6 dc of other ring. Turn work.

Row 4: Ch 1, sc in 1st 4 sc of Row 3, ch 3, skip 2 sc, sl st in next sc, ch 3, skip 2 sc, sc in last 4 sc. Turn work.

Row 5: Ch 1, sc in 1st 4 sc, 6 sc in ch3-sp, sc in center sl st, 6 sc in ch3-sp, sc in last 4 sc. Turn work.

Row 6: Ch 1, sc in 1st 6 sc, 2 sc-dec, skip next sc, 2 sc-dec, sc in last 6 sc. Turn work.

Row 7: Ch 1, sc in each sc to end. 16 sts. Turn work.

Row 8: Ch 6 (counts as 1 tr and 1 ch2-sp), skip 1st 3 sc, tr in next sc, [ch 2, skip next 2 sc, tr in next sc] 4 times.

Turn work.

Row 9: Ch 1, [sc in tr, sc in each ch of ch-2] 4 times, sc in tr, sc in each of next 3 ch. 16 sts. Turn work.

Row 10: Ch 1, sc in each sc to end. Do not turn work.

Rotate work 90 degrees clockwise; next row will be worked along side edge of skull.

Row 11: Ch 1, work 1 sc in edge of each sc row, 5 sc in tr, 1 sc in edge of each row to base of eye, dc in 1st 18 dc along 1st eye, sc in next 5 dc; hold edges of eyes together, insert hook into next dc *and* corresponding dc on other eye, sl st to join; sc in next 5 dc of 2nd eye, dc in next 18 sc, 1 sc in edge of each sc row to ch3-sp, 5 sc in ch3-sp, 1 sc in edge of rem 2 sc rows. Break yarn, draw through last st and pull tight.

Count 8 sts up right eye from sl st which connects eyes. Sl st to rejoin yarn to this dc.

Row 12: Working towards center, sl st in next 2 sts, sc in next 3 sts, sc-dec, sc-dec in adjacent sts of other eye, sc in next 3 sts, sl st in next 3 sts. Turn work.

Row 13: Skip 1st sl st, sl st in next 2 sl st, sc in next 2 sc, 2 sc-dec, sc in next 2 sc, sl st in next 2 sts. Turn work.

Row 14: Skip 1st sl st, sl st in next 2 sts, sc in next 4 sts, sl st in next 2 sts. Break yarn, leaving a long tail.

Sew yarn tail into skull and use it to sew gap between eyes closed.

Block as described for sweater. Use lots of pins; you can shape and mold the expression on the skull's face in many subtle ways!

Cozy Peacoat

by Robyn Chachula

How often do you go looking for a winter coat that is stylish and warm, yet says something about you? How often do you find a great coat, but it's not warm enough? Or a coat that is warm enough, but you know at least 10 people who own it, too. This winter coat is for those like me that want a coat you can stylize to your own desires. The winning combination for this coat is the sturdy wool yarn mixed with a spicy cotton yarn. After you master the basic form of the coat that hugs your curves, you can add on as many embellishments as you wish. Now stop looking and get hooking!

Project Rating: Summer Fling

Cost: Approximately $80 - $120

Necessary Skills: ch (page 7); sc (page 10); sl st (page 16); sewing ends (page 24)

Abbreviations: sc-dec: Insert hook into 1st st, pull up a loop, insert hook into second st, pull up a loop, yarn over, pull through all 3 loops on hook. 1 st decreased.

ch-sp: the space made in the previous row by chaining one or more times between stitches.

Finished Size

S[M, L, XL]

Chest (when closed and buttoned): 34 [36, 40, 44] inches

Length: 20.25 [20.75, 22.5, 23] inches

Materials

- ♦ MC1: Uros Aran, Peruvian Collection by Elann.com (50g, 91yd/ 83m, 50 percent Highland Wool, 50 percent llama), Color: #1477 Peridot–16, [17, 19, 22] balls
- ♦ MC2: Luna, Endless Summer Collection by Elann.com (50g, 109yd/ 100m, 57 percent viscose, 43 percent cotton), Color: #5052 Fresh Cream –14 [14, 16, 18] balls

- ♦ CC: Berroco Suede [50g, 120yd/111m, 100 percent nylon], Color: #3769 Sundance Kid - 1 ball

Note: Sample jacket uses yarn-covered buttons. If you wish to make this type of button, purchase an extra ball of yarn.

- ♦ Substitution: for MC1 and MC2, look for an aran weight wool blend yarn, and a DK weight cotton yarn. Approx. 1460 [1520, 1760, 1990]yd/1355 [1390, 1610, 1820]m of each are needed. Choose an aran weight yarn with an interesting texture for CC; have fun with this one!
- ♦ Ball band for aran weight yarn will indicate a knitted gauge of 17 sts = 4 inches/10cm; ball band for dk weight yarn will indicate a knitted gauge of 22 sts = 4 inches/10cm.
- ♦ US K / 6.5mm crochet hook
- ♦ US H / 5.0mm crochet hook
- ♦ Yarn needle
- ♦ 8 large buttons
- ♦ 1 large hook and eye

A Note about the Buttons: The yarn-covered buttons for this jacket were made using the directions found here: www.crochetme.com/easy-crocheted-button-covers.

Gauge

Gauge is measured over Seed Stitch using US K / 6.5mm hook, and with 1 strand each of MC1 and MC2 held together. To make a swatch, ch 20 and work at least 4 inches in Seed Stitch (see directions below). Block swatch and measure the number of sts over a 4-inch section in center of swatch.

16 sts = 4 inches/ 10cm

17 rows = 4 inches / 10cm

Note: When counting stitches, each sc and ch1-sp is counted as a stitch.

Schematics

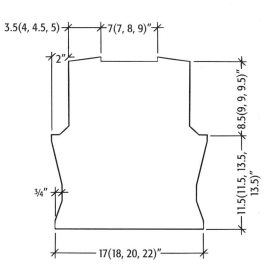

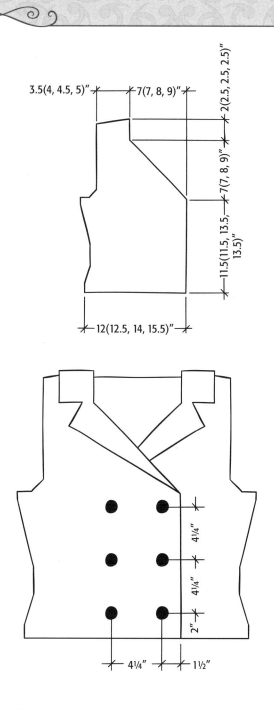

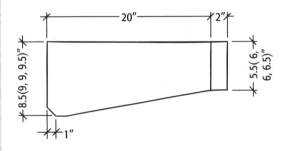

Seed Stitch Pattern

Ch an even number of sts (desired number of sts + 1).

Set-up Row: Sc in 2nd ch from hook, [ch 1, skip next ch, sc in next ch] to end.

Row 1: Ch 1, sc in 1st sc, sc in ch1-sp, [ch 1, skip next sc, sc in ch1-sp] to last ch1-sp, sc in last sc.

Row 2: Ch 1, sc in 1st sc, [ch 1, skip next sc, sc in ch1-sp] to last ch1-sp, ch 1, skip next sc, sc in last sc.

Repeat rows 1 and 2 for Seed Stitch.

Instructions

See note under Gauge re. counting stitches.

Back:

Using US K / 6.5mm hook, and with 1 strand each of MC1 and MC2 held together, Ch 66 [70, 78, 86].

Work 4 [4, 8, 8] rows in Seed Stitch, including set-up row. Row 1 of Seed Stitch Pattern has just been worked. 65 [69, 77, 85] sts.

First Decrease Row: Ch 1, sc in 1st sc, skip next sc, sc in ch1-sp, [ch 1, skip next sc, sc in ch1-sp] to last ch1-sp, skip next sc, sc in last sc. 2 stitches decreased. 63 [67, 75, 83] sts.

Work Row 2 of Seed Stitch.

Work 2 more rows in Seed Stitch.

Second Decrease Row: Ch 1, sc-dec in 1st sc and ch1-sp, [ch 1, skip next sc, sc in ch1-sp] to next-to-last ch1-sp, ch 1, sc-dec in last ch1-sp and last sc. 2 sts decreased. 61 [65, 73, 81] sts.

Work Row 1 of Seed Stitch.

Work 2 more rows in Seed Stitch.

Third Decrease Row: Ch 1, sc in 1st sc, skip next sc, sc in ch1-sp, [ch 1, skip next sc, sc in ch1-sp] to last ch1-sp, skip next sc, sc in last sc. 2 stitches decreased. 59 [63, 71, 79] sts.

Work Row 2 of Seed Stitch.

Work 8 more rows in Seed Stitch. Row 2 has just been worked.

Work *Increase Row: Ch 1, sc in 1st sc, ch 1, sc in ch1-sp, [ch 1, skip next sc, sc in ch1-sp] to last ch1-sp, ch 1, sc in last sc. 2 sts increased. 61 [65, 73, 81] sts.

Work Row 1 of Seed Stitch.

Work 3 more rows in Seed Stitch.*

Repeat from * to * 4 times more. 69 [73, 81, 89] sts.

(Sizes L and XL Only)

Work 4 more rows in Seed Stitch.

(All Sizes)

Shape armholes as follows:

Next Row: Sl st in 1st 4 sts, ch 1, sc in next sc, sc in ch1-sp, [ch 1, skip next sc, sc in ch1-sp] 29 [31, 35, 39] times, sc in next sc. Leave last 4 sts unworked. 61 [65, 73, 81] sts remain (not including sl sts).

Armhole Decrease Row: Ch 1, sc in 1st sc, skip next sc, sc in ch1-sp, [ch 1, skip next sc, sc in ch1-sp] to last ch1-sp, skip next sc, sc in last sc. 2 stitches decreased. 59 [63, 71, 79] sts.

Repeat this row 3 times more. 53 [57, 65, 73] sts.

Work Row 2 of Seed Stitch.

Work 31 [33, 35, 35] more rows in Seed Stitch. Row 1 has just been worked.

Shape Shoulders and Back Neck:

For the next row: **Sl st in 1st 4 sts, ch 1, sc in ch1-sp, [ch 1, skip next sc, sc in ch1-sp] 4 [5, 6, 7] times, sc in next sc. Leave remaining sts unworked.

Next Row: Ch 1, sc in 1st sc, [ch 1, skip next sc, sc in ch1-sp] 2 [3, 4, 5] times, sl st in next 4 sts. Break yarn, draw through last st and pull tight.**

Use a sl st to rejoin yarn to work at other armhole edge. Repeat from ** to ** as for first shoulder.

Right Front:

Using US K / 6.5mm hook, and with 1 strand each of MC1 and MC2 held together, Ch 48 [50, 56, 62].

Work 4 [4, 8, 8] rows in Seed Stitch, including set-up row. Row 1 of Seed Stitch Pattern has just been worked. 47 [49, 55, 61] sts.

First Decrease Row: Ch 1, sc in 1st sc, skip next sc, sc in ch1-sp, [ch 1, skip next sc, sc in ch1-sp] to last ch1-sp, ch 1, skip next sc, sc in last sc. 1 st decreased. 46 [48, 54, 60] sts.

Next Row: Ch 1, sc in 1st sc, sc in ch1-sp, [ch 1, skip next sc, sc in ch1-sp] to last ch1-sp, ch 1, skip next sc, sc in last sc.

Repeat this row once more.

Buttonhole Row: Ch 1, sc in 1st sc, sc in ch1-sp, ch 1, skip next sc, sc in ch1-sp, ch 5, skip next 5 sts, sc in next ch1-sp (buttonhole made), cont in patt to end.

Second Decrease Row: Ch 1, sc-dec in 1st sc and ch1-sp, [ch 1, skip next sc, sc in ch1-sp] to last ch1-sp before buttonhole, ch 1, skip next sc, sc in 1st ch of ch5-sp, [ch 1, skip next ch, sc in next ch] twice, ch 1, skip next sc, sc in ch1-sp, ch 1, skip next sc, sc in last sc. 1 st decreased. 45 [47, 53, 59] sts.

Work Row 1 of Seed Stitch.

Work 2 more rows in Seed Stitch.

Third Decrease Row: Ch 1, sc in 1st sc, skip next sc, sc in ch1-sp, [ch 1, skip next sc, sc in ch1-sp] to last ch1-sp, ch 1, skip next sc, sc in last sc. 1 st decreased. 44 [46, 52, 58] sts.

Next Row: Ch 1, sc in 1st sc, sc in ch1-sp, [ch 1, skip next sc, sc in ch1-sp] to last ch1-sp, ch 1, skip next sc, sc in last sc.

Repeat this row 8 times more.

First Increase Row: Ch 1, sc in 1st sc, ch 1, sc in ch1-sp, [ch 1, skip next sc, sc in ch1-sp] to last ch1-sp, ch 1, skip next sc, sc in last sc. 1 st increased. 45 [47, 53, 59] sts.

Work Row 1 and Row 2 of Seed Stitch.

Work Buttonhole Row.

Next Row: Ch 1, sc in 1st sc, [ch 1, skip next sc, sc in ch1-sp] to last ch1-sp before buttonhole, ch 1, skip next sc, sc in 1st ch of ch5-sp, [ch 1, skip next ch, sc in next ch] twice, ch 1, skip next sc, sc in ch1-sp, ch 1, skip next sc, sc in last sc.

Second Increase Row: Ch 1, sc in 1st sc, sc in ch1-sp, [ch 1, skip next sc, sc in ch1-sp] to last ch1-sp, ch 1, sc in last sc. 1 st increased. 46 [48, 54, 60] sts.

Next Row: Ch 1, sc in 1st sc, sc in ch1-sp, [ch 1, skip next sc, sc in ch1-sp] to last ch1-sp, ch 1, skip next sc, sc in last sc.

Repeat this row 3 times more.

Third Increase Row: Ch 1, sc in 1st sc, ch 1, sc in ch1-sp, [ch 1, skip next sc, sc in ch1-sp] to last ch1-sp, ch 1, skip next sc, sc in last sc. 1 st increased. 47 [49, 55, 61] sts.

Work Row 1 of Seed Stitch.

Work 3 more rows in Seed Stitch.

Fourth Increase Row: Ch 1, sc in 1st sc, sc in ch1-sp, [ch 1, skip next sc, sc in ch1-sp] to last ch1-sp, ch 1, sc in last sc. 1 st increased. 48 [50, 56, 62] sts.

Next Row: Ch 1, sc in 1st sc, sc in ch1-sp, [ch 1, skip next sc, sc in ch1-sp] to last ch1-sp, ch 1, skip next sc, sc in last sc.

Repeat this row 3 times more.

Fifth Increase Row: Ch 1, sc in 1st sc, ch 1, sc in ch1-sp, [ch 1, skip next sc, sc in ch1-sp] to last ch1-sp, ch 1, skip next sc, sc in last sc. 1 st increased. 49 [51, 57, 63] sts.

Work Buttonhole Row.

Next Row: Ch 1, sc in 1st sc, [ch 1, skip next sc, sc in ch1-sp] to last ch1-sp

before buttonhole, ch 1, skip next sc, sc in 1st ch of ch5-sp, [ch 1, skip next ch, sc in next ch] twice, ch 1, skip next sc, sc in ch1-sp, ch 1, skip next sc, sc in last sc.

Work Row 1 of Seed Stitch.

❊❊❊

(Sizes S and M Only)

Work 1 more row in Seed Stitch.

Begin armhole shaping as follows:

Next Row: Ch 1, sc in 1st sc, sc in ch1-sp, [ch 1, skip next sc, sc in ch1-sp] 21 [22, —, —] times, sc in next sc. Leave remaining 4 sts unworked. 45 [47, —, —] sts.

(Size L Only)

Work 2 more rows in Seed Stitch.

Begin neckline shaping as follows:

First Neckline Decrease Row: Ch 1, sc in 1st sc, [ch 1, skip next sc, sc in ch1-sp] to last ch1-sp, skip next sc, sc in last sc. 1 st decreased. 56 sts.

Second Neckline Decrease Row: Ch 1, sc in 1st sc, skip next sc, sc in ch1-sp, [ch 1, skip next sc, sc in ch1-sp] to last ch1-sp, sc in last sc. 1 st decreased. 55 sts.

Work First Neckline Decrease once more. 54 sts.

Begin armhole shaping as follows:

Next Row: Ch 1, sc in 1st sc, skip next sc, sc in ch1-sp, [ch 1, skip next sc, sc in ch1-sp] 23 times, sc in next sc. Leave remaining 4 sts unworked. 49 sts.

(Size XL Only)

Begin neckline shaping as follows:

First Neckline Decrease Row: Ch 1, sc in 1st sc, [ch 1, skip next sc, sc in ch1-sp] to last ch1-sp, skip next sc, sc in last sc. 1 st decreased. 62 sts.

Second Neckline Decrease Row: Ch 1, sc in 1st sc, skip next sc, sc in ch1-sp, [ch 1, skip next sc, sc in ch1-sp] to last ch1-sp, sc in last sc. 1 st decreased. 61 sts.

Repeat these 2 rows once more, then work First Neckline Decrease Row once more. 58 sts.

Begin armhole shaping as follows:

Next Row: Ch 1, sc in 1st sc, skip next sc, sc in ch1-sp, [ch 1, skip next sc, sc in ch1-sp] 25 times, sc in next sc. Leave remaining 4 sts unworked. 53 sts.

(All Sizes)

Shape neckline and armhole as follows:

Armhole Decrease Row: Ch 1, sc in 1st sc, skip next sc, sc in ch1-sp, [ch 1, skip next sc, sc in ch1-sp] to last ch1-sp, skip next sc, sc in last sc. 2 stitches decreased. 43 [45, 47, 51] sts.

Repeat this row 3 times more. 37 [39, 41, 45] sts.

Continue neckline shaping as follows:

First Neckline Decrease Row: Ch 1, sc in 1st sc, [ch 1, skip next sc, sc in ch1-sp] to last ch1-sp, skip next sc, sc in last sc. 1 st decreased. 36 [38, 40, 44] sts.

Second Neckline Decrease Row: Ch 1, sc in 1st sc, skip next sc, sc in ch1-sp, [ch 1, skip next sc, sc in ch1-sp] to last ch1-sp, sc in last sc. 1 st decreased. 35 [37, 39, 43] sts.

Repeat these 2 rows 10[10, 10, 11] times more, then work First Neckline Decrease Row once more. 14 [16, 18, 20] sts.

Next Row: Ch 1, sc in 1st sc, [ch 1, skip next sc, sc in ch1-sp] to last ch1-sp, sc in last sc.

Repeat this row 8 [10, 10, 10] times more.

Next Row: Sl st in 1st 4 sts, ch 1, sc in ch1-sp, [ch 1, skip next sc, sc in ch1-sp] 4 [5, 6, 7] times, sc in next sc.

Next Row: Ch 1, sc in 1st sc, [ch 1, skip next sc, sc in ch1-sp] 2 [3, 4, 5] times, sl st in next 4 sts. Break yarn, draw through last st and pull tight.❊❊❊

Left Front:

Using US K / 6.5mm hook, and with 1 strand each of MC1 and MC2 held together, ch 48 [50, 56, 62].

Work 4 [4, 8, 8] rows in Seed Stitch, including set-up row. Row 1 of Seed Stitch Pattern has just been worked. 47 [49, 55, 61] sts.

First Decrease Row: Ch 1, sc in 1st sc, skip next sc, sc in ch1-sp, [ch 1, skip next sc, sc in ch1-sp] to last ch1-sp, ch 1, skip next sc, sc in last sc. 1 st decreased. 46 [48, 54, 60] sts.

Next Row: Ch 1, sc in 1st sc, sc in ch1-sp, [ch 1, skip next sc, sc in ch1-sp] to last ch1-sp, ch 1, skip next sc, sc in last sc.

Repeat this row twice more.

Second Decrease Row: Ch 1, sc-dec in 1st sc and ch1-sp, [ch 1, skip next sc, sc in ch1-sp] to ch1-sp, ch 1, skip next sc, sc in last sc. 1 st decreased. 45 [47, 53, 59] sts.

Work Row 1 of Seed Stitch.

Work 2 more rows in Seed Stitch.

Third Decrease Row: Ch 1, sc in 1st sc, skip next sc, sc in ch1-sp, [ch 1, skip next sc, sc in ch1-sp] to last ch1-sp, ch 1, skip next sc, sc in last sc. 1 st decreased. 44 [46, 52, 58] sts.

Next Row: Ch 1, sc in 1st sc, sc in ch1-sp, [ch 1, skip next sc, sc in ch1-sp] to last ch1-sp, ch 1, skip next sc, sc in last sc.

Repeat this row 8 times more.

First Increase Row: Ch 1, sc in 1st sc, ch 1, sc in ch1-sp, [ch 1, skip next sc, sc in

ch1-sp] to last ch1-sp, ch 1, skip next sc, sc in last sc. 1 st increased. 45 [47, 53, 59] sts.

Work Row 1 of Seed Stitch.

Work 3 more rows in Seed Stitch.

Second Increase Row: Ch 1, sc in 1st sc, sc in ch1-sp, [ch 1, skip next sc, sc in ch1-sp] to last ch1-sp, ch 1, sc in last sc. 1 st increased. 46 [48, 54, 60] sts.

Next Row: Ch 1, sc in 1st sc, sc in ch1-sp, [ch 1, skip next sc, sc in ch1-sp] to last ch1-sp, ch 1, skip next sc, sc in last sc.

Repeat this row 3 times more.

Third Increase Row: Ch 1, sc in 1st sc, ch 1, sc in ch1-sp, [ch 1, skip next sc, sc in ch1-sp] to last ch1-sp, ch 1, skip next sc, sc in last sc. 1 st increased. 47 [49, 55, 61] sts.

Work Row 1 of Seed Stitch.

Work 3 more rows in Seed Stitch.

Fourth Increase Row: Ch 1, sc in 1st sc, sc in ch1-sp, [ch 1, skip next sc, sc in ch1-sp] to last ch1-sp, ch 1, sc in last sc. 1 st increased. 48 [50, 56, 62] sts.

Next Row: Ch 1, sc in 1st sc, sc in ch1-sp, [ch 1, skip next sc, sc in ch1-sp] to last ch1-sp, ch 1, skip next sc, sc in last sc.

Repeat this row 3 times more.

Fifth Increase Row: Ch 1, sc in 1st sc, ch 1, sc in ch1-sp, [ch 1, skip next sc, sc in ch1-sp] to last ch1-sp, ch 1, skip next sc, sc in last sc. 1 st increased. 49[51, 57, 63] sts.

Work Row 1 of Seed Stitch.

Work 2 more rows in Seed Stitch.

Work from *** to *** as for Right Front.

Sleeves (Make 2):

Using US K / 6.5 mm hook, and with 1 strand each of MC1 and MC2 held together, ch 44 [48, 48, 52].

Work 7 rows in Seed Stitch, including set-up row. Row 2 of Seed Stitch Pattern has just been worked. 43 [47, 47, 51] sts.

Work *Increase Row: Ch 1, sc in 1st sc, ch 1, sc in ch1-sp, [ch 1, skip next sc, sc in ch1-sp] to last ch1-sp, ch 1, sc in last sc. 2 sts increased. 45 [49, 49, 53] sts.

Work Row 1 of Seed Stitch.

Work 5 more rows in Seed Stitch.*

Repeat from * to * 10 times more. 65 [69, 69, 73] sts.

Work Increase Row once more. 67 [71, 71, 75] sts.

Work Row 1 of Seed Stitch.

Work 3 more rows in Seed Stitch. Work measures approx. 21 inches.

Note: Cuffs will be turned back approx. 2 inches during finishing. If longer sleeves are desired, work extra rows at this point.

Decrease Row: Ch 1, sc-dec in 1st sc and ch1-sp, [ch 1, skip next sc, sc in ch1-sp] to next-to-last ch1-sp, ch 1, skip next sc, sc-dec in last ch1-sp and last sc. 2 sts decreased. 65 [69, 69, 73] sts.

Repeat Decrease Row 3 times more. 59 [63, 63, 67] sts.

Break yarn, draw through last st and pull tight.

Collar:

First Half

Ch 12.

Work 48[52, 56, 60] rows in Seed Stitch, including Set-up Row. Row 1 of Seed Stitch pattern has just been worked. 11 sts.

Now, #Ch 1, sc in 1st sc, ch 1, skip next sc, sc in ch1-sp, ch 9.

Next Row: Sc in 2nd ch from hook, sc in next ch, [ch 1, skip next ch, sc in next ch] 3 times, ch 1, skip next sc, sc in ch1-sp, sc in last sc. 11 sts.

****

(Sizes S and M Only)

First Decrease Row: Ch 1, sc in 1st sc, skip next sc, sc in ch1-sp, [ch 1, skip next sc, sc in ch1-sp] to last ch1-sp, ch 1, skip next sc, sc in last sc. 1 st decreased. 10 sts.

Next Row: Ch 1, sc in 1st sc, sc in ch1-sp, [ch 1, skip next sc, sc in ch1-sp] to last ch1-sp, ch 1, skip next sc, sc in last sc.

Repeat this row twice more.

Second Decrease Row: Ch 1, sc-dec in 1st sc and ch1-sp, [ch 1, skip next sc, sc in ch1-sp] to last ch1-sp, ch 1, skip next sc, sc in last sc. 1 st decreased. 9 sts.

Work Row 1 of Seed Stitch.

Work 2 rows in Seed Stitch.****

Repeat from **** to **** 3 times more. 3 sts.

Next Row: Ch 1, sc-dec in 1st 2 sts, sc in last sc. 2 sts.

Next Row: Ch 1, sc in each sc.

Repeat this row twice more.

Next Row: Ch 1, sc-dec in remaining 2 sc. 1 st.

Next Row: Ch 1, sc in sc.

Repeat this row 3 times more.

Sl st in sc. Break yarn, draw through last st and pull tight. #

****

(Size L Only)

First Decrease Row: Ch 1, sc in 1st sc, skip next sc, sc in ch1-sp, [ch 1, skip next sc, sc in ch1-sp] to last ch1-sp, ch 1, skip next sc, sc in last sc. 1 st decreased. 10 sts.

Next Row: Ch 1, sc in 1st sc, sc in ch1-sp, [ch 1, skip next sc, sc in ch1-sp] to last ch1-sp, ch 1, skip next sc, sc in last sc.

Repeat this row 3 times more.

Second Decrease Row: Ch 1, sc in 1st sc, sc in ch1-sp, [ch 1, skip next sc, sc in ch1-sp] to last ch1-sp, skip next sc, sc in last sc. 1 st decreased. 9 sts.

Work Row 2 of Seed Stitch.

Work 3 rows in Seed Stitch.****

Repeat from **** to **** 3 times more. 3 sts.

Next Row: Ch 1, sc-dec in 1st 2 sts, sc in last sc. 2 sts.

Next Row: Ch 1, sc in each sc.

Repeat this row 3 times more.

Next Row: Ch 1, sc-dec in remaining 2 sc. 1 st.

Next Row: Ch 1, sc in sc.

Repeat this row 3 times more.

Sl st in sc. Break yarn, draw through last st and pull tight. #

****

(Size XL Only)

First Decrease Row: Ch 1, sc in 1st sc, skip next sc, sc in ch1-sp, [ch 1, skip next sc, sc in ch1-sp] to last ch1-sp, ch 1, skip next sc, sc in last sc. 1 st decreased. 10 sts.

Next Row: Ch 1, sc in 1st sc, sc in ch1-sp, [ch 1, skip next sc, sc in ch1-sp] to last ch1-sp, ch 1, skip next sc, sc in last sc.

Repeat this row 3 times more.

Second Decrease Row: Ch 1, sc in 1st sc, sc in ch1-sp, [ch 1, skip next sc, sc in ch1-sp] to last ch1-sp, skip next sc, sc in last sc. 1 st decreased. 9 sts.

Work Row 2 of Seed Stitch.

Work 4 rows in Seed Stitch.

Third Decrease Row: Ch 1, sc in 1st sc, sc in ch1-sp, [ch 1, skip next sc, sc in ch1-sp] to next-to-last ch1-sp, ch 1, skip next sc, sc-dec in last ch1-sp and last sc. 1 st decreased. 8 sts.

Next Row: Ch 1, sc in 1st sc, sc in ch1-sp, [ch 1, skip next sc, sc in ch1-sp] to last ch1-sp, ch 1, skip next sc, sc in last sc.

Repeat this row 3 times more.

Fourth Decrease Row: Ch 1, sc-dec in 1st sc and ch1-sp, [ch 1, skip next sc, sc in ch1-sp] to last ch1-sp, ch 1, skip next sc, sc in last sc. 1 st decreased. 7 sts.

Work Row 1 of Seed Stitch.

Work 4 rows in Seed Stitch.****

Repeat from **** to **** once more. 3 sts.

Next Row: Ch 1, sc-dec in 1st 2 sts, sc in last sc. 2 sts.

Next Row: Ch 1, sc in each sc.

Repeat this row 3 times more.

Next Row: Ch 1, sc-dec in remaining 2 sc. 1 st.

Next Row: Ch 1, sc in sc.

Repeat this row 3 times more.

Sl st in sc. Break yarn, draw through last st and pull tight. #

Second Half:

Use sl st to rejoin yarn to **first** st of foundation chain.

Work Row 1 of Seed Stitch.

Work from # to # as for First Half.

Back Belt:

Ch 48[50, 56, 62].

Work 8 rows in Seed Stitch. Break yarn, draw through last st and pull tight.

Finishing Instructions

Sew in ends.

Note: Whip stitch is recomended for sewing seams.

Sew Fronts to Back at shoulder seams.

Sew Sleeves into armholes.

Sew sleeve and side seams.

Sew Collar to neckline edge of jacket, matching pointed ends of collar to beginning of neckline shaping on fronts.

Using US H / 5mm hook and CC, work 1 row of sc around all edges of jacket and back belt.

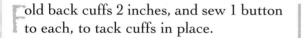

Fold back cuffs 2 inches, and sew 1 button to each, to tack cuffs in place.

Try on jacket and determine best placement for back belt; pin in place.

Sew 1 button near each end through both belt and jacket, to hold belt in place.

Sew 3 buttons to Left Front, opposite buttonholes.

Sew 3 buttons to Right Front, using photo as a guide.

Sew hook to Left Front, at point where collar ends.

Sew eye to inside of Right Front, opposite hook.

Variation

To make a jacket for a warmer climate, substitute a worsted weight cotton or acrylic yarn for the wool-blend yarn.

Alternately, a bulky-weight, boucle or novelty yarn can be substituted for the MC yarns. Just be certain to get the right gauge! The fabric for this coat should be denser and stiffer than the fabric for most sweaters.

Chapter Nine

◆◆◆

Put Your Hook Where Your Heart Is: Great Gifts to Crochet

Granny's Been in the Bourbon Again: A Drunken Throw

A new twist on an old ripple.

Classic Street Page Boy

Sexy meets sweet in this spunky newsboy hat.

Daisy Chain Neck Warmer

Tie this garland loosely around your neck for a bit of warmth and a lot of style.

Lucy-Lou and Tim Bob, Too

This pair may just be the new "Bonnie and Clyde". In any case, you'll make the lucky giftee feel like a million buckaroonies.

Woven Fringe Scarf

It's all about texture with this mohair and ribbon scarf.

Bubble Belt

Faux-suede crocheted into a hip-worthy belt.

Who Hat

Avoid the Grinch, Seuss-style, with this baby cap.

Granny's Been in the Bourbon Again: A Drunken Throw

Who said the afghan needs to be indestructible acrylic in indescribably ugly colors? Instead, choose a luscious palette of yarns from a fine yarn dyer for a one-of-a-kind accent to the most chic décor.

Project Rating: Summer Fling

Cost: Upwards of $200, as shown.

Necessary Skills: ch (page 7); dc (page 13); sewing ends (page 24)

Abbreviations: dc-2dec: Work 1st dc until 2 loops remain on hook, work 2nd dc until 3 loops remain on hook (including 2 loops from 1st dc), work 3rd dc until 4 loops remain on hook, yarn over, draw through all 4 loops on hook. 2 sts decreased.

Finished Size

Length: approx. 58 inches
Width: approx. 44 inches

Materials

All Yarns from Curious Creek Fibers in color "Purple Haze"

- A: Samburu (50g–108 yards /98m, 55 percent mohair, 45 percent Merino)–4 skeins
- B: Abuko (50g–88 yards/80m, 100 percent nylon)–3 skeins
- C: Shira (50g–86 yards/78m, 54 percent Mohair, 23 percent silk, 18 percent wool, 5 percent nylon)–4 skeins
- D: Kalahari (50g–87 yards/79m, 100 percent nylon)–3 skeins

- E: Etosha (50g–220yards/200m, 90 percent Kid Mohair, 10 percent nylon)–2 skeins
- Substitution: Select four or five different yarns with different textures to obtain a similarly eclectic appearance.
- Ball bands should indicate a knitted gauge ranging from 12-10 sts = 4 inches / 10 cm.
- US J10 / 6.0mm crochet hook
- Yarn needle

Gauge

8 dc = 4 inches/10 cm using Samburu

Note: Exact gauge isn't critical for this project. A looser gauge or a bigger yarn will result in a larger throw. A tighter gauge or smaller yarn will create a smaller throw. Additionally, because of the various textures and thicknesses of yarn, your gauge will slightly vary between yarns.

Instructions

Using A, ch 130.

Set-up Row: Dc in 4th ch from hook, [dc in next 5 ch, dc-2dec, dc in next 5 ch, 3 dc in next ch] 8 times, dc in next 5 ch, dc-2dec, dc in next 5 ch, 2 dc in last ch. 127 sts (ch-3 at beg of row counts as 1st dc).

Work next row using B:

Pattern Row: Ch 3 (counts as 1st dc), dc in 1st dc, [dc in next 5 dc, dc-2dec, dc in next 5 dc, 3 dc in next dc] 8 times, dc in next 5 dc, dc-2dec, dc in next 5 dc, 2 dc in 3rd ch of initial ch-3. 127 sts.

Repeat Pattern Row, working as follows:

3 rows C

1 row D

2 rows A

3 rows E

1 row C

2 rows B

2 rows D

1 row E

3 rows A

1 row B

2 rows E

1 row B

3 rows C

2 rows D

3 rows A

1 row E

2 rows C

1 row D

3 rows B

2 rows A

2 rows D

1 row C

3 rows E

3 rows A

At end of last row, break yarn, draw through last st and pull tight.

Finishing Instructions

Sew in ends securely.

Variation

Not a fan of the ripple? Make a stunning variation by substituting any stitch pattern. (Hint: This is where Chapter 2's stitch gallery comes in handy!) Or, make horizontal stripes instead by casting on fewer stitches and working from the bottom up. Be sure to ch a multiple of 14 sts + 4 ([14 sts + 1] + 3 sts for turning chain).

You can also switch up the stripes. The "Drunken Afghan" above uses a random non-pattern of yarn and repeats. Instead, invent your own!

Same Technique, Different Yarn

Many times, the old-fashioned stitches we love to hate can be renewed and remade simply by selecting a gorgeous, modern yarn. For example, the Drunken Throw is just a new take on Granny's old ripple afghan. Instead of pure indestructible acrylic, I chose a selection of hand dyed and hand spun yarns in luscious textures and colors.

Next time you're at a big box craft store or a vintage market, instead of just laughing at the hideous color combos found in vintage patterns, try to imagine what the stitch would look like in your favorite yarn. Can you see the possibilities? Is it worth a second look? Sometimes the best stitches are the most classic.

Classic Street Page Boy

by Jennifer Hansen

The simple styling of this classic hat has been created with crochet stitches worked "around the post" of the stitch on the previous row. Typically, working around the post of crochet stitches is done to create highly textured crochet fabrics and ribbing. However, this design illustrates how working around the post of crochet stitches can create a knit-looking fabric that is simple, sturdy, and very fun to do!

Project Rating: Summer Fling

Cost: Approximately $40–$50 as shown.

Necessary Skills: sl st (page 16); ch (page 7); Yo (page 13); sc (page 10); dc (page 13); sewing ends (page 24)

Abbreviations: BPdc: Back Post double crochet: Yarn over, insert hook into row below from back to front, then around the "post" of the next st in the previous row, to the back of the work. Pull up a loop and continue to work dc as normal.

FPdc: Front Post double crochet: Yarn over, insert hook into row below from front to back, then around the "post" of the next st in the previous row, to the front of the work. Pull up a loop and continue to work dc as normal.

BPsc: Back Post single crochet: Insert hook into row below from back to front, then around the "post" of the next st in the previous row, to the back of the work. Pull up a loop and continue to work sc as normal.

FPsc: Front Post single crochet: Insert hook into row below from front to back, then around the "post" of the next st in the previous row, to the front of the work. Pull up a loop and continue to work sc as normal.

BPdc-dec: Work next BPdc until 2 loops remain on hook, work following BPdc until 3 loops remain on hook (including 2 loops from 1st BPdc), yarn over, draw through remaining 3 loops on hook. 1 st decreased.

Sc-dec: Insert hook into 1st st, pull up a loop, insert hook into 2nd st, pull up a loop, yarn over, pull through all 3 loops on hook. 1 st decreased.

Sc-2dec: Insert hook into 1st st, pull up a loop, insert hook into 2nd st, pull up a loop, insert hook into 3rd st, pull up a loop, yarn over, pull through all 4 loops on hook. 2 sts decreased.

Finished Size

Finished hat will fit most adults.

Materials

- Curious Creek Oban (95g; fifty percent Silk, fifty percent Merino Wool, 205 yards/185m); Color: Autumn in New England-2 hanks
- Substitution: Approx. 400 yards/366m of worsted weight yarn. Use a silk/wool blend to acheive the same drape as the sample garment.
- Ball band will indicate a knitted gauge of 20 sts = 4 inches / 10cm.

- US H / 5mm crochet hook or size to obtain gauge
- US G / 4.5mm crochet hook or size to obtain gauge
- A clean plastic milk or water jug (used to make the brim)
- Yarn needle

Gauge

14 dc and 9 rows = 4 inches / 10cm using larger hook

Instructions

Make a ring of yarn around 2 fingers, with the working yarn (the length of yarn which leads to the ball) leading off to the right, from the top of the ring. Insert the larger hook into this ring and pull up a loop, then ch 1.

Round 1: Ch 3 (counts as 1st dc), work 7 dc in ring, pull short yarn tail to tighten ring, sl st in 3rd ch of initial ch-3 to join. 8 sts.

Round 2: FPsc in 1st dc, ch 2 (counts as 1st FPdc), BPdc around same st, [FPdc, BPdc] in next st and in each st to end, sl st in 2nd ch of initial ch-2 to join. 16 sts.

Round 3: FPsc in 1st dc, ch 2 (counts as 1st FPdc), work 2 BPdc in 2nd dc, [FPdc in next dc, 2 BPdc in next dc] to end, sl st in 2nd ch of initial ch-2 to join. 24 sts.

Round 4: FPsc in 1st dc, ch 2 (counts as 1st FPdc), 2 BPdc in 2nd dc, BPdc in 3rd dc, [FPdc in next dc, 2 BPdc in next dc, BPdc in next dc] to end, sl st in 2nd ch of initial ch-2 to join. 32 sts.

Round 5: FPsc in 1st dc, ch 2 (counts as 1st FPdc), BPdc in 2nd dc, BPdc in 3rd dc, 2 BPdc in 4th dc, [FPdc in next dc, BPdc in next 2 dc, 2 BPdc in next dc] to end, sl st in 2nd ch of initial ch-2 to join. 40 sts.

Round 6: FPsc in 1st dc, ch 2 (counts as 1st FPdc), 2 BPdc in 2nd dc, BPdc in next 3 dc, [FPdc in next dc, 2 BPdc in next dc, BPdc in next 3 dc] to end, sl st in 2nd ch of initial ch-2 to join. 48 sts.

Round 7: FPsc in 1st dc, ch 2 (counts as 1st FPdc), BPdc in each dc to last dc before next FPsc, 2 BPdc in next dc, [FPdc in next dc, BPdc in each dc to last dc before next FPsc, 2 BPdc in next dc] to end, sl st in 2nd ch of initial ch-2 to join. 8 sts increased.

Round 8: FPsc in 1st dc, ch 2 (counts as 1st FPdc), 2 BPdc in 2nd dc, BPdc in each dc to next FPdc, [FPdc in next dc, 2 BPdc in next dc, BPdc in each dc to next FPdc] to end, sl st in 2nd ch of initial ch-2 to join. 8 sts increased.

Repeat Rounds 7 and 8, 5 times more. 144 sts.

First Decrease Round: FPsc in 1st dc, ch 2 (counts as 1st FPdc), BPdc in each dc to last 2 BPdc before next FPdc, BPdc-dec, [FPdc in next dc, BPdc in each dc to last 2 BPdc before next FPdc, BPdc-dec] to end. 8 sts decreased.

Second Decrease Round: FPsc in 1st dc, ch 2 (counts as 1st FPdc), BPdc-dec, BPdc in each dc to next FPdc, [FPdc in next dc, BPdc-dec, BPdc in each dc to next

FPdc] to end, sl st in 2nd ch of initial ch-2 to join. 8 sts decreased.

Repeat these 2 rounds 4 times more. 64 sts remain.

Edging:

Next Round: Using smaller hook, FPsc in 1st dc, ch 2 (counts as 1st FPdc), BPdc in 2nd dc, [FPdc in next dc, BPdc in next dc] to end, sl st in 2nd ch of initial ch-2 to join.

Repeat this round twice more. Break yarn, draw through last st and pull tight.

Brim (Make 2):

Using larger hook, ch 10.

Row 1: Sc in 2nd ch from hook and in each ch to end. 9 sts.

Rows 2 and 3: Ch 1, 2 sc in 1st sc, 2 sc in 2nd sc, 1 sc in each sc to last 2 sc, 2 sc in second-last sc, 2 sc in last sc. 4 sts increased. 17 sts at end of Row 3.

Rows 4–7: Ch 1, 2 sc in 1st sc, sc in each sc to last sc, 2 sc in last sc. 2 sts increased. 25 sts at end of Row 7.

Row 8: Ch 1, sc in 1st sc and in each sc to end.

Row 9: Ch 1, 2 sc in 1st sc, sc in each sc to last sc, 2 sc in last sc. 2 sts increased. 27 sts.

Rows 10 and 11: Work as for Rows 8 and 9. 29 sts.

Row 12: Work as for Row 8.

Shape Side of Brim:

Row 13: Ch 1, sc in first 11 sc. Turn work. Side of Brim will be worked over these 11 sts.

Row 14: Skip 1st sc, do not work turning chain; sc-dec, sc in next 7 sc, 2 sc in last sc. 10 sts.

Row 15: Ch 1, sc in first 8 sc, sc-dec. 9 sts.

Row 16: Skip 1st sc, do not work turning chain; sc-dec, sc in each sc to end. 7 sts.

Row 17: Ch 1, sc in first 5 sts, sc-dec. 6 sts.

Row 18: Ch 1, sc-dec, sc in next 3 sc, 2 sc in last sc. 6 sts.

Row 19: Ch 1, sc in first 4 sc, sc-dec. 5 sts.

Row 20: Ch 1, sc-dec, sc in each sc to end. 4 sts.

Row 21: Ch 1, sc in first 2 sc, sc-dec. 3 sts.

Row 22: Ch 1, sc-dec, sc in last sc. 2 sts.

Row 23: Ch 1, sc in each sc. 2 sts.

Row 24: Ch 1, sc-dec. 1 st.

Row 25: Ch 1, sc. Break yarn, draw through last st and pull tight.

Use a sl st to rejoin yarn to opposite side of Brim and shape remaining side in the same way.

Finishing

Sew in ends.

Cut a plastic milk or water jug so that you have a flat piece of plastic. Lay one Brim piece flat on this piece of plastic, and trace the brim shape. Cut out the piece of plastic, slightly smaller than the crocheted brim piece.

Hold the crocheted brim pieces together and work 1 row of sc around the curved outer edge. Break yarn, leaving a 1-yard tail; draw through last st and pull tight. Insert the plastic brim piece inside the pocket formed by the joined brim pieces.

Fit hat to wearer's head, and hold up brim so that it squarely spans 4 hat segments. Mark brim attachment points on hat edge with safety pins — the hat fabric will need to be stretched to fit to brim during sewing of brim to hat. Use the long yarn tail to sew brim to hat through both upper and lower brim pieces, securely enclosing the plastic stiffener. Sew in remaining ends.

Variation

Not into the "brimmed" look? Create this hat without the brim and you will have a sassy little beret that is big on style.

Want the page boy look yet want to soften the boyish edge? Grab a rhinestone brooch and pin it to the hat just above the edge of the brim to add some girly flair to this boyish hat.

Daisy Chain Neck Warmer

Wrap this soft alpaca vine around your neck to bring a bit of spring into even the chilliest season.

Project Rating: Summer Fling

Cost: Approximately $20–$30 as shown, however, the yarn required will be plenty for two scarves.

Necessary Skills: ch (page 7); sc (page 10); dc (page 13); sewing ends (page 24)

Abbreviations: ch-sp: the space made in the previous row by chaining one or more times between stitches.

Finished Size

Length: approx. 14 inches, not including ties. One size fits most.

Materials

- Frog Tree Alpaca Sport Weight (50g, 118m/ 130 yards, 100 percent Alpaca), 1 ball each color
- MC: Color #46
- CC1: Color #31
- CC2: Color #82
- Substitution: Look for a soft, sport weight yarn. Approx. 55 yards/50m of MC and 33 yards/30m each of CC1 and CC2 are needed.
- Ball band will indicate a knitted gauge of 24 sts = 4 inches / 10cm.
- US H / 5.0mm crochet hook
- US C / 2.75mm crochet hook
- Yarn needle

Gauge

20 sc = 4 inches /10 cm using smaller hook

Note: Exact gauge isn't critical for this project. A looser gauge or a bigger yarn will simply make a wider necktie.

Instructions:

Large Daisy (Make 1):

Using larger hook and one strand each of CC1 and CC2 held together, ch 4. Sl st in 1st ch to form a ring.

Ch 1, work 10 sc into ring, sl st in 1st sc to join.

First Petal: Ch 3 (counts as 1 dc), dc in 1st sc, dc in 2nd sc. Turn work.

Ch 3 (counts as 1 dc), dc in 1st dc, dc in 2nd dc, dc in 3rd ch of initial ch-3. Turn work.

Ch 1, sc into each dc to end. Rotate work 90 degrees clockwise.

Ch 1, work 4 sl st along edge of petal, sl st in next sc of ring. This sc will be the 1st sc of the next petal.

Work 4 more petals in the same manner as the first, working the last sl st of the last petal into the 1st sc of the ring. Break yarn, draw through last st and pull tight.

Small Daisy (Make 2 of CC1 and 2 of CC2):

Using US C /2.75mm hook and one strand of yarn, work as for Large Daisy.

Note: While you can decide in advance which colors you like for the flowers, it's also fun to keep it random and decide as you go. Each daisy only takes a few moments to whip up.

Finishing Instructions

Do not yet sew in ends. Using MC and 5.0mm hook, ch 100.

Ties (Make 2):

Turn and sl st 30. Fold cord to form a loop as pictured. The loop should be approximately 15 sl st long. Insert hook through next ch on working ch and through top of edge of loop to form another sl st. Sl st 10 more, then fold again and join to the corner of the previously made loop. Continue to sl st to the end of the chain.

Attach Flowers:

String the first CC1 flower onto one tie, and slide it along until it lays flat next to the circle loop in the tie. Tie a knot in the cord to prevent the flower from slipping off, and pull the end of the cord back through the center of the flower.

Attach the first CC2 flower in the same way, leaving a 1-inch space between flowers.

Attach the remaining small flowers to the other tie in the same way.

Pull both ties through the center of the large flower, from back to front. Tie a square knot using both ties. Use a crochet hook to pull the ends back through the first (sc) round of the flower. This will secure the flower on the ties.

Sew in ends, using the end to more securely fasten the flowers to the ties.

Variation

Crocheted flowers are delicate and versatile. As you saw in the previous instructions, simply changing yarn thickness and hook size gives a dramatically different look to the bloom. Flowers, on their own, make great adornments for jackets, shawls, bags, or hats. Try making one of the flowers and adding to the crocheted toque (see It's Called a Toque, Eh in chapter 7).

Lucy-Lou & Tim-Bob, Too

by Kim Piper Werker

Lucy-Lou looks demure and quiet, but when the lights go down she's a mad-scientist aerobics instructor who can't stop shakin' it to *Sweating to the Oldies*. Tim-Bob, her little sidekick, tried to be French but ended up wearing a pill-box hat instead. He looks innocent, but he once heisted a cool million from a Swiss bank. And he has no arms.

Project Rating: Summer Fling

Cost: Approximately $35–$45, but you'll have enough yarn to make four (or more) Lucy-Lous and Tim-Bobs too!

Necessary Skills: ch (page 7); sc (page 10); sl st (page 16); whip stitch (page 23); sewing ends (page 24)

Abbreviations: sc-dec: Insert hook into 1st st, pull up a loop, insert hook into 2nd st, pull up a loop, yarn over, pull through all 3 loops on hook. 1 st decreased.

Finished Size

Height:
Lucy-Lou: 7 inches
Tim-Bob: 6.5 inches

Materials

- Cascade 220 [100g; 220 yards/201m; 100 percent Peruvian highland wool]; 1 skein each color
- C1: Color: #9444 Orange
- C2: Color: #7822 Brown
- C3: Color: #8021 Tan
- C4: Cascade 220 Quattro; Color: #9438 Salmon
- Substitution: You will require approx. 50 yards/45m of worsted weight yarn in each color (or any color you want!)
- Ball band will indicate a knitted gauge of 20 sts = 4 inches / 10cm.
- US G / 4.5mm crochet hook
- Safety pin or split ring marker
- Yarn needle
- Polyfill (polyester stuffing)
- Small dried beans
- Embroidery needle (thinner than a yarn needle)
- 8mm doll or bear eyes
- Small amount of embroidery floss for facial features
- 0.5-inch pompom maker (Lucy-Lou only)
- Scrap of craft felt and 3 small buttons (Tim-Bob only)

Gauge

20 sc = 1 inch / 10cm

A note about gauge: Gauge is relatively unimportant in this pattern. It is more important to make sure your stitches are fairly tight. Feel free to use a lighter-weight yarn and smaller hook to make smaller dolls, or a bulkier yarn and larger hook to make bigger dolls.

Stitch Pattern

Spike stitch: Work the next stitch as follows: Insert your hook into the space below the next stitch in the previous round, pull up a loop, yarn over, and draw the yarn through both loops on your hook.

Instructions

Note: Rounds are not joined, but are worked in a spiral. Place a safety pin or split ring marker in the first stitch of the second round to mark the beginning of the round. Remove this marker when working the first stitch of each round, and replace it immediately into the stitch you just made.

Lucy-Lou

Head:

Using C2, *make a ring of yarn around 2 fingers, with the working yarn (the length of yarn which leads to the ball) leading off to the right, from the top of the ring. Insert the hook into this ring and pull up a loop, then ch 1.

Round 1: Work 6 sc into ring. Pull yarn tail to tighten ring.

Round 2: Work 2 sc in each sc. 12 sts. Place marker in first st of round.

Round 3: [Sc in next sc, 2 sc in next sc] to end. 18 sts.

Round 4: [Sc in next 2 sc, 2 sc in next sc] to end. 24 sts.

Round 5: [Sc in next 3 sc, 2 sc in next sc] to end. 30 sts.

Round 6: [Sc in next 4 sc, 2 sc in next sc] to end. 36 sts.

Round 7: [Sc in next 5 sc, 2 sc in next sc] to end. 42 sts.*

Rounds 8–9: Using C3, sc in each sc.

Round 10: [Sc-dec, sc in next 5 sc] to end. 36 sts.

Round 11: [Sc-dec, sc in next 4 sc] to end. 30 sts.

Round 12: [Sc-dec, sc in next 3 sc] to end. 24 sts.

Rounds 13–14: Sc in each sc.

Round 15: [Sc-dec, sc in next 2 sc] to end. 18 sts.

Sl st in next st. Break yarn, leaving a 10-inch tail. Draw through last st, pull tight.

Body:

Using C4, work from * to * as for Head.

Round 8: [Sc in next 6 sc, 2 sc in next sc] to end. 48 sts.

Round 9: Sc in back loop of each sc.

Rounds 10–12: Sc in each sc.

Round 13: [Sc-dec, sc in next 6 sc] to end. 42 sts.

Rounds 14–15: Sc in each sc.

Round 16: [Sc-dec, sc in next 5 sc] to end. 36 sts.

Rounds 17–18: Sc in each sc.

Round 19: [Sc-dec, sc in next 4 sc] to end. 30 sts.

Round 20: Using C1, [sc in next sc, spike st in next sc] to end.

Round 21: Sc in each sc.

Round 22: Using C4, [sc-dec, spike st in next sc, sc in next st, spike st in next st] to end. 24 sts.

Rounds 23–24: Sc in each sc.

Round 25: [Sc-dec, sc in next 2 sc] to end. 18 sts.

Rounds 26–27: Using C3, sc in each sc.

Sl st in next st. Break yarn, draw through last st and pull tight.

Finishing Instructions

Make two 0.5-inch pompoms using C2, and sew them to either side of the head, using photo as a guide.

Stuff the head with Polyfill. Fill the bottom 1.5 inch of the body with small, dried beans. Fill the rest of the body with Polyfill, packing it tightly to keep the beans in place. Lining up the slip stitches of both pieces, sew head and body together, matching stitches all the way around.

Sew on the eyes, securing and hiding the yarn behind the pompoms. Embroider the mouth.

Tim-Bob

Head:

For the head, **using C1, make a ring of yarn around 2 fingers, with the working yarn (the length of yarn which leads to the ball) leading off to the right, from the top of the ring. Insert the hook into this ring and pull up a loop, then ch 1.

Round 1: Work 6 sc into ring. Pull yarn tail to tighten ring.

Round 2: Work 2 sc into each sc. 12 sts. Place marker in first st of round.

Round 3: [Sc in next sc, 2 sc in next sc] to end. 18 sts.

Round 4: [Sc in next 2 sc, 2 sc in next sc] to end. 24 sts.

Round 5: [Sc in next 3 sc, 2 sc in next sc] to end. 30 sts.

Round 6: [Sc in next 4 sc, 2 sc in next sc] to end. 36 sts.**

Rounds 7–9: Sc in each sc.

Round 10: [Sc-dec, sc in next 4 sc] to end. 30 sts.

Round 11: [Sc-dec, sc in next 3 sc] to end. 24 sts.

Round 12: [Sc-dec, sc in next 2 sc] to end. 18 sts.

Round 13: [Sc-dec, sc in next sc] to end. 12 sts.

Rounds 14–15: Sc in each sc.

Sl st in next st. Break yarn, leaving a 10-inch tail. Draw through last st, pull tight.

Body:

Work from ** to ** as for Head.

Round 7: [Sc in next 5 sc, 2 sc in next sc] to end. 42 sts.

Round 8: Sc in back loop of each sc.

Rounds 9–11: Sc in each sc.

Round 12: [Sc-dec, sc in next 5 sc] to end. 36 sts.

Rounds 13–14: Sc in each sc.

Round 15: [Sc-dec, sc in next 4 sc] to end. 30 sts.

Rounds 16–17: Sc in each sc.

Round 18: [Sc-dec, sc in next 3 sc] to end. 24 sts.

Rounds 19–20: Sc in each sc.

Round 21: [Sc-dec, sc in next 2 sc] to end. 18 sts.

Rounds 22–23: Sc in each sc.

Round 24: [Sc-dec, sc in next sc] to end. 12 sts.

Round 25: Sc in each sc.

Sl st in next st. Break yarn, draw through last st and pull tight.

Hat:

Using C2, work from ** to end of Round 4 as for Head. 24 sts.

Round 5: Sc in back loop of each sc.

Round 6: Sc in each sc.

Sl st in next st. Break yarn, draw through last st and pull tight.

Finishing Instructions

Stuff the head with Polyfil. Fill the bottom 1.5 inch of the body with small, dried beans. Fill the rest of the body with Polyfill, packing it tightly to keep the beans in place.

Cut a small oval of felt for face, using photo as a guide. Sew to head using blanket stitch. Mark eye placement and attach eyes. If the eyes you're using protrude in the back where the hole is, cut a small slit in the felt so the protrusion can be hidden inside the head. Embroider mouth. Sew buttons to body, using photo as a guide.

Lining up the slip stitches of both pieces, sew head and body together, matching stitches all the way around. Sew on hat. Sew in ends.

Variation

Dolls are super easy to customize. Most simply, you can substitute any colors you'd like. For Lucy-Lou, you can make the whole body striped instead of just working the one strip of spike stitch, or you can make the spikes more dramatic by inserting your hook two or three rounds below the working round. You can also vary your gauge. You can make tiny dolls by using fingering weight yarn and a much smaller hook, or huge dolls by using super bulky yarn and a very large hook. And then there are the embellishments! You can make dolls that are dressed all prissy-like, dolls that are punk rockers, and dolls that are ticked off at their deadbeat boyfriends. Go nuts!

Organic versus Synthetic

When stuffing toys, crafters love the debate between organic stuffing and synthetics. Although it's possible to find synthetic beads that will provide the weight of dried beans, many crafters appreciate that the plastic weights will not carry bacteria and mold. However, most of us grew up on bean-stuffed toys and games and came out no worse for wear. It's up to you!

If you'd like to use synthetic beads for weight in your Lucy Lou or Tim-Bob, choose beads that are large enough to not escape through the holes between crochet stitches. Or, sew them into a small fabric pouch, just as you would a bean bag.

Woven Fringe Scarf

by Mandy Moore

Simple single crochet stitches are unexpectedly beautiful when worked in a softer-than-soft hand-dyed mohair yarn. Dyed-to-match ribbon is woven through the ends of the scarf and knotted into a shimmering, cascading fringe.

Project Rating: Flirtation

Cost: Approximately $40–$50 as shown.

Necessary Skills: ch (page 7); sc (page 10); sewing ends (page 24)

Finished Size:

Length: approx. 72 inches (not including fringe)

Width: approx. 6 inches

Materials

- All yarns from Curious Creek Fibers in color "Rock Grotto"; 1 skein each color.
- [MC] Etosha [50g; 220 yards/200m; 90 percent Kid Mohair, 10percent Nylon]
- [CC] Kalahari [50g; 87 yards/79m; 100percent Nylon]
- Substitution: Choose a worsted-weight mohair-blend yarn for MC, and any ribbon yarn that is approx 0.25–0.5 inch wide. 220 yards/200m of MC and 28 yards/26m of CC are needed.
- Ball band for MC should indicate a knitted gauge ranging from 14-22 sts = 4 inches / 10cm. Mohair yarns can be worked at many different gauges, and the recommended gauge for yarns of similar thicknesses may vary widely depending on the preferences of the manufacturer.
- US L / 8.0mm crochet hook
- Yarn needle
- Ruler (a yardstick would be best)

Gauge

10 sc = 4 inches / 10cm using MC

Instructions

Using MC, ch 15.

Row 1: Sc in 2nd ch from hook, and in each ch to end. 14 sts.

Row 2: Ch 1, sc in each sc to end.

Repeat this row until work measures 72 inches, or desired length. Break yarn, draw through last st and pull tight.

Finishing Instructions:

Sew in ends.

Fringe:

Cut 28 1-yard pieces of CC.

Thread one piece on yarn needle. Weave this strand in and out through one column of stitches, beginning at end of scarf and working 3-6 inches up length of scarf.

Weave length of CC back down through same column of stitches to

end of scarf. (If yarn was woven over a stitch on the first pass, it will be woven under that stitch on the second pass, and vice-versa.)

Adjust woven strand so that ends which extend to form fringe are the same length. Knot ends close to end of scarf.

Weave all CC strands in the same way, varying lengths of woven section randomly. The fringe will not all be the same length; trim ends if desired (the fringe of the sample scarf was not trimmed).

Variation

This scarf could be made using many different combinations of yarn. What about making the scarf in a chunky wool yarn and weaving strands of eyelash into the ends? Why not use several different kinds of yarn for the fringe, instead of just one? Try weaving the CC yarn along the whole length of the scarf, instead of just the ends.

Bubble Belt

by Robyn Chachula

Imagine this: you are having your perfect shopping day, and you happen upon your perfect bohemian skirt. It is perfect because you are going to a party later that same day, but one problem, you don't have a bohemian belt to pair it with. Do you chance the shopping gods and try to scour the mall for a belt? Or do you head home to your yarn stash? You're smart. You head home and whip up this little number in an afternoon, and still have time to do your nails.

Project Rating: Flirtation

Cost: Less than $15.

Necessary Skills: ch (page 7); sl (page 16); dc (page 13); sewing ends (page 24)

Finished Size:

Width: 2 inches
Length: Sized to fit

Materials

- ♦ Lion Brand Lion Suede [85g, 122 yards/110m, 100 percent polyester),
- ♦ Color: #210-126 Coffee – 1 ball

Note: If you want a belt that measures longer than 46 inches, buy 2 balls.

- ♦ Substitution: Look for a smooth, lightweight, chunky yarn.
- ♦ Ball band will indicate a knitted gauge of 12 sts = 4 inches / 10cm.
- ♦ US H / 5.0mm crochet hook
- ♦ Yarn needle
- ♦ Large silver lobster keyring and 9mm metal loop

Gauge

Large Motif = 2 inch diameter

Gauge is unimportant for this project.

Instructions

Note: After first motif is worked, subsequent motifs are worked in sequence, each only half-completed, until the desired length is reached. The end motif is worked, then the rest of the motifs are completed. Do not break yarn after working each motif.

First (Large) Motif:

Ch 9, sl st in 1st ch to form ring.

Ch 3, work 19 dc in ring, sl st to 3rd ch of initial ch-3 to join.

Second (Small) Motif:

Ch 8, sl st in 5th ch from hook to form ring.

Ch 2, sl st in 1st dc of first motif, work 5 dc in ring.

*Next Large Motif:

Ch 12, sl st in 9th ch from hook to form ring.

Ch 2, sl st in last dc of previous motif, work 9 dc in new ring.

Next Small Motif:

Ch 8, sl st in 5th ch from hook to form ring.

Ch 2, sl st in last dc of previous motif, work 5 dc in new ring.*

Repeat from * to * until work measures 2 inches less than desired length.

End Motif:

Ch 12, sl st in 9th ch from hook to form ring.

Ch 2, sl st in last dc of previous motif, work 18 dc in new ring, sl st to top of ch at beginning of ring.

Complete Remaining Motifs:

Work 5 dc in ring of next motif, sl st to top of ch at beginning of ring.

Next, **work 9 dc in ring of next motif, sl st to top of ch at beginning of ring.

Work 5 dc in ring of next motif, sl st to top of ch at beginning of ring.**

Repeat from ** to ** until all motifs have been completed.

Break yarn, draw through last st and pull tight.

Finishing Instructions

Sew in ends.

Sew loop to lobster keyring and end of belt (see photo).

Variation

Try using different yarn types for different effects. Use a hook at least one size smaller then what the label recommends. Have the wool left over from the Cozy Peacoat? Why not whip one up for a perfect matching scarf? Or try using cotton thread and continue the pattern for a long necklace. Want a snazzier belt, add beads to the yarn before starting. Then pull up a bead at each intersection of each circle, for a little jewel to your belt.

Who Hat

by Mandy Moore

Inspired by Dr. Seuss' wonderful characters, the Whos, this whimsical hat makes an adorable and unique baby gift. It's worked in a wool/acrylic blend yarn that is soft and easy to care for, with a touch of nylon to make it durable. It incorporates a fun and unique tassel which is worked from side to side, then stitches are worked around the bottom of the tassel, and the hat is worked in the round from the top down.

Project Rating: Flirtation

Cost: Approximately $15–$20 as shown. Since only bits of CC1 and CC2 are used, you'll be able to use the leftovers for another project. Try making some flowers from the Daisy Chain Neck Warmer!

Necessary Skills: sl st (page 16); ch (page 7); sc (page 10); dc (page 13) ; sewing ends (page 24)

Finished Size:

Circumference: 16.5 inches

Materials

- Sirdar Country Style DK (100g, 45 percent Acrylic, 40 percent Nylon, 15 percent Wool; 347 yards/318m); 1 ball each color
- [MC] Color: #538 Olive
- [CC1] Color: #506 Bilberry
- [CC2] Color: #517 Cranberry
- Substitution: Look for a soft DK weight yarn. 100 percent cotton yarns are not recommended, as they will not maintain the correct shape. Acrylic or washable wool blends are practical choices. Approx. 100 yards/110m of MC and small amounts of CC1 and CC2 are needed.

- Ball band will indicate a knitted gauge of 22 sts = 4 inches / 10cm.
- US F / 4mm crochet hook or size to obtain gauge
- Yarn needle

Gauge

16 sc = 4 inches / 10cm

Instructions

Tassel:

Using MC, ch 7.

Row 1: Work 9 sc in 2nd ch from hook, then 1 sc in each ch to end.

Row 2: Ch 1, sc in 1st and 2nd sc only.

Row 3: Ch 7, work 9 sc in 2nd ch from hook, then 1 sc in each ch and sc to end.

Row 4: Ch 1, sc in 1st and 2nd sc only.

Row 5: Ch 5, work 9 sc in 2nd ch from hook, then 1 sc in each ch and sc to end.

Hat:

Round 1: Turn tassel 90 degrees clockwise. Ch 1, work 6 sc along lower edge of tassel, sl st in 1st sc to join.

Round 2: Ch 1, sc in each sc to end, sl st in 1st sc to join. 6 sts.

Round 3: Ch 1, sc in 1st sc, 2 sc in 2nd sc, [sc in next sc, 2 sc in next sc] to end, sl st in 1st sc to join. 9 sts.

Round 4: Ch 1, sc in 1st and 2nd sc, 2 sc in 3rd sc, [sc in next 2 sc, 2 sc in next sc] to end, sl st in 1st sc to join. 12 sts.

Round 5: Ch 1, sc in first 3 sc, 2 sc in 4th sc, [sc in next 3 sc, 2 sc in next sc] to end, sl st in 1st sc to join. 15 sts.

Round 6: Ch 1, sc in first 4 sc, 2 sc in 5th sc, [sc in next 4 sc, 2 sc in next sc] to end, sl st in 1st sc to join. 18 sts.

Round 7: Ch 1, sc in first 5 sc, 2 sc in 6th sc, [sc in next 5 sc, 2 sc in next sc] to end, sl st in 1st sc to join. 21 sts.

Round 8: Ch 1, sc in first 6 sc, 2 sc in 7th sc, [sc in next 6 sc, 2 sc in next sc] to end, sl st in 1st sc to join. 24 sts.

Round 9: Ch 1, sc in first 5 sc, 2 sc in 6th sc, [sc in next 5 sc, 2 sc in next sc] to end, sl st in 1st sc to join. 28 sts.

Round 10: Ch 1, sc in first 6 sc, 2 sc in 7th sc, [sc in next 6 sc, 2 sc in next sc] to end, sl st in 1st sc to join. 32 sts.

Round 11: Ch 1, sc in first 7 sc, 2 sc in 8th sc, [sc in next 7 sc, 2 sc in next sc] to end, sl st in 1st sc to join. 36 sts.

Round 12: Ch 1, sc in first 8 sc, 2 sc in 9th sc, [sc in next 8 sc, 2 sc in next sc] to end, sl st in 1st sc to join. 40 sts.

Round 13: Ch 1, sc in first 7 sc, 2 sc in 8th sc, [sc in next 7 sc, 2 sc in next sc] to end, sl st in 1st sc to join. 45 sts.

Round 14: Ch 1, sc in first 8 sc, 2 sc in 9th sc, [sc in next 8 sc, 2 sc in next sc] to end, sl st in 1st sc to join. 50 sts.

Round 15: Ch 1, sc in first 9 sc, 2 sc in 10th sc, [sc in next 9 sc, 2 sc in next sc] to end, sl st in 1st sc to join. 55 sts.

Round 16: Ch 1, sc in first 4 sc, 2 sc in 5th sc, [sc in next 4 sc, 2 sc in next sc] to end, sl st in 1st sc to join. 66 sts.

Rounds 17–19: Ch 1, sc in each sc to end, sl st in 1st sc to join.

Shell Round (Round 20): [Skip first 2 sc, work 5 dc in front loop of next sc, skip 2 sc, sl st in front loop of next sc] to end. 11 shells made. Break yarn, draw through last st and pull tight.

Round 21: Use sl st to join CC1 to back loop of 3rd st of row 19, ch 1, sc in back loop of each sc to end, sl st in 1st sc to join. 66 sts.

Rounds 22–23: Ch 1, sc in each sc to end, sl st in 1st sc to join.

Joining Round (Round 24): Ch 1, insert hook into 3rd dc of 1st shell of Shell Round then into 1st sc, work sc; insert hook into 4th dc of 1st shell then into 2nd sc, work sc; sc in next 4 sc, [insert hook into 3rd dc of next shell then into next sc, work sc; insert hook into 4th dc of same shell then into next sc, work sc; sc in next 4 sc] to end.

Round 25: Work Shell Round.

Round 26: Use sl st to join CC2 to back loop of 3rd st of row 24, ch 1, sc in back loop of each sc to end, sl st in 1st sc to join. 66 sts.

Rounds 27–28: Ch 1, sc in each sc to end, sl st in 1st sc to join.

Round 29: Work Joining Round.

Rounds 30–33: Ch 1, sc in each sc to end, sl st in 1st sc to join.

Round 34: Work Shell Round.

Round 35: Use sl st to join MC to back loop of 3rd st of row 33, ch 1, sc in back loop of each sc to end, sl st in 1st sc to join. 66 sts.

Rounds 36–37: Ch 1, sc in each sc to end, sl st in 1st sc to join.

Round 38: Work Joining Round.

Round 39: Work Shell Round, working into both loops of each stitch. Break yarn, draw through last st and pull tight.

Finishing Instructions:

Sew edges of base of tassel together for approx. 0.5 inch.

Sew in ends.

Variation

This yarn has a great color palette; have fun choosing colors to suit the taste of the recipient! It would be lovely worked in pastel tones.

This hat could also be easily worked with four different colors, or even five.

To use five colors, work the tassel and Rounds 1-20 using the first color; work Rounds 21-25 three times using a different color each time, then work rounds 35-39 using the fifth color.

Chapter Ten

◆◆◆

Bucking Tradition

Straight-Laced Tank and Shrug

Appliqued and embroidered ready-to-wear is all the rage, and thankfully, easy to do at home! With a bit of yarn and some creativity, you can whip up a couture-worthy tank in a single evening. This project uses two basic motifs to jazz up a store-bought tank top. The diagram and instructions are based on a scoop neck fine rib tank. However, since the motifs are crocheted and then sewn in place, they can be easily positioned to suit nearly any top. Crochet the matching shrug, and you'll be set for a night on the town.

Project Rating: Summer Fling

Cost: Approximately $35–$50 as shown, including cost of base tank.

Necessary Skills: ch (page 7); sc (page 10); sl st (page 16); dc (page 13); tr (page 14); sewing ends (page 24)

Abbreviations: dc-dec: Double Crochet Decrease. Yarn over, insert hook into next stitch and pull up a loop, yarn over and pull through first 2 loops on hook, yarn over, insert hook into following stitch and pull up a loop, yarn over and pull through first 2 loops on hook, yarn over, pull through remaining 3 loops on hook. One stitch decreased.

Finished Size

Length of shrug (cuff to cuff): 32 inches
Sleeve width: 13 inches

Materials

- Lorna's Laces Swirl DK (50g, 150yd/138m, 85 percent Wool, 15 percent Silk); Color: Black Purl
- For Tank: 1 skein
- For Shrug: 2 skeins

- Substitution: Approx. 100m dk weight yarn for tank motifs, approx 260m for shrug. Choosing a thicker (or thinner) yarn for the motifs will simply change the size of the motifs. Choosing a thicker yarn for the shrug will make a looser and larger shrug.
- For Dk weight yarn, ball band will indicate a knitted gauge of 22 sts = 4 inches / 10cm.
- US D / 3.0mm crochet hook
- Yarn needle
- Sewing needle and thread to match color of tank
- 1 tank top or tee in your size. Shown in black.

Gauge

Motif B is 5 inches in diameter
15 tr = 4 inches / 10cm

Instructions

Tank Instructions

Make 3 of Motif A and 1 of Motif B.

Motif A

Ch 4, sl st in 1st ch to join in a ring.

Round 1: Ch 1, 12 sc in ring, sl st in 1st sc to join.

Round 2: Ch 1, sc in backloops of each sc to end, sl st in 1st sc to join.

Note: The next round involves working into stitches 2 rows down. The stitches in Row 3 will be worked in the same loops in which the stitches of Row 2 were worked. Reach the hook *behind* the stitches of Row 2 before inserting the hook into the loop.

Round 3: Ch 6, skip 1st sc, dc in back loop of 2nd sc of Row 1, [ch 3, skip 1 sc, dc in back loop of row below] 4 times. Turn work.

Note: The next row is worked with the wrong side facing. When instructed to work into the front loop of a stitch, work into the loop closest to you; it would be the back loop if the right side was facing.

Round 4: Ch 1, [4 sc in ch3-sp] 4 times, 9 sc in ch6-sp, sc in front loop of sc at base of ch, sc in front loops of next 3 sc, 5 sc in dc, sl st in 1st sc to join.

Break yarn, draw through last st and pull tight. Sew in ends.

Motif B

Ch 4, sl st in 1st ch to join in a ring.

Round 1: Ch 3 (counts as 1st dc), 10 dc in ring, sl st in 3rd ch of initial ch-3 to join.

Round 2: Begin working into 2nd st as follows: [5 hdc in next dc, sl st in next dc] 5 times, sl st in sl st from end of last round.

Round 3: Ch 9 (counts as 1 dc and 1 ch6-sp), [skip next 5 hdc, dc in next sl st, ch 6] 4 times, sl st in 3rd ch of initial ch-9.

Round 4: Ch 1, 10 sc in each ch6-sp to end, sl st in 1st sc to join. 50 sts.

Round 5: Ch 9 (counts as 1 dc and 1 ch6-sp), [skip next 4 sc, dc in next sc, ch 6] 9 times, sl st in 3rd ch of initial ch-9.

Round 6: Ch 1, 9 sc in each ch6-sp to end, sl st in 1st sc to join.

Break yarn, draw through last st and pull tight. Sew in ends.

Once all motifs have been made, join the three A motifs as follows:

Place the motifs next to each other, right sides facing, with the straight edges up and corners touching. If necessary, slightly shift the sc sts worked on the ch9-sp of the motifs, so that there are 14 sc along the straight edge of each motif.

Use a sl st to attach yarn to the sc at the top right corner of the 3 motifs.

Row 1: Ch 3 (counts as 1st dc), dc in 1st sc, [hdc in next sc, sc in next 10 sc, hdc in next sc, dc-dec to join last sc of this motif and 1st sc of next motif] twice, hdc in next

sc, sc in next 10 sc, hdc in next sc, 2 dc in last sc. 42 sts. Turn work.

Row 2: Ch 2, hdc in 1st and 2nd sts, sc in next st, sl st in next 10 sts, sc in next st, dc in next 2 sts, sc in next st, sl st in next 8 sts, sc in next st, dc in next 2 sts, sc in next st, sl st in next 10 sts, sc in next st, hdc in last 2 sts.

Break yarn, draw through last st and pull tight.

Sew in ends.

Finishing Instructions:

Block motifs, pinning to acheive desired shape.

Use sewing needle and thread to sew in place on tank.

Shrug Instructions:

Note: As written the sleeves of this shrug are 13 inches wide. If you want wider sleeves, ch a multiple of 6 more sts than the number given (eg. 58, 64, or 70 sts). Every 6 extra sts will add approx. 1.5 inches to width of sleeves. Remember to buy more yarn if you are making wider sleeves!

First Cuff:

Ch 52.

Row 1: Dc in 4th ch from hook and in each ch to end. 49 sts (ch-3 at beginning of row counts as 1 dc).

Row 2: Ch 3 (counts as 1st dc), dc in 2nd dc and each dc to end.

Row 3: Ch 3 (counts as 1st dc), 2 dc in 1st dc, skip 2 dc, sc in 4th dc, [skip 2 dc, 6 dc in next dc, skip 2 dc, sc in next dc] to last 3 sts, skip 2 dc, 3 dc in last dc.

Row 4: Ch 1, sc in first dc, ch 3, skip 2 dc, dc in 1st sc, [ch 6, skip 6 dc, dc in next sc] to last sc, ch 3, skip 2 dc, sc in 3rd ch of inital ch-3.

Note: If you have added extra sts to the sleeves, work more stitches on Row 5 so that you end up with a multiple of 6 sts + 1.

Row 5: Ch 1, 3 sc in ch3-sp, 7 sc in each ch6-sp, 3 sc in last ch3-sp. 55 sts.

Rows 6 and 7: Ch 3 (counts as 1st dc), dc in 2nd sc and in each sc to end.

Row 8: Ch 3 (counts as 1st dc), 2 dc in 1st dc, skip 2 dc, sc in next dc, [skip 2 dc, 6 dc in next dc, skip 2 dc, sc in next dc] to last 3 sts, skip 2 dc, 3 dc in last dc.

Break yarn, draw through last st and pull tight.

Sleeves and Back:

Next row will be worked into the back of the foundation chain from the First Cuff.

Use a sl st to rejoin yarn to 1st st of foundation chain.

Row 1: Ch 4 (counts as 1st tr), tr in 2nd ch and in each ch to end. 49 sts.

Row 2: Ch 4 (counts as 1st tr), tr in 2nd tr and in each tr to end, working last tr in 4th ch of initial ch-4.

Repeat Row 2, 34 times more.

Second Cuff:

Next Row: Ch 3 (counts as 1st dc), dc in 2nd tr and in each tr to end, working last dc in 4th ch of initial ch-4.

Work Rows 2-8 as for First Cuff.

Finishing Instructions:

Sew in ends.

Sew sleeve seams, beginning at cuff edge of each sleeve and working inwards, leaving a 23-inch opening in the center. Try on shrug before ending seams to ensure a good fit! It is much easier to make the seams longer or shorter at this point, than after you have finished them and worked the edging.

Edging:

Use a sl st to attach yarn at one seam edge of opening.

Work 1 row of sc around body opening, working 4 sc for each tr row; sl st in 1st sc to join round.

Break yarn, draw through last st and pull tight. Sew in remaining ends.

Variation

Couturize your own wardrobe by applying crocheted motifs. They're great on denim, skirts, blouses, and more. Use these motifs or adapt your own from the stitch guide in chapter 2. The shrug can easily be altered to make longer sleeves by working additional repeats of the triple crochet rows and trying it on as you go.

DIY: Freeform Crochet

"Freeform Crochet," though it sounds all arty and mysterious, is really one of the easiest ways to experiment with crochet. Just take a few colors or textures of yarn and a suitable hook and get going.

Start with a chain loop of 6 stitches or so, just as for the top of the toque in chapter 6. Try working a few stitches into the chain to start a circle. And then see where the inspiration takes you.

Want to veer off on an angle? Do you think a change of color is called for? Go for it! The beauty of freeform is that you can do what you want when you want. If you don't like it, it's easy to rip back and try something new. Don't forget to work three dimensionally. Crochet can grow up and down just as easily as it can spread from side to side.

The Wowie Zowie Eco-Tote

by Marcia Wentela

Marcia's named this bag the "wow" tote, because everyone whom you meet will say "Wow! You made that out of shopping bags?" We love it because it takes wimpy plastic bags and makes a sturdy plastic tote; great for the beach or just bumming around. The best part? When you want the crochet fix but are low on cash, you can improvise your "yarn" from the kitchen cabinet.

Project Rating: Flirtation

Cost: Approximately $10 for the handles.

Necessary Skills: ch (page 7); sc (page 10); sl st (page 16); sewing ends (page 24)

Finished Size

Width: 10 inches

Height: 7 inches (not including handles)

Materials

- Approx. 18 plastic shopping bags
- US K / 6.5mm crochet hook
- Sharp scissors
- Large yarn needle
- 1 set plastic purse handles, available from large craft stores

Note: The handles used for this bag have square metal rings at the bottom, which make it easy to attach them to the bag. The instructions are written for attaching this kind of handle.

Gauge

Approx. 9 sc = 4 inches

Gauge isn't crucial for this project. Just be sure the fabric is tightly crocheted, to prevent stretching and holes.

"Yarn" Preparation

Before crocheting, you'll need to cut the plastic bags into strips, and join them into a long, continuous strip.

Lay a bag flat on a table and remove any creases by smoothing with your hands. Fold the bag in half lengthwise, so that the sides of the bag are together. Fold in half lengthwise again.

Cut off the top straps and the bottom bag seam. Cut the folded bag horizontally, into 1-inch strips. When the bag is unfolded, these will be loops, each the width of the bag.

Lay 2 loops next to each other. Overlap the left loop over the right loop. With your right hand, reach up through the right loop, then reach down into the left loop and grasp the portion of the right loop which lays beneath it. Grasp the left loop with your left hand, and pull with both hands; the loop will form a knot.

Continue to join the loops in this way until you have used up all your bags. You'll need to begin to wind the "yarn" into a ball after a few loops have been joined.

Instructions

Ch 21.

Row 1: Sc in second ch from hook, and in each ch to end. 20 sts.

Rows 2–4: Ch 1, sc in each sc to end.

Row 5: Ch 1, sc in 1st st and mark this st as beginning of round. (Marcia recommends slipping a bobby pin onto the stitch. Bobby pins will be removed when the bag is done.) Sc in each sc to end, rotate work 90 degrees clockwise, 2 sc in end st of Row 4, sc in end sts of Row 3 and Row 2, 2 sc in end st of Row 1, sc in 20 ch of foundation chain (hold "yarn" tail along chain and crochet over it as you work these sts; no end to sew in later!), 2 sc in end st of Row 1, sc in end sts of Row 2 and Row 3, 2 sc in end st of Row 4, sl st in 1st sc to join round. 52 sts.

Rounds 6–19: Ch 1, sc in each sc to end, sl st in 1st sc to join. Move marker up for each new row, to help keep track of placement of row end.

Round 20: Center the bag handles on the sides of the bag. Hold the handle upside down against the outside of the bag, with the metal ring touching the top edge of the bag. Work this round in sc as you have worked previous rounds, attaching the handles as follows when you work the stitches that correspond with the location of the handle ends:

Insert hook into metal ring and into next sc, work sc as usual.

Depending on the width of the metal rings, you will work 2 or 3 sts this way for each ring.

Round 21: Ch 1, sc in each sc to end.

Round 22: Sl st in each sc to end. Draw "yarn" tail through last st and pull tight.

Finishing Instructions

Sew in ends with yarn needle.

Variation

Now that you have the hang of it, experiment! Cast on more stitches and make your next bag larger and taller if you like. Add a flap and use a great button. Embellish with a crocheted flower. The possibilities are endless!

Crocheted Bling

Tell your friends, and they may not believe you; this sea-glass inspired choker necklace is actually crochet! Use a variety of beads and some silver wire. The stitch is just chain stitch. By now, you could do this in your sleep!

Project Rating: Flirtation

Cost: Approximately $15–$50 for either the choker or the bracelet. Exact cost depends on the types and qualities of beads chosen.

Necessary Skills: ch (page 7); sewing ends (page 24)

Finished Size
Sized to fit.

Materials
- 28 gauge silver beading wire; 15 yards/13.5m per spool; 1 spool will make two or three chokers
- One silver toggle clasp
- Approx. 36 transparent glass beads of various sizes and colors.
- As shown: 14 square clear beads, 4 larger clear beads, 9 lime green beads, and 9 turquoise blue beads.
- Two silver jump rings, one for each end of the strand.
- Beading pliers for working with findings (??? Is this what they are called???)
- US 8/1.5mm steel crochet hook

Gauge
It's a necklace. Gauge doesn't matter.

Instructions
String the beads onto the wire.

To replicate the pattern as shown, use the following color pattern: [1 clear, 1 blue, 1 clear, 1 green] to end. Use a random pattern of sizes and shapes for the most natural appearance. I recommend stringing some smaller beads first, as these beads will be worked last and will end up near the toggle clasp. If the choker toggle is attached too close to a large bead, you won't be able to fit the toggle through the fastener.

With crochet hook, make a slipknot and chain 2.

Next, *slide first bead up the wire until it is next to hook. Rotate hook to grab wire and complete another chain stitch, catching the bead in the stitch. Work one chain st without a bead.*

Repeat from * to * until all beads have been placed. Doesn't look long enough? You can hold it up to your neck to check.

Work an additional 5 or 6 chain stitches to leave enough room to attach the toggle clasp.

Fold your strand into thirds. Secure one of the jump rings to the outer edges of the chain stitches on one side of the piece and one side of the toggle clasp.

Attach the second jump ring to the outer edges of the chain stitches on the other side of the piece and the other side of the toggle clasp. Voilà, you now have a fibbity fab bauble to show off your advanced-variety skills.

Variation

Instead of one, consider a three-strand necklace...or how about a bracelet? Just make three strands and attach them all to the clasps. This design would be stunning in pseudo-pearl baubles!

Jewelry Design and Resources

Working with wire and beads can be as complex and artful as you choose. If the Sea Glass Choker has you *hooked*, check out Kate Welsh's beading book, *Not Your Mama's Beading*. For crochet-specific projects, take a look at *Bead Crochet* by Bethany Barry (Interweave Press). Or, your local bead shop will be thrilled to help. Most feature classes and work-shops to get you going.

When the Jeans Don't Fit: A Recycled Denim Rug

We all have this problem from time to time. The jeans may still be stylish, but they sure don't fit. Or, they're left over from the acid wash '80s. Now, there's a solution. Cut up jeans make great crocheting material. It's sturdy; it's cozy; it's perfect for a charming accent rug. Select a variety of denim colors to make a striped rug, or crochet all from the same shade... it's up to you!

Project Rating: Summer Fling

Cost: Stick to your own closet or a second hand shop, and you'll keep the cost under $20.

Necessary Skills: ch (page 7); sc (page 10); sewing ends (page 24)

Finished Size

5 pairs of women's size 10s make a 36 inch × 24 inch foot oval rug.

Materials

- Good fabric shears
- 4-6 pairs of jeans

Note: Get creative – you don't have to stick to just jeans! Skirts work well too. You may need more or fewer to make a rug of the same size. If jeans are frayed or holey, you'll need to be careful when cutting into strips.

- US Q / 15mm crochet hook
- Safety pin
- Thread and sewing needle

Gauge

Approx 4 sc to 4 inches; however, gauge doesn't matter. Just keep it tight so the rug will wear well.

"Yarn" Preparation

Before crocheting, you'll need to make yarn from your jeans. Begin at one lower leg hem and cut a 1.5-inch strip that spirals up the pant leg. When reaching the bum part of the jeans, cut straight across the lower bum and begin to spiral down the opposite leg until you reach the hem. In this way, you'll be able to make one long strip from each garment.

Because denim comes in a wide range of colors and textures, consider planning your color pattern in advance. To crochet a rug as shown, alternate between contrasting colors of denim. Because of the size and length variations, color changes are not specified in the pattern. Instead, treat the denim strips as you would balls of yarn, switching to a new one when you're close to running out.

Note: Due to the thickness of the "yarn", turning chains are not worked in this pattern. Rather, the rounds are worked in a spiral; keep track of the first stitch of each round by placing a safety pin in it.

Instructions

Ch 6.

Round 1: Sc in 2nd ch from hook and in each sc to end, rotate work 180 degrees, 4 sc in 1st ch of foundation chain, sc in next 4 ch, 3 sc in last ch. 16 sts.

Note: For all remaining rows, work into back loops only.

Round 2: [Sc in next 5 sc, 2 sc in next sc, sc in next sc, 2 sc in next sc] twice. 20 sts.

Round 3: [Sc in next 7 sc, [2 sc] in next 3 sc] twice. 26 sts.

Round 4: [Sc in next 9 sc, 2 sc in next sc, sc in next 2 sc, 2 sc in next sc] twice. 30 sts.

Round 5: [Sc in next 12 sc, [2 sc] in next 3 sc] twice. 36 sts.

Round 6: [Sc in next 15 sc, [2 sc] in next 3 sc] twice. 42 sts.

Round 7: [Sc in next 18 sc, [2 sc] in next 3 sc] twice. 48 sts.

Round 8: [Sc in next 21 sc, [2 sc] in next 3 sc] twice. 54 sts.

Cut "yarn", draw through last st and pull tight.

Finishing Instructions

Using your fingers, weave the yarn ends through neighboring stitches. This is where the firmness of the fabric is important: The tighter your stitches, the more difficult it will be for the ends to come loose.

Using thread and a sharp sewing needle, secure the ends by sewing together.

Variation

Instead of jeans, use old tee shirts or bath towels for a softer, less hardy feel. A mat crocheted from old towels would be great for your bathroom floor!

Deliberate Shrinkage Sack

Remember when dad would do the laundry and his favorite wool sweater would come out doll sized? The same principals of shrinkage can work for you to create durable and water-resistant items, such as this sweet purse.

Project Rating: Summer Fling

Cost: Approximately $15–$20 as shown.

Necessary Skills: ch (page 7); sc (page 10); hdc (page 31); sl st (page 16); sewing ends (page 24)

Finished Size:

Before felting:
Height: 9 inches
Width: 9 inches

After Felting:
Height: 7.5 inches
Width: 6.5 inches

Materials

- Noro Kureyon [50g, 110 yards /100m, 100 percent Wool], Color: #92; 2 balls
- Substitution: Choose an aran weight, 100 percent wool, yarn, or wool blended with a small amount of mohair. Be certain to choose wool which has not been treated to be machine washable! If it says "Superwash", it is machine washable and will not felt.
- Ball band will indicate a knitted gauge of 18 sts = 4 inches / 10cm.
- US J / 6mm crochet hook
- Washing machine and pillowcase for felting

Gauge

Approx. 10 hdc = 4 inches / 10cm before felting, but exact gauge is not important. Just be sure to keep stitches loose!

Instructions

Ch 36.

Row 1: Hdc in 3rd ch from hook and in each ch to end. 34 sts.

Row 2: Ch 2, hdc in 1st hdc and in each hdc to end.

Work Row 2, 16 times more.

Fold work in half lengthwise, so that top edge and foundation chain are folded.

Insert hook into back loop of first and last sts of last row, sl st together; work all sts of last row together in this way. Break yarn, draw through last st and pull tight.

Working from fold towards corners, seam opposite side in the same way; do not break yarn. Rotate work 90 degrees

clockwise; next row will be worked around opening of bag, working into row ends from previous section.

Round 1: Ch 2, hdc in seam, 22 hdc across first side of bag, hdc in other seam, 22 hdc across remaining side of bag, sl st in 2nd ch of initial ch-2 to join.

Round 2: Ch 2, hdc in each hdc to end, sl st in 2nd ch of initial ch-2 to join.

Repeat Round 2, 4 times more.

Next Row: Sl st in 1st 3 hdc; turn work.

Handle:

Next Row: Ch 1, sc in each sl st and in next 3 hdc. 6 st.

Next Row: Ch 1, sc in each sc to end.

Repeat Row 3 until strap measures 32 inches.

Break yarn, leaving a long tail, draw through last st and pull tight.

Use yarn tail to sew end of strap to opposite edge of bag.

Sew in ends.

Finishing Instructions

Sew in all loose ends. Put the bag into an old pillowcase and knot the top. This prevents too much wool fluff from getting into your washing machine and potentially clogging the pipes. Put the pillowcase in the wash with some old jeans; maybe before you cut them to make a rug! (You can also use an old pair of tennis shoes, although anything that heavy may cause damage to your washing machine.) Since you'll be washing on *hot*, anything may shrink, so choose your items carefully. The idea is to provide a lot of agitation. Putting the purse in the wash alone will take quite a bit longer to achieve maximum feltage.

Include a small bit of washer soap and set to *hot*. Check the wash every five or ten minutes until the bag has shrunk down to its desired fabric and size. Kureyon takes a notoriously long time to felt. In a standard washing machine, you may have to put it through two or three full wash cycles. In an energy-efficient front-loader, it may take even longer. To speed things up a bit, between hot cycles, rinse with ice water. The intense temperature change shocks the wool into shrinking more quickly.

After the bag has shrunk to your desired texture, manipulate the strap and body of the bag while they are still wet. This is the time to push, prod, pull, or otherwise manipulate the item into a pleasing and even shape. It's also a good time to pull on the strap to stretch it.

Lay the bag on an old towel or two and air dry. After the bag has dried, the shape will be set. Sometimes Kureyon gets fairly furry in the wash. If a hairy purse leaves you less than thrilled, take a disposable razor to the surface to remove extra fuzz. You can also use a pair of scissors, or just leave it hairy.

Variation

Ah, the thrills of felting. The bag shown was crocheted in a self-striping wool. You can do the same pattern in two colors of solid wool...just switch when you change directions for the top part of the bag. Or, add a pocket by crocheting a square and sewing it to the front before felting.

Is It Felt? Is It Fulled?

Contrary to popular belief, the term *felting* doesn't really pertain to the process of shrinking a crocheted or knit item. Instead, it refers to taking raw wool and using heat and agitation to pound it into a flat and dense fabric. The Mongolian nomads use felt to line and insulate the walls of their portable gers.

More correctly, *fulling* refers to the process we explore in this chapter. A crocheted or knit scarf, bag, hat, and so on, is then fulled by applying hot water and agitation and results in a fabric very similar to the felt produced by working with the raw animal fleece.

Is this book wrong? Sort of. In recent years, pattern designers and crafters have begun to use the term felting to describe either process. If we were to call the bag a *fulled bag*, you may just think we were full of it!

Felted Trellis Scarf

by Mandy Moore

Another quick felted project, this scarf is so fun and unique you'll want to make more than one. They make great gifts, and can look very different depending on the yarn used. Different yarns can felt very differently. For example, the accent yarn for this scarf was a softly spun, single-ply yarn, which shrunk into little squiggly spikes when felted. Mandy has made other scarves with different accent yarns, which have shrunk into little worms instead. Don't be afraid to experiment! You never know what you'll come up with, but it will almost certainly be cool.

Project Rating: Flirtation

Cost: Approximately $25-$35 as shown.

Necessary Skills: ch (page 7); sc (page 10); tr (page 14); sewing ends (page 24)

Finished Size:

Before felting:
Length: 84 inches
Width: 6 inches

After Felting:
Length: 66 inches
Width: 4.5 inches

Materials

- [MC] Noro Kureyon [50g, 110 yards /100m, 100 percent Wool], Color: #51; 2 balls
- [CC] Manos del Urguay Variegated Wool [100g, 138 yards /126m, 100 percent Wool], Color: Bramble; 1 skein (approx. 17 yards/15.5m used)
- Substitution: Choose an aran weight, 100 percent wool, yarn, or wool blended with a small amount of mohair. *Be certain to choose wool which has not been treated to be machine washable! If it says "Superwash", it is machine washable and will not felt.*

- Ball band will indicate a knitted gauge of 18 sts = 4 inches / 10cm.
- US M / 9mm crochet hook
- Washing machine and pillowcase for felting

Gauge
Gauge is unimportant for this project.

Instructions

Ch 18.

Row 1: Sc in 2nd ch from hook, and in each ch to end.

Row 2: Ch 5 (counts as 1 tr and 1 ch1-sp), skip 2 sc, tr in 3rd sc, [ch 1, skip next sc, tr in next sc] to end.

Row 3: Ch 5 (counts as 1 tr and 1 ch1-sp), skip 1st tr and ch1-sp, [tr in next tr, ch1] 7 times, tr in 4th ch of initial ch-5.

Repeat Row 3 until work measures 84 inches or desired length.

Last Row: Ch 1, sc in each tr and ch until 17 sc have been worked. Break yarn, draw through last st and pull tight.

Apply Accent Yarn:

Cut approx. 200 6-inch pieces of CC.

Tie these pieces randomly to different parts of the scarf. The sample scarf has fairly even coverage, but the accent yarn could be concentrated at the ends, or along one long edge, for example.

Finishing Instructions

See the Deliberate Shrinkage Sack (page 174), for felting instructions.

Immediately after felting, remove the scarf from the pillowcase and shape it with your fingers, pulling and tugging to open the grid pattern, separate pieces of accent yarn that have become slightly joined, and shape the ends and edges. The shape will be a little weird and wonky from the felting process, but it will also be very malleable, and can be bent to your will!

Once you have acheived the shape you want, hang the scarf or lay it flat to dry.

Variation

Why not try a wrap? The Felted Trellis pattern worked over, say, 75 or 95 stitches (any large, odd number) would make a fabulous, funky stole. Try adding the shell edging from the Lace Edged Tank in this chapter, or roses like the ones from the Rose Jacket pattern in chapter 8, or add a frill to the ends, worked like the Getting Dizzy Scarf in chapter 7. . . .

Creatures of the Wooly Deep

by Zak Greant

A real eel or octopus might be a little more than your cat could handle, but these quick-to-make, wooly renditions should be just her size. They can be felted or not, depending on your preference; the eel shown is felted, but not the octopus. Both have met with the approval of the test kitten.

One safety note: Keep an eye on the toys, and discard them when they get too frayed. Yarn can be dangerous to feline digestive systems.

Project Rating: Flirtation

Cost: Approximately $10 for both toys.

Necessary Skills: ch (page 7); hdc (page 31); sc (page 10); sl st (page 16); sewing ends (page 24)

Abbreviations: sc-dec: Insert hook into 1st st, pull up a loop, insert hook into 2nd st, pull up a loop, yarn over, pull through all 3 loops on hook. 1 st decreased.

Finished Size

Octopus: Approximately 5 inches in width from tentacle to tentacle
Eel: Approximately 5 inches in length

Materials:

- Noro Kureyon [50g, 110 yards/100m, 100 percent wool], Color: #128; 1 ball will make both toys
- Substitution: Look for an aran weight yarn. If you plan to felt your cat toys, look for a 100 percent wool yarn, which has not been treated to be machine washable.
- Ball band will indicate a knitted gauge of 18 sts = 4 inches / 10cm.

- US G / 4.5mm crochet hook
- Yarn needle
- Safety pin

Gauge

Gauge is unimportant for this project.

Instructions

Octopus

Tentacles:

First, *ch 14.

Sl st in first 5 ch, sc in next 4 ch, 2 hdc in each rem ch to end. Do not break yarn.*

Repeat from * to * 7 times more; 8 tentacles have been worked. Sl st in 1st ch of foundation ch of 1st tentacle, to join in a ring.

Body:

Ch 1.

Round 1: Working into the edge of the last hdc of each tentacle, work 2 sc in 1st tentacle, [3 sc in each of next 2 tentacles, 2 sc in next tentacle] twice, 3 sc in last tentacle, sl st in 1st sc to join. 21 sts.

Round 2: Ch 1, [sc-dec, sc in next sc] to end, sl st in 1st sc to join. 14 sts.

Round 3: Ch 1, [sc-dec] to end, sl st in 1st sc to join. 7 sts.

Rounds 4-5: Ch 1, sc in each sc to end, sl st in 1st sc to join.

Round 6: Ch 1, [sc in next sc, 2 sc in next sc] 3 times, sc in last sc, sl st in 1st sc to join. 10 sts.

Round 7: Ch 1, sc in each sc to end, sl st in 1st sc to join.

Round 8: Ch 1, [sc in next sc, 2 sc in next sc] to end, sl st in 1st sc to join. 15 sts.

Rounds 9-10: Ch 1, sc in each sc to end, sl st in 1st sc to join.

Round 11: Ch 1, [sc in next 3 sc, sc-dec] to end, sl st in 1st sc to join. 12 sts.

Round 12: Ch 1, [sc-dec] to end, sl st in 1st sc to join. 6 sts.

Round 13: Ch 1, [sc-dec] to end, sl st in 1st sc to join. 3 sts. Break yarn, leaving a 6-inch tail; draw through last st and pull tight.

Finishing Instructions:

Thread yarn tail on needle and sew small hole on top of Octopus closed.

Sew in ends.

Felt if desired (see the Deliberate Shrinkage Sack, for felting instructions).

Eel

Body

Ch 16.

Row 1: Sc in 2nd ch from hook and in each ch to end. 15 sts.

Rows 2–3: Ch 1, sc in each sc to end.

Row 4: Fold work lengthwise, so that foundation ch and last row of work meet. Ch 1, [insert hook into next st of next row, then into corresponding ch of foundation ch, work sc] to end. Work has been joined into a small tube.

Row 5: Ch 1, sc in front loops of each sc to end.

Rows 6–9: Ch 1, sc in each sc to end.

Row 10: Roll tube towards back of work and up, until back loops of Row 4 meet top of Row 9. Ch 1, [insert hook into next sc, then into back loop of corresponding loop of st from Row 4, work sc] to end.

Row 11: Ch 1, sc in front loops of each sc to end.

Rows 12–19: Ch 1, sc in each sc to end.

Row 20: Roll body towards back of work and up, until back loops of Row 10 meet top of Row 19. Ch 1, [insert hook into next sc, then into back loop of corresponding loop of st from Row 10, work sc] to end. Do not break yarn.

Ends:

First, **ch 1.

Row 1: Work 1 sc into edge st of each row around one end of Body, sl st in 1st sc to join. 9 sts.

Row 2: Ch 1, skip 1st sc, [sc-dec] to end, sl st in 1st sc to join. 4 sts.**

Break yarn, draw through last st and pull tight.

Use sl st to rejoin yarn to opposite end of body, and work from ** to ** to form head. Do not break yarn.

Fin:

Row 1: Work 2 sl st along edge of head, towards end of Row 20; work 1 sc in each sc of Row 20; work 2 sc along edge of tail end; work 1 sc in end of tail end, and mark this st with a safety pin; work 2 sc along edge of tail end, work 15 sc along edge of body, work 2 sc along edge of head, sl st in end of head. Turn work.

Row 2: Skip sl st, sl st in first 3 sc, sc in each sc to marked st, 3 sc in marked sc, mark the center sc of these 3 sc, sc to last 3 sc, sl st in next sc. Turn work.

Row 3: Skip sl st, sl st in first 3 sc, sc in each sc to sc before marked sc, 2 sc in next sc, 3 sc in marked sc, 2 sc in next sc, sc in each sc to last 3 sc, sl st in last 3 sc and next sl st. Break yarn, draw through last st and pull tight.

Finishing Instructions:

Sew in ends.

Use a piece of yarn from another (contrasting color) part of the ball of Kureyon to embroider eyes for your eel, hiding ends deep in the eel's body.

Felt if desired (see page 174, Deliberate Shrinkage Sack, for felting instructions).

Variation

As written, the octopus makes an ideal friend for your kitty to playfully murder, but it can easily be stuffed with bits of shredded paper and catnip, then sewn shut to form a catnip toy.

If you have a child (or adult!) in your life who loves sea creatures (or Spongebob Squarepants™), the eel is an easy beast to size up. Use the basic technique, working more layers over more stitches, to make a human-sized toy, or even a bolster pillow. Want a bigger octopus? Use bulky-weight yarn and a larger hook to scale up this beguiling cephalopod.

· Part Three ·

Resources and Appendices

Chapter Eleven

◆◆◆

History of the Hook

Because crochet's origins are about as fuzzy as fur novelty yarn, at times it seems that the art of the hook spontaneously developed worldwide. Numerous sources cite potential evidence of crochet from the sixteenth century in diverse cultures including China, Peru, and Arabia.

Some historians presume that in non-European cultures, a bent forefinger was used with strands of animal hair or plant matter to essentially crochet ropes. However, these theories are inconclusive. Since hand-spinning tools, textiles, and woven fabrics have been found dating back to the Neolithic period, it's presumable that if crochet were indeed a known craft from this time, some evidence would have survived.

In fact, the first verifiable reports of crochet, as we know it today, only date back to early nineteenth century Europe. In an 1812 book, *The Memories of a Highland Lady,* Scottish author Elizabeth Grant describes "shepherd's knitting" as a means of using a hook to make warm garments from handspun wool. Unfortunately, no earlier writings or artifacts indicate this as a long-known craft. In 1824, the first published pattern that we now recognize as crochet appeared in a Dutch ladies magazine. However, the term "crochet" was not used this early.

The word crochet itself is a derivative of the Middle French word for hook, *croc* or *croche*, indicating that perhaps the tools now used as crochet hooks were developed during the fourteenth and fifteenth centuries. In early years, many publications used the variation *crotchet*. One such early book of needlework patterns, printed in first edition in 1847, eventually switched to the term crochet in late 1848.

No Primitive Art

Historians and crochet geeks have long wondered, "What took so long?" Why would significantly more complex textile arts, including knitting and weaving, be the first to develop, even among ancient cultures? Woven artifacts have been found from nearly every prehistoric culture. Knitting developed some 400 years before crochet. But crochet only turned up immediately before the Industrial Revolution evolved crafts into hobbies.

If you knit, you may have realized by now that crochet uses a much larger quantity of material to produce a fabric of the same size. Due to the thick construction of a crochet stitch, it's no economical technique. Before machines took over from humans for fabric production, the fabric needed to be constructed in the cheapest way possible. Wasting yards and yards of wool or cotton was simply not an option.

For the home crafter, prior to the early nineteenth century, all thread or wool would need to be handspun prior to use. But after machines were able to spin thread and thin yarns quickly and relatively cheaply, it's probably no surprise that thriftiness was no longer the prime concern. And so, excited by the new wealth of materials, nineteenth century women jumped on the crochet bandwagon on its first pass.

Many of the first crochet hooks were simple implements carved from hardwoods. Some specimens remain that were hand-crafted of brass, silver, or ivory. In the early twentieth century, the first mass-produced crochet hooks were made from steel, very similar to the ones still available today.

Let Them Single Crochet!

Since the Renaissance, artfully handmade lace was reserved for only the wealthiest classes. Initially, the cost and time required to make such detailed work from handspun yarn made lace unaffordable for anyone outside the nobility. But, as the spinning wheel developed, the cost of thread declined, and the cost of lace declined as well. To prevent merchants and other commoners from dressing in the fashion of the nobility, many countries actually passed laws to restrict what people wore. Subsequent centuries were focused on creating lace so fine, so extravagant, that years and years could be spent on a single small piece.

In the nineteenth century, crochet was mostly used to imitate the intricate and fine lacework previously created through more expensive and time-intensive methods. Some historians believe crochet gained somewhat of a knock-off reputation that was disdained by the upperclasses. But, just like fake Louis Vuittons, crochet couldn't be stopped. To alleviate the poverty in Ireland in the 1840s, schools were established to teach the art of crocheted lace for export to wealthier cultures. These charitable organizations not only taught the skills but arranged the sales of the finished pieces and distributed the profit. England's Queen Victoria purchased large amounts of this Irish crochet lace and learned to crochet herself. Soon, fashionable ladies, especially among the middle class, followed the trend. Buying lace, although still a luxury, could actually be considered charitable.

By the end of the nineteenth century, not only spinning but lace-making machines were invented, allowing beautiful but inexpensive decorative fashion to be available to nearly everyone. A modern take on this tradition, the Uber-femme Capelet in chapter 8 is an example of lacework.

Purely Puritanical

As European settlers fled the Old World for the New, many brought the art of crochet along for the journey. Functional and straightforward sewing was standard, but crochet was viewed as art and entertainment rolled into one. Even the most basic cotton pillowcase could be gentrified by the addition of a simple border of elegant crochet lace. For women surviving and thriving on the frontier, adding a bit of frivolous handiwork to their houses helped bring an element of civilization to their harsh surroundings.

Famed author and early settler Laura Ingalls Wilder (1867–1957) not only includes several references to crochet in her *Little House on the Prairie* series, but examples of her own Irish lace crochet still survive in the Midwest. Notable sites include her childhood home in Burr Oak, Iowa, and the museum in Walnut Grove, Minnesota.

In addition to decorative thread crochet, women in the harsh prairie climates also used thicker wool to crochet scarves, capes, shawls, even underwear—anything to keep warm. In contrast to knitting's smooth and even fabric, the intertwined layers of crocheted thread made perfect insulation.

As machine-produced cotton fabrics became available in North America, creative women took large hooks to strips of fabric leftover from sewing and crocheted rag rugs, the earliest of which date to the 1840s.

Nomadic Stitching: Crochet in Present-Day Mongolia

In today's Mongolia, crochet is a valued art form. Taking up precious little cargo weight, a hook and some simple thread allow women (and men) to enjoy a decorative hobby during the dark winters. On my latest visit to the countryside north of Ulaan Baatar, the capital, I encountered a nomadic woman who had adorned her *ger* (tent) with filet crochet borders of her own design. Not only creating images of flowers and standard decorations, she had used the eyelets to sketch out images of her sheep and goats, the livelihood of her family.

Crochet Negligée?

After the end of World War I, women found themselves with time on their hands to return to hobbies that made the world around them more beautiful. While women's clothing became more plain and business-like, crocheters quickly adapted the dainty lace techniques for creating and adorning undergarments.

Books featuring trims and insets for boudoir apparel flew off the shelves. Rather than simply recreating the laces of the previous century, designs from this time were sleek and feminine, mirroring the fashions popular in the roaring '20s. If sleek and tailored appeals to your inner girl, check out the Pseudo-Kimono wrap in chapter 8.

Designers today are even going back to this period of exquisite hand-work. White Lies Designs, a pattern and kit company founded by Joan McGowan-Michael, features lovely kits and patterns for hand crocheted and knit lingerie. Interested in making a little something-something? Check out her site at www.whiteliesdesigns.com.

Hippy Hookers at Woodstock

As delicate knit fashion in the '50s morphed into the freewheeling spirit of the '60s and '70s, crochet went along for the ride. Suddenly, the scrap-yarn Granny Square, first patterned in the early twentieth century, was used in a never-ending technicolor spectrum of the new easy-care 100 percent acrylic yarns. Breaking out of the square, designers realized that any number of shapes were possible.

In part inspired by the knit color work of the Missoni family design house in Milan, crocheted garments featured an unbelievable number of colors in simple stitch patterns.

In many ways, crochet and hippy fashion went hand in hand. Big fringe, texture, and color are all ideally suited to the funky and sturdy art of crochet. Flirty openwork made from circular motifs are perfect for the shawls, ponchos, and tunics so synonymous with the pre-disco '70s.

Many of these patterns are still available in vintage stores and on eBay. And, with the current fashions trending toward eclectic, it's not much of a stretch to adapt them to modern styles with color and fiber selections.

But, just as the spirit of free love tambourines faded into a disco and new wave drumbeat, fashion choices morphed as well into synthetic man-made spandex and neon nylon. And crochet, not so suited to pegged jeans and three-tiered hot pink skirts, was relegated to baby blankets and afghans made by well-meaning grandmothers.

The Rebirth of Cool Crochet

Somewhere in the late '90s, crochet and knitting had a mass-market resurgence. Suddenly, glossies were calling knitting "the new yoga." Hip high-end yarn boutiques were popping up in ritzy locales from WeHo to Soho. Although the focus at first was on providing current and fashionable designs for hand knitting, crochet soon followed. Major yarn companies on every scale began publishing crochet patterns to flatter and fit a modern generation of crafters.

Instead of finding only mile-a-minute afghan patterns and slippers designed for Phentex acrylic tape, crafters soon had as wide a range of choice as in stores at the local mega-mall.

Crochet is everywhere these days. With most major crafting publications producing crochet-specific magazines and new books springing up every Tuesday, crochet has evolved from a much-maligned outsider art into the mainstream of needlecrafts once again.

In the world of blogging, too, crochet has been popping up more and more frequently, both from dedicated crochet fanatics and from life-long knitters who have more recently discovered the magic of the hook. As of February 2005, the Fiber Arts Blog Ring had almost 700 members. A ring devoted to crochet had 250. Just do a search on Google for "crochet blog" and you'll get more than 2 million results. Searching on "crochet patterns" retrieves more than 4 million. For some of my favorite links, see chapter 12's sections on blogs and online resources.

Crochet on the Catwalk

Spend a few minutes with the latest *Vogue, InStyle,* or *Elle* and you're likely to find some drool-worthy crochet. Especially as the interest in hand-crafted garments has surged, crochet has become a viable design medium. Quick, architectural, and free-form, crochet allows designers to think outside the row.

Designers as diverse as Michael Kors and BCBG are using crochet from trims on shirts and denim to creating lacy and textured boleros, sweaters, and skirts.

Want inspiration? Just stop by Anthropolgie (www.anthropologie.com) or the designer boutiques at BlueFly (www.bluefly.com). Pick up any fashion magazine. Watch fashion television or go shopping in your local mall. You'll see crochet everywhere, after you know what you're looking for.

I defy anyone to suggest that crochet is passé.

Chapter Twelve

◆◆◆

Surf 'n Turf: Crochet Resources Online and on Land

As discussed in chapter 11, crochet resources are everywhere; from your local library to your favorite newsstand, to the computer in your loft. You can talk, listen, read, and learn crochet 24 hours a day in nearly any language.

Webzines and Pattern Sources

Like me, many of you are probably from the generation who remembers the first time the word blog was mentioned in the mainstream press. Less than a decade later, and there are blogs on every imaginable subject, and a few you'd rather *not* imagine!

Many of this book's talented contributors have sites to feature their work. Don't forget to check out their biographies in the Designer Bios section on page 212.

- ◆ *CrochetMe* (www.crochetme.com). *CrochetMe* magazine, started in 2004, features hip and urban patterns in modern yarns. Published mostly bi-monthly, the CrochetMe Web site also features an active bulletin board forum for asking questions, posting photos of your works in progress, and connecting with other crocheters.

- ◆ *Crochet Pattern Central* (www.crochetpatterncentral.com). Updated weekly, this site may be the Web's largest collection of free crochet patterns. Rather than simply hosting the patterns, you'll also find links to other crochet sites, organized by type of patterns.

- *Crochet with Dee* (**members.aol.com/crochetwithdee**). Dee has been crocheting and teaching crochet long enough to answer your questions before you get a chance to ask them. Her site is a treasure of crochet information, from patterns to instructions on obscure crochet techniques.
- *Crochet911* (**www.crochet911.com**). Produced by the Craft Yarn Council of America, Crochet911 provides illustrations and written instructions for common crochet techniques.

Blogs

Blogs can be one of the best ways to get inspiration and check out what other crochet geeks are stitching, especially if you don't know any other crocheters in real life.

- **Crochetblogs Webring (www.yarntomato.com/crochetblogs/).** Crochetblogs, with more than 250 members, is the Web's largest ring of blogs with a crochet focus. Going to the ring's home page will allow you to navigate through all the member sites.
- **The Crochet Dude (thecrochetdude.blogspot.com).** Rosy Grier, ex-NFLer crochets. So does Drew Emborsky, "The Crochet Dude." Drew's patterns can be found in numerous publications, including the "Crochet Pattern a Day" calendars for 2006 and 2007. His Web site also features a set of free original crochet patterns.
- **MonsterCrochet (www.monstercrochet.com).** MonsterCrochet has a stellar blog, plus an army of self-designed crochet vegetables called the Vegetable Liberation Army. They even have buggy and blood-shot crocheted eyes!
- **The Yarn Harlot (www.yarnharlot.ca/blog/).** Although not limited to crochet, Stephannie Pearl-McPhee's writings on yarn and yarnaholic behaviors have placed her work on the shelves of many yarn addicts worldwide. Her blog is updated almost daily and is a great way to feed your fiber addiction when away from your yarn stash.
- **Jodi Green (www.jodigreen.ca/blog/).** Jodi, an art student in Georgia, blogs about knitting, crochet, and art at JodiGreen.ca.
- **ModeKnit/The Knitting Heretic (www.modeknit.com/blog/).** Annie Modesitt, designer of the "Ramblin' Rose Cardie" on page 117, blogs and showcases her workshops.
- **Yarnageddon (www.yarnageddon.com/).** Blog of our most talented technical editor and designer extraordinaire, Mandy Moore, Yarnageddon features Mandy's crochet, knitting, and life in Vancouver. Not only the best technical editor in the world, Mandy also does amazing things with yarn and rarely ever works a pattern exactly as written.
- **Catie Berger (www.herself75.blogspot.com).** Catie Berger, designer of the "S^3 Sari Silk Shrug" on page 114, blogs about crochet, knitting, and life, with frequent free pattern posts.

Get Connected: Start Your Own Blog!

Want a blog? With free online blogging software, it's easier than ever. Without knowing a lick of Web code, you can get set up and online within minutes. Check out these fully hosted sites for more information:

Blogger: www.blogger.com

Blogspot: www.blogspot.com

Typepad: www.typepad.com

LiveJournal: www.livejournal.com

Xanga: www.xanga.com

If you already have a Web site and would like to start a blog, many Web hosts now include popular blogging software along with your hosting package. Check out some of these open-source favorites:

GreyMatter: www.noahgrey.com/greysoft

MoveableType: www.moveabletype.org

WordPress: www.wordpress.org

After you're up and running, consider joining a Web ring to get noticed and get readers. Check out RingSurf, the Web's most popular ring system, at www.ringsurf.com.

♦ **Robyn Chachula (www.crochetbyfaye.blogspot.com).** Get inside the mind of a designer at Robyn Chachula's blog. Robyn writes and photographs crochet projects and original designs throughout the creative process. For more of Robyn's work, don't miss her Peacoat (page 128), Bubble Belt (page 157), and Pseudo-Kimono (page 107).

Crochet Groups and Communities

Crocheting all by your lonesome in front of a good DVD can be a satisfying stress-reliever. But, sometimes a gal wants to hook with others! Even if you know no other yarn addicts in your local community, you can find them online through these great forums!

♦ **Crochetville (www.crochetville.org).** Also founded in 2004, Crochetville's online forum is an active community that provides support and inspiration for crocheters of all experience.

♦ **Craftster (www.craftster.org).** Focusing on all types of handwork, craftster is one of the largest online forums focusing on crafting. Be sure to check out the crochet corner!

- ♦ **Knitter's Review (www.knittersreview.com).** Yes, it says "Knitter's Review," But this handy site, run by Clara Parkes, features weekly yarn, product, and book reviews, articles on other yarn crafts, and an uber-helpful online forum where crafters around the world connect.

- ♦ **Yahoo! Groups (groups.yahoo.com/).** Do a search on Yahoo! Groups for "crochet," and you'll find more than 1200 ready and waiting to join. Several of this book's designers mentioned "crochetlist" as a particularly active group. For charity crochet, check out "hugsandstitches." Or, start your own and soon hook up with other like-minded crocheters from around the globe.

- ♦ **Meetup (www.meetup.com).** An online collection of offline groups, Meetup can help you find a local crochet or knitting group and, after you sign up, will send you meeting reminders and updates. Can't find one in your location? Start one! Meetup can help with all the details.

Local Guilds

Most cities or towns have at least one guild dedicated to the fiber arts. In large cities, you may have more than one to choose from! Guilds tend to charge a small annual membership fee in exchange for meetings, contents, classes, and discounts on supplies and materials.

Stitching for the Greater Good

Want to put your hook to good use? Charity crochet is a rewarding reason to put hook to yarn. Many local charities are thrilled to receive hand-crocheted blankets and clothing. Check with your local hospitals and shelters to find the best way to help. Don't forget animal shelters! Animals in need also love to snuggle into a warm blanket.

For national and worldwide charities, check on the Web. Several directories list programs that welcome your handwork. For a great starter list, check out this site: crochet.about.com/od/charities/.

The Dulaan Project is a handwork charity promoted by knitblogger Ryan Morris. To help impoverished families survive the harsh Mongolian winters, the Dulaan Project is collecting warm items of all kinds to be shipped *en masse* to Mongolia every summer. For more information, or to join, visit Ryan's blog, Mossy Cottage, at www.nwkniterati.com/MovableType/MossyCottage/.

Don't think you need to buy new yarn and patterns for charity crochet. Scrap blankets made from odds and ends can bring color into someone's life. Save your scraps and crochet colorful (and simple) granny squares to be sewn into a larger blanket. Make it a group project by collecting squares from your crochet friends. Need inspiration? Check out the square motifs in chapter 2.

Although the character of each guild is largely determined by its members, in general guilds are a wonderful way to connect with other crochet fans locally. Usually made of a large variety of generations and experience levels, it's delightful to see that sometimes it **is** your mama's (or grandmother's) crochet.

Need to find a guild? Check with your local yarn shop. They'll have a good idea of the local groups, when they meet, and how to become a member.

The Glossies

Like knitting magazines, crochet magazines have undergone a beast-to-beauty transformation over the past few years. Not only are more and more of the big name textile arts mags featuring crochet designs, but crochet-specific special issues are being published semi-annually.

Some bookstores import magazines from Europe and other locations. Translated into English, these can be great resources for designs that are on the edge of current fashion. When crocheting from foreign magazines, be careful to make sure that you're speaking the same language. Remember, British and American patterns use the same terms in different ways. If working from a British pattern, check out the handy translation chart on page 207 in Appendix A.

♦ *Interweave Knits (and Crochet)* (www.interweave.com/knit/). Also the publishers of a variety of textile arts magazines, *Interweave Knits* has long focused on wearable and creative designs that highlight and enhance the craftsperson's skills. Since 2005, *Interweave* has also published an exciting semi-annual crochet-only issue, only available on newsstands and by order through their Web site.

KnitScene, another special format magazine, is *Interweave's* experimental younger sister. As of press time, two issues have been published, with fans hoping for more. The patterns in *KnitScene* focus on a collaboration between different textile techniques. You'll find knit and crochet working as one, embroidery, sewing, and more. All with a fashion focus that appeals to many generations.

♦ *Vogue Knitting* (www.vogueknitting.com). *Vogue* now publishes three separate magazines. *Vogue Knitting* is published four times per year. It features mostly knit designs with a smattering of crochet thrown in for good measure. Each issue tends to feature a design or two by Fifth Ave fashion houses.

Run by the same publisher, *Knit Simple* and *Knit.1* are two new magazines geared more toward Gen X and Gen Y. With thicker yarn and quicker projects, these magazines occasionally offer crochet. We've even heard plans of a new crochet-specific magazine coming down the pipeline in the next year—keep your eyes open!

♦ *Family Circle Easy Knitting (Plus Crochet)* (www.fceasyknitting.com). Even though the "plus crochet" is in a tiny circle next to the magazine's title, this quarterly regularly features classic crochet designs and instruction. Geared toward beginners, the pattern section publishes a "refresher" guide in each issue, with illustrations of common crochet and knitting techniques.

Other Books

You've already purchased one book...why do you need another? While *Not Your Mama's Crochet* gives you great instruction, patterns, and resources, if you're hooked on crochet, you'll probably want more.

In general, crochet books can be broken down into three main categories: instructional, pattern, and stitch reference.

- ◆ **Instructional Books** These books focus on a specific technique. General crochet knowledge, you'll get from this book. But if you want to learn Tunisian crochet, hairpin lace, Irish crochet, or Tapestry crochet, you're best off to find a book specific to those topics. Great instructional books can be found nearly anywhere books are found: at the library, at your local independent book store, at your favorite mall outlet or chain store, and at your local yarn store.

- ◆ **Pattern Books** Books that focus more on patterns than on instructions are also easy to come by. Look for a book with a few designs that catch your eye, and then read the patterns a bit to see if you gel with the author's writing style. Although you may be interested in checking out the yarn choices and colors, remember, that part is usually easy to substitute.

  Pattern books are sometimes published by major publishers and sometimes produced by yarn companies. In general, the yarn company books will be available only through shops that stock their yarns.

- ◆ **Stitch Reference Books** Want to design a blanket or scarf? Want to experiment with new stitch combinations? You're in luck. Every year, many stitch reference books, guides, and even calendars are put on the shelves. Some focus on certain types of stitches: circular motifs, afghan stitches, or lace. Others are broken down into sections, such as what we did in chapter 2.

  When selecting a stitch guide, look for clear photographs or illustrations. Also see how they've printed the instructions. Do you work best from a symbolcraft diagram? If so, unless you're in love with a particular complicated stitch, don't buy the book that only has written-out instructions.

  Stitch references make up a large part of my personal library. Even if I rarely use them as is, they provide fantastic inspiration.

Indie Designers

In no particular order, these crochet designers consistently push the envelope on the art form. Visit their sites for inspiration or shopping. Of course, this is an incomplete list. Knitting and crochet magazines are constantly featuring new designers. You'll find it's rare to see designers who only work in crochet. Rather, most folks tend to use either knitting or crochet, depending on the design concept.

- ♦ **Annie Modesitt (www.anniemodesitt.com).** Designer of the "Ramblin' Rosie Cardie" on page 117, Annie not only designs for major books and magazines, but offers her own line of knitting and crochet patterns for sale on her Web site.

- ♦ **Stitch Diva Studios (www.stitchdiva.com/).** Jennifer Hansen, designer of the fabulous "Classic Street Page Boy" on page 144, features an original line of crochet patterns under the label "Stitch Diva." Available for sale online or in local shops, she's one of the few designers to work with hairpin lace and Tunisian crochet. Want to learn more? Her site features handy tutorials.

- ♦ **Teva Durham (www.loop-d-loop.com).** Designer Teva Durham has been featured in *Vogue Knitting, Interweave Crochet, Rowan Magazine,* and more. She's recently launched her own Web site featuring a gallery of her innovative designs in knit and crochet.

- ♦ **White Lies Designs (www.whiteliesdesigns.com).** Joan McGowan-Michael's White Lies Designs features nice and naughty crochet and knitting patterns. Want to crochet a gorgeous silk camisole? This is the place to go. From her Web site, Joan sells the individual patterns as well as kits that include all the yarn you'll need.

- ♦ **Prudence Mapstone (www.knotjustknitting.com).** Prudence Mapstone specializes in free-form crochet designs that make the most of crochet's more spontaneous side. Rather than publishing books of patterns, Prudence's slim volumes teach you the theory behind free-form crochet. She is also an active traveling teacher. If you're interested, check out her tour and class schedule on her Web site.

- ♦ **indiKnits (www.indiknits.com).** This Web site is brought to you by your dear friend (and this book's author), Amy Swenson. indiKnits offers crochet, knitting, and felting patterns with unusual yarns.

Chapter Thirteen

◆◆◆

Safe S.E.X.: Stash-Enhancing eXcursions

Talk to any avid crocheter and you're likely to hear more than one thinly veiled complaint about the size of his or her stash, proving once again, size *does* matter. *My stash has taken over my kitchen! My boyfriend says my stash has more closet space than he does! My mom says if I steal from her stash one more time, I'm out on the street.*

Stashing more yarn than one could hope to crochet that month, year, or lifetime isn't for everyone. But, with a bit of time, it's likely that even the most stash-conscious crocheters have a shoebox or two of scraps to be saved for that scrap afghan or charity project.

Although the hording instinct may vary from crocheter to crocheter, most hook-loving gals and guys can't resist the lure of new yarn. Even though yarn may be chosen with a specific project in mind, sometimes the yarn itself is the reason for shopping.

Psychologists have likely studied this impulse. But yarnaholics know that new yarn isn't just an impulse buy or an obsession. This unassuming ball of blue two-ply wool can turn into a cozy hat, a felted bag, a pair of socks, or a fun toy for your favorite nephew. That shelf of hand-dyed silk might make a lovely freeform shawl. Then again, wouldn't it be fun to pick up some of that shiny pink cotton and make a feminine and flirty cape, like the one on page 101?

New yarn is, quite simply, *possibility.*

The Big Box Stores

You know which stores I'm talking about. They have "Mart" in the name. Or "Super." They're as big as several football fields and allow you to buy your lacy underwear, all-seasons tires, and fresh pesto from the same checkout line. So, are you really surprised they usually also stock yarn and crochet accessories?

Enter the craft section of these stores and you'll find mass-market brands such as Bernat, Patons, Red Heart, and Lion Brand. Although these companies occasionally feature a few wool-blend yarns, most of the fiber you'll find is 100 percent acrylic. Yarn is typically packaged in huge "super-saver" balls of 100g or more. Here you'll find great deals for everyday items that take a lot of abuse and a lot of yarn: throw blankets come to mind. You can also find some varieties of novelty yarn that can be fun for scarves and silly gifts. Prices are low, but you'll be unlikely to find a real person who can answer your crochet queries.

LYS: Local Yarn Stores

Chances are your town has at least one true yarn shop. Unless you live in a yarn mecca, these tend to be small, family-run businesses with an emphasis on personal interaction. It's hard to overstate the benefits of a good yarn shop.

Not only will you find a great selection of yarns in all fibers, colors, and gauges, but you'll typically find incredibly knowledgeable staff who are happy to help when you run into trouble. Books and online resources are a great place to start, but you run into complicated instructions you don't quite understand; there's nothing like a real person to talk you through it.

Every yarn store has its own schtick. Some focus on the highest-end yarns, for which it's not uncommon to pay $30 for a single ball that has been carefully and artfully hand dyed. Others feature raw fleeces, dyes, and spinning supplies for DIY yarnaholics. Still others span the widest range of budgets, offering some of the same yarns you find in the big box stores on the same shelf as pricier imported merino.

Aside from products and supplies, yarn stores offer a range of classes and events geared to both knitters and crocheters. These classes can be a fantastic way of connecting with other crochet fans in your own town.

Finding the Ever-elusive LYS

Local yarn stores can be elusive beasts. They're rarely found at common retail watering holes such as mega-malls and tend to gather in offbeat areas that include historic districts, upscale shopping streets, and warehouse districts. Just driving around is rarely effective.

The first place to check is the your local telephone directory. Look not only under "Yarn" but also under "Wool-Retail." In some locales, "Wool" is used as a generic term for yarn.

On the Web, Woolworks (www.woolworks.org) maintains a world-wide listing of retail yarn shops, along with (mostly) unbiased reviews. Although the listings can be slightly out of date, it's a nice place to get more information than you'd get from your standard telephone directory ad.

If you're on the road and are looking for a shop in a strange city, ask your hotel front desk, concierge, or hostel workers. They may know. If not, they may be able to give you the phone number of a similar shop. Quilt stores are more common and tend to be "in the loop" as far as other crafting stores are concerned.

Finally, if you have a favorite brand of yarn, try the manufacturer's Web site. Most keep a comprehensive list of all stores that stock their products. Major knitting magazines do the same.

Trying a LYS on for Size

Not all yarn stores are one-size-fits-all. If your city has several, you'll notice different products, attitudes, and a certain *je ne sais quoi* from each. Chances are, one will fit just right and the others will be less satisfying. If your first visit to a store is deflating, try to take a look at why you were disappointed.

Not enough crochet patterns? Suggest a few designers that you've read about in this book or online. No crochet classes? If you feel confident enough, offer to teach an introductory crochet class that covers the principles discussed in chapter 1. Yarn selection disappointing? Suggest the yarn you'd like to see and give some reasons why it would be a good fit for the store. Because ordering may be done infrequently, don't expect changes overnight. But, the owner may not know there's a demand for a product or service unless you ask.

Maybe, on the day you visited, the shopkeeper was less than welcoming. Although it's impossible to condone outright rudeness, everyone knows bad days happen. Try visiting on a different day of the week and see whether the atmosphere is friendlier.

Perhaps most unfortunately for the industry is an antiquated attitude that if you're under 40, you're not serious about the craft and, therefore, not willing to spend money. Fortunately, with the increase in Gen X crafters, you're now less likely to run into these folks than in years past. Still, I've been followed around stores as if under suspicion of shoplifting. I've been ignored, and I've been told there's nothing for me in the store. But remember *Pretty Woman*? With a little persistence and a positive attitude, you'll find a place that welcomes your enthusiasm and energy as much as they welcome your hard-earned cash. And sometimes, it only takes a few kind words about the latest issue of *Interweave Crochet* to show them that you are, indeed, a serious "hooker."

Falling in Love with a LYS

It's happened to everyone. Maybe in your own city or while on vacation. You fall in love. Not with a boy. Not with a girl. With a LYS. You spend a few hours browsing its shelves, chatting with its friendly staff, and you never want to leave. If the store is in your town, you're in luck! You can make a weekly date to attend a stitch 'n bitch night. You can sign up for classes or special events. If they're hiring, you can even pick up a part time job to earn a little cash and a nice discount on the yarn you were planning on buying anyway.

If you're far from home on vacation or a work trip, don't think the brief fling is doomed. Although you won't be able to simply pop in, a good yarn store, local or not, should be valued.

Take a business card, bookmark the Web site, or whatever you have to do. It's rare to find a store that can't (or won't) do mail order by phone or email. And, who knows when you'll be back to visit? One of my favorite not-so-local yarn shops is "Wool & Company" (www.woolandcompany.net) in Geneva, Illinois, only 15 minutes from my parents' house. Luckily, holidays have me visiting a few times a year, so I always stop in to chat with the owner, Lesley Edmonson, and see what's new.

Of course, if you want to chat with the author of this here book, you can visit my very own yarn shop in Calgary, AB. I opened "Make One Yarn Studio" (www.make1yarns.com) in March 2006 with my partner Sandra. Since then, we've taught loads of newbies and avid knitters about the lure of the crochet hook. Consider this your open invitation to drop by if you're ever in my neck of the woods.

Online Yarn Stores

Local (and not-so-local) yarn shops are a place to get more than supplies. You get support, knowledge, and inspiration. But sometimes, you just want yarn. And you want to order it *now*. 24/7, you can feed your yarn addiction in the privacy of your own home by visiting one of the thousands of Internet yarn shops.

Some brick-and-mortar stores also have an online store feature where you can browse the same stock and place orders for delivery or pickup. But, one of the newest developments in the world of yarn are the e-tailers that run online shops without the retail storefront.

Discounters

The Internet is a great place to find a bargain, especially when you check out one of the many yarn discounters. Specializing in closeout yarns that have been discontinued, you can find quality wool, silk, and cotton at prices that even the Big Box stores can't beat.

Some even produce their own branded yarn lines. Elann.com (www.elann.com) and KnitPicks (www.knitpicks.com) are featured in the pattern chapters for their house branded yarns. Since house brand yarns are only available through a single Web site, the price is typically lower than yarns that were manufactured, then resold to a yarn company for branding, then resold to a distributor, and then finally resold to your local yarn shop. If you're on a budget, this is a great way to work with alpaca, silk, and cashmere without breaking the bank.

Indie Yarn Companies

Yarn companies aren't all huge multi-national organizations. Fiber artists much like you are dyeing their own yarn for sale online. These yarns are typically limited runs. When they're gone, they're gone, never to be duplicated. Search for "hand-dyed yarn" for some good options.

eBay, Stash Swaps, and De-Stashing

Delve into the world of knit and crochet blogs, and it won't be long before you see evidence of "de-stashing" from longtime yarnaholics. Sometimes, perfectly good unused yarn winds up on eBay at unbelievable discounts. Or, bloggers will post personal stash sales on their Web sites. Keep your eyes open for deals, but if you're sensitive to smoke, make sure that the yarn comes from a non-smoking household. Although you could crochet with stinky yarn and wash the finished garment, you probably won't enjoy the process.

Stash-swapping is also a favorite, both online and among knitting and crocheting friends. Trading with others is a great way to swap less-than-thrilling yarn for something shiny and new. It's also a great way to pass along pattern books you're not planning on using.

The Bottom Line

Shopping online has trade-offs. No matter how good your monitor, colors in real life (and real light) are never exactly what they seem online. Without visiting a LYS, you'll miss out on the personal interaction that accompanies any visit. Sometimes, this means you won't receive advice on how to work with a particularly slippery mohair. Online, you have more risk of being disappointed when the yarn finally arrives. There's also the delayed gratification of waiting for the box to be delivered.

On the plus side, you can take advantage of a seemingly endless selection. You can price-compare across town, across continents, and across the world. To find that discontinued yarn specified in last year's magazine, going online is the only way to go. And, the pleasure of coming home after work to find a luscious box of yarn sometimes more than makes up for the wait.

Yarn Companies

Ah. Yarn. Color, texture, and spin coming together to help you create a beautiful fabric. These yarn companies, all featured in the patterns section, produce some of the most beautiful yarns in North America. For more information or to see their other products, check out their Web sites, as listed here in alphabetical order.

- ♦ Art Yarns www.artyarns.com
- ♦ Cascade Yarns www.cascadeyarns.com
- ♦ Curious Creek Fibers www.curiouscreek.com
- ♦ Debbie Bliss Yarns www.debbieblissonline.com
- ♦ Eisaku Noro Distributed by www.knittingfever.com and www.diamondyarn.com
- ♦ Elann: Peruvian Collection www.elann.com
- ♦ Elsebeth Lavold Designer's Choice Distributed by www.knittingfever.com and www.diamondyarn.com
- ♦ Jade Sapphire www.jadesapphire.com
- ♦ KnitPicks www.knitpicks.com
- ♦ Lion Brand Yarn Company www.lionbrand.com
- ♦ Lorna's Laces www.lornaslaces.net
- ♦ Rowan Yarns www.knitrowan.com

It's In the Bag

Of course, with the increase in yarn arts comes the increase in yarn accessories. You suddenly have a lot of yarn to carry around. Of course, you could just use your backpack or purse, but it's just that much more fun to have a yarn-specific bag and crochet in style.

These companies either offer online ordering or will refer you to a store in your area.

Offhand Designs

www.offhanddesigns.com

Based in Oakland, California, Offhand Designs uses the highest quality materials and hand-crafts each bag and case. Because vintage or rare fabrics are the foundation of their designs, each style is a limited edition. Aside from being beautiful, each bag undergoes rigorous testing to make sure that it can stand up to everyday abuse, including your subway commute.

The Organized Knitter

www.organizedknitter.com

Don't be fooled by the company name. Designer Megan Reardon makes a sleek and handy crochet-hook case that'll help you organize your hooks in style. Choose from her line of fabrics; each case is handmade to order.

Jordana Paige

www.jordanapaige.com

Jordana's conservative designs put the work into "handiwork." Suitable with a sharp suit, her knitting and crochet bags feature pockets and zippered compartments for staying organized.

Know Knits

www.knowknits.com

Knit designer Jennifer Lippman developed a lightweight nylon yarn pouch specifically to allow her to continue knitting through the most crowded commute hours. Ideal for taking small projects on the go, the GoKnit pouch straps to your belt, bag, or wrist, and feeds the yarn smoothly through a small guide.

Lexie Barnes

www.lexiebarnes.com

Go mod-retro with Lexie Barnes' fun fabric prints. From the sleek "Flo" to a bowling-night inspired "Lady B," you'll find a size to suit your current crochet obsession.

Festivals, Fairs, and Events

Want to pet a sheep? Want to see exhibits of crocheted works? Want to go yarn shopping in a festival atmosphere or take classes on Tunisian crochet from a published author? Every year across the globe, festivals, fairs, and events provide loads of fiber-related fun.

This is by no means a comprehensive list. For up-to-date listings, watch your favorite knitting or crochet magazines and Web sites, as well as local newspapers.

Stitches—East, West, and Midwest

Three times a year, XRX, the publishers of *Knitter's Magazine,* host consumer trade-shows. Featuring world-class speakers and instructors, plus a marketplace of hundreds of drool-worthy stalls, Stitches is, in many ways, the crème de la crème of yarn events. Watch their Web site at www.knittinguniverse.com for dates and exact locations.

Sheep and Wool Festivals

Wool and fiber producers attend sheep and wool festivals to promote their flocks, win awards, and interact with crocheters, spinners, and knitters. Although nearly every state and province has an annual wool festival, some of the most prominent include Salt Spring Island's Fibre Festival (www.fibrefestival.com), the Maryland Sheep and Wool Festival (www.sheepandwool. org), and the New York Sheep and Wool Festival, also known as Rhinebeck (www.sheepandwool. com). Most of the major magazines feature ads for the larger festivals. Smaller home-town fests may only be advertised in your local newspapers. If all else fails, check with your LYS for details and dates.

Local Events and DIY

Your LYS is the best way to learn about local events. From book readings to trunk shows to crochet-a-thons or yarn tasting parties, you can crochet with company every month of the year. Or, host your own crochet party! Find some interested friends, provide some nonstaining munchies and cool beverages, and be the hostess who hooks!

Chapter **Fourteen**

◆◆◆

Weaving Ends

You've made it to the end, and hopefully have had some fun along the way. This, my friend, is the beginning of many years of fun with a little yarn and a little hook.

When you crochet, people in your life may try to get all serious on you. They may insist that every project needs to be finished promptly. They may claim that you need to use the exact yarn called for in the pattern. They may hint that only knitting is sexy, that crochet belongs to purple-haired ladies and dusty living rooms. Don't let them. Define your crochet for yourself. Make what you love to wear and trust your gut; it tends to be right 99 percent of the time.

Join (or start) a crocheting circle. Read the mags and blogs. Get to know your local yarn shop owners. Somewhere along the way, you'll probably run into a cool purple-haired lady who can teach you a thing or two about creativity. And she may just love this book as much as you have.

Now, I'm about to get cheesy. Bear with me. The neat thing about yarn arts, at least as I've observed, is that just as we weave loops together to make fabric, the yarn actually loops people together, forges a common ground between people who seem to be polar opposites.

Here in Calgary, we have a knitting activist organization that wants to spread a message of peace and understanding through knitting. When I watch the crocheters and knitters at our shop events, I can't help but think they're on the right track. The group spans 60 years of life and craft experience. We're married, divorced, gay, straight, male, and female. We're pierced and tattooed. We have pink hair and gray hair. We are yogis, software engineers, lawyers, and nurses. We are health nuts and couch potatoes.

But as different as we are, we have one thing in common. We're all drawn to a sometimes impractical and old craft because we find joy in taking a tradition and molding it into something new, something modern, something irresistible. We all love this strange process of twisting yarn together to make something whole.

Whatever your reasons for picking up this book, I hope you found more than you had expected. I hope you've not only learned a few new stitches, but also a new way of looking at the craft, and a new appreciation for the fine designers who work so hard. Who knows? Maybe in a few years, you'll be one of them.

Crochet. Be happy.

Appendix A

◆◆◆

A Crochet Reference

To promote consistency across patterns, this book uses the Craft Yarn Council of America's standards and guidelines for crochet patterns. For more information on yarn standards, see the CYCA website at www.yarnstandards.com.

Common Abbreviations

Most patterns will provide you with a list of any specific abbreviations used in the instructions. Here are the ones you'll encounter most often.

alt	Alternate, i.e., every other		ch-sp	Chain space, i.e., the space formed by one or more chain stitches.
beg	Beginning			
bet	Between		cont	Continue
BL	Back loop, i.e., the loop furthest away from you.		dc	Double crochet
			dc2tog	Double decrease by working two dc together
BP	Back Post, i.e., the stitch on the row below, worked from back to front.		dec	Decrease, generic term
			Fl	Front loop, i.e., the loop closest to you.
BPdc	Back post double crochet			
BPsc	Back post single crochet		FP	Front post, i.e., the stitch on the row below, worked from front to back.
CC	Contrasting color			
ch	Chain stitch			
			FPdc	Front Post double crochet

FPsc	Front Post single crochet		sl st	Slip St
hdc	Half double crochet		sp	Space or spaces
inc	Increase, generic term		st	Stitch or stitches
MC	Main color		tch	Turning chain
RS	Right Side		tr	Triple Crochet
sc	Single crochet		WS	Wrong Side
sk	skip		YO	Yarn over

British/American Terminology

As noted in chapter 1, the same crochet terms are used in British patterns, but they often describe very different stitches. Note the pattern origin and use the following chart to make sure you're working the right stitches.

American Term	British Term
Slip Stitch	Single Crochet
Single Crochet	Double Crochet
Half Double Crochet	Half Treble Crochet
Double Crochet	Treble Crochet
Triple or Treble Crochet	Double Treble Crochet

US/Metric Hook Sizing

Because not all hooks are produced with the same standards, the US size labels may vary slightly. Additionally, it's possible to find a hook labeled G instead of G6 or G7. When in doubt, check to see if a Metric size, in millimeters, is also provided.

US Size	Metric Size
B-1	2.25mm or 2.5mm
C-2	2.75mm
D-3	3.25mm
E-4	3.5mm
F-5	3.75mm

continued

continued

US Size	Metric Size
G-6	4mm
G-7	4.5mm
H-8	5mm
I-9	5.5mm
J-10	6mm
K-10.5	6.5mm
L-11	8mm
M or N-13	9mm
N or P-15	10mm
P or Q	15mm
Q	16mm
S	19mm

Yarn Weight and Gauge Chart

Some patterns prefer a tighter (or looser) fabric, and so recommended hook size may vary from the CYCA chart below. When selecting the right hook for the job, first start with the pattern's recommendations. Then do a gauge swatch to make sure your gauge is right on the mark!

Types of Yarn	Knit Gauge (number of sts per 4 inches)	Crochet Gauge (number of sc to 4 inches)	Metric Hook	US Hook
Fingering, Sock	27 to 32 sts	21 to 28 sts	2.25 to 3.5mm	B-1 to E-4
Sport	23 to 26 sts	16 to 20 sts	3.5 to 4.5mm	E-4 to G-7
DK, Double Knitting	21 to 24 sts	12 to 17 sts	4.5 to 5.5mm	G-7 to I-9
Worsted, Aran	18 to 20 sts	11 to 14 sts	5.5 to 6.5mm	I-9 to K-10.5
Chunky	12 to 15 sts	8 to 11 sts	6.5 to 9mm	K-10.5 to M13
Bulky, Super Bulky	Fewer than 11 sts	5 to 9 sts	9mm and up	M-13 and up

Appendix B

◆◆◆

Worksheets and Forms

Instead of writing in this book, you can copy the following worksheets and keep them in your crochet notebook or binder. Make multiple copies of each to keep on hand. When things change, you can always make another copy!

Measurement Worksheet

Custom Measurements for:

Head Circumference
Wrap the measuring tape around your head as if it's a
close fitting hat.

Head Height
Take the tape from the top of one ear to the other ear,
over the top of the head. Divide
this by two.

Neck Circumference
At the top of your shoulders, wrap the tape around your
neck comfortably.

Shoulder Width
Measuring across the back of your neck, stretch the tape
from the tip of one shoulder to the tip of the other.

Arm Circumference
Wrap the tape around your bicep at its widest point. You
may wish to take the measurement of each arm separately
and choose the larger of the two to ensure a comfortable fit.

Wrist Circumference
Wrap the tape around your wrist at its smallest point.

Arm Length
With the tape positioned in your underarm, measure to the
smallest point on your wrist. This measurement will be
compared to your desired sleeve length. For example, if I
like my sleeves to hit mid-hand, I'll add 2 inches to my
sleeve length when working the pattern.

Chest Circumference
Wrap the tape around the widest part of your chest.

Waist Circumference
Wrap the tape around the smallest part of your waist.

Torso Height
Measure from the top of your shoulders to the smallest
part of your waist.

Hip Circumference
Wrap the tape around the widest part of your hips. No,
it's not ok to fudge this one!

Ankle Circumference
For socks, wrap the tape around the top of your ankle.
If your calves are well developed, take the calf measurement
instead.

Foot Length
Measure your foot sole from end of heel to tip of longest toe.

Project Log

Project Name: _____

Source: _____

Yarn: _____

Gauge: _____ on hook: _____

Size: _____

Date Started: _____ Date Finished: _____

General Notes:

Designer Bios

Catie Berger Catie has been crocheting so long she doesn't remember learning. She crochets to unwind and relax. Crocheting is a form of meditation, and giving away the final product is the ultimate joy! When she's not crocheting, she is a civil engineer and mother of three. Her engineering background makes it difficult to follow a pattern without redesigning it. No wonder she prefers to design her own! You can follow her cyber-fiber on her blog: www.herself75.blogspot.com.

Robyn Chachula Robyn has only been crocheting for a short time, but crafting her own style for years. Her older sister used to tell everyone that she was going to have her own fashion line one day. Her day job is designing structural renovations and restorations of existing buildings, which may seem like a far cry from crochet fashion design. But for Robyn, they are one and the same. They both use her ability to take a big project, break it down into little items, and then piece them back together for the overall big picture. More of Robyn's architecturally inspired pieces can be found at www.crochetbyfaye.blogspot.com.

Zak Greant Zak Greant works in the information technology field harvesting bits and bytes in the summer and then saving them up for the long hard Canadian winters. He lives in Vancouver, Canada with his wife, their cat, and several large and affectionate dust bunnies. He sometimes blogs at zak.greant.com — but mostly just about technology.

Jodi Green Jodi Green is a displaced Canadian currently dividing her time between her home in Windsor, Ontario, and Athens, Georgia, where she is a candidate for a master's degree in printmaking at the University of Georgia. It's amazing how much knitting and crocheting she manages to get done while she's up to her elbows in ink half the time.

Jennifer Hansen Jennifer Hansen lives in Fremont, California, where she is a full-time designer, teacher, and writer. Her innovative work has been featured in various books and magazines including *Vogue Knitting, Interweave Crochet,* and *The Happy Hooker.* She also publishes designs through her company, Stitch Diva Studios. Stitch Diva Studios' patterns are available for download and may be purchased at yarn stores nationwide. You can visit Stitch Diva Studios online at www.stitchdiva.com to view more of Jennifer's designs.

Annie Modesitt Annie Modesitt was taught to knit at age 6 by a family friend and has loved it ever since. She especially enjoys the sculptural nature of crochet and the fact that beautiful fabric can be made using just a hook and a string — like catching a fish! Annie's taught her own kids to crochet, but at this point they're finding it hard to work beyond the 'miles of chain' phase of crochet love. Annie's designs and essays about knitting can be found in several books and magazines, including *Interweave Crochet, Family Circle,* and *Easy Knitting.* Annie is the editor of the 2006 & 2007 Accord Crochet Pattern A Day Calendars.

Marcia Wentela Marcia learned to crochet from her sister Shirley at the age of 7. She never saw her grandmother without a crochet project in her hands. She is eternally grateful to these women in her life who have passed along a passion for all things fiber. Marcia lives in Marquette, Michigan, where she is married to a wonderful man, is the mother of three, and works as an obstetrics nurse by day. Her family is very supportive of her love of crocheting, knitting, and quilting. Her mother and daughter even helped make the "yarn" for her Plastic Purse project!

Kim Piper Werker Kim is the founder and editor of *crochetme.com,* the wickedly cool online mag. She likes sushi, hardcover books, thunderstorms, and the smell of clean laundry. Her youthful dream of being a fighter pilot was dashed when she ended up an astigmatic pacifist. She lives in Vancouver, British Columbia, with her husband and their dog.

 **Mandy Moore** (Technical Editor) Mandy Moore lives in Vancouver, BC with her small family of husband and cat. She is, among other things, the technical editor for Knitty.com, and she was the technical editor for *Big Girl Knits* (Potter Craft, 2006). She enjoys crocheting and knitting because they are engaging to both sides of her brain, and technical editing because she is a control freak. She honed her skills by working in yarn stores for several years as salesperson, teacher and general know-it-all. She is a hardcore making-things evangelist, and will probably try to convince you that you should try (crocheting, knitting, sewing, painting) too! You can find her online at yarnageddon.com.

Index

hooks
  construction, 62
  difficulty inserting, 26
  history, 183–184
  sizes, 58, 62–64, 207–208
hook sizing tools, 63, 64

I

increasing, 19–20
Interweave Knits (and Crochet),
  193
ironing, 25
itchiness, yarn, 46

J

jackets, 128–139
Japan, crocheting/knitting in,
  113
jewelry-making, 170. *See also*
  necklaces
Jodi Green blog, 190
Jordana Paige, source for
  project bags, 202

K

kimono, 107–112
Knit.1, 193
KnitPicks, 199
KnitScene, 193
Knit Simple, 193
Knitter's Review, 60, 192
knitting, 2, 5–6, 184, 186
Know Knits, source for project
  bags, 202
Kool-Aid, dyeing yarn with, 55

L

lace-making, 184–185
lace-weight yarn, 52
lacy flower stitch, 37
Lexie Barnes, source for project
  bags, 202
light weight yarn, 52
linen, 48
loose threads on surface, 26
love o' your life projects,
  described, 2
Lucy-Lou & Tim-Bob, Too,
  150–154

M

macramé, 9
magazines, crochet, 193
Make One Yarn Studio, 199
Market Bag, 86–87
measurement chart, 210
measurements, body, 66–67, 210
medium-weight yarn, 52
Meetup, 192
The Memories of a Highland Lady
  (Grant),.183
men, crochet patterns for, 72–73
mercerized cotton, 48
merino wool, 45, 46
metric system for yarn
  measurement, 56
microfiber, 49
mistakes, fixing, 25–28, 75
ModeKnit/The Knitting Heretic
  blog, 190
mohair, 42, 45, 92, 93
moisture-wicking fibers, 47
MonsterCrochet blog, 190
motifs. *See* appliqués
multiple ply yarn, 40

N

necklaces
  Bubble Belt variation, 158
  Crocheted Bling, 169–170
  Daisy Chain Neck Warmer,
    148–149
new age fibers, 48
notebooks, project, 58, 64, 211
Not Your Mama's Beading (Welsh),
  170
nylon fibers, 49

O

Offhand Designs, source for
  project bags, 201–202
The Organized Knitter, source
  for project bags, 202

P

Pashmina, 45
pattern instructions
  Alien Skull, 126–127
  beret (variation on Classic
    Street Page Boy), 147
  Bubble Belt, 158
  cardigan (variation on Sari
    Silk Shrug), 116
  Chunky Monkey Scarf, 99
  Classic Street Page Boy,
    144–147
  Cozy Peacoat, 128–139
  Creatures of the Wooly
    Deep, 178–180
  Crocheted Bling, 169–170
  crocheted flowers, 149
  Daisy Chain Neck Warmer,
    148–149

About the Author

Amy Swenson learned to crochet when she was still young enough to make blankets for her dolls. She promptly forgot everything about needlework until she turned 23 and suddenly fell back in love with the idea of creating fabric. Since 2003, Amy has developed and distributed her own line of original patterns for knitting and crochet, IndiKnits (www.indiknits.com), which can be found in more than 120 shops across North America.

Amy is thrilled to have worked on several textile arts projects, including writings and designs for Interweave Knits, Knitty.com, "Knit Wit," "Big Girls Knits," "Stitch and Bitch Nation," "Knitgrrl," and "Knitting for Dogs." *Not Your Mama's Crochet* is her first book-length publication.

When not doing crazy things with yarn, Amy loves to travel. The photo of her was taken outside the Gobi Cashmere Factory in Ulaan Baatur, Mongolia, where Amy risked any shred of human dignity to try to buy as much cashmere yarn as she could carry. In 2007, Amy plans on leading Adventure Knitting trips to places such as Mongolia and Peru.

In early 2006, Amy opened Make One Yarn Studio (www.make1yarns.com), a textile arts shop focusing on fine yarns for knitting and crochet. Amy lives and designs in Calgary, Alberta, where she and her partner are the proud humans of four cats who, thankfully, leave the yarn alone.

Notes

Notes

Notes

Notes

Notes

Notes

Notes

Notes

There's lots more in store with *Not Your Mama's*™ Craft Books!

Hip and savvy *Not Your Mama's* books are designed for confident crafters like you who don't need to start at the beginning and don't want to go back to basics and slave over every pattern and page. These books get right to the point so you can jump right into real projects. With easy-to-follow instructions plus hints, tips, and steps for customizing projects, you'll quickly have something to show for your efforts—fun, trendy items to add sass and class to your wardrobe or home.

0-471-97382-3

0-471-97381-5

0-471-97380-7

It's knitting with a trés chic attitude. Projects include Pirate Socks, Boot-i-licious (boot jewelry), Girly (a sexy cardigan), Macho Picchu (a man's sweater), Techno Bag (a laptop case), Pampered Pooch Pullover, Hearts & Stars (cushions), and more.

Creative crochet is in today! Patterns include an Uber-Femme Capelet, Pseudo Kimono, Daisy Chain Neck Warmer, When the Jeans Don't Fit (recycled denim rug), Straight-Laced Tank and Shrug, Wowie Zowie Eco-Tote, Crocheted Bling, two super-cute plush toys, and more.

Do the bling thing. Projects include Financial Freedom (recycled credit card necklace), Tough Cuff, Catch Your Own Bouquet ring, Tipple Rings (wine stem markers), Girls Gone Bridaled (a tiara), Security Anklet, push pins with pizzazz, and more.

All *Not Your Mama's*™ Craft Books
$14.99 US/$17.99 CAN/£9.99 UK • Paper • 240–264 pp.
7 3/8 x 9 1/4 • Lots of illustrations and color photos

Available wherever books are sold.

Wiley, the Wiley logo, and Not Your Mama's are trademarks or registered trademarks of John Wiley & Sons, Inc. and/or its affiliates in the United States and other countries.

WILEY
Now you know.
wiley.com